In Justice

Inside the Scandal That Rocked the Bush Administration

DAVID IGLESIAS
WITH
DAVIN SEAY

WILEY

John Wiley & Sons, Inc.

Published by John Wiley & Sons, Inc., Hoboken, New Jersey
Published simultaneously in Canada

For general information about our other products and services, please contact our
Customer Care Department within the United States at (800) 762-2974, outside the
United States at (317) 572-3993 or fax (317) 572-4002.

Wiley also publishes its books in a variety of electronic formats. Some content that
appears in print may not be available in electronic books. For more information
about Wiley products, visit our web site at www.wiley.com.

Library of Congress Cataloging-in-Publication Data:

Iglesias, David, date.
    In justice : inside the scandal that rocked the Bush administration / David
Iglesias with Davin Seay.
      p. cm.
    Includes index.
    ISBN 978-0-470-26197-2 (cloth)
      1. Iglesias, David, 1958-   2. Public prosecutors—United States—Biography.
3. Lawyers—New Mexico—Biography.   4. Public prosecutors—Resignation—
United States—History.   5. United States. Dept. of Justice—Officials and
employees—Resignation—United States—History.   I. Seay, Davin.   II. Title.
    KF373.I38A3 2008
    345.73'01—dc22   2008009569

Printed in the United States of America

10 9 8 7 6 5 4 3 2 1

*To my wife, Cynthia, who unwaveringly
stood beside me before, during,
and after the tempest.*

CONTENTS

ACKNOWLEDGMENTS

You know who your friends are in times of trouble. This book could not have happened without the encouragement, support, and prayers of the following people: my four wonderful daughters, Claudia, Amanda, Marisa, and Sophia Iglesias; my beloved parents, Reverend Claudio and Margaret Iglesias; the best big sister in the world, Lorie Iglesias Heydenburk, and her husband, Bill, and their family; my incredibly supportive in-laws, Frank and Jann Corrick, Betty Sears, and Rusty Kuhns; my courageous fellow former U.S. Attorneys who cared enough about the rule of law to speak out, Dan Bogden, Margaret Chiara, Paul "Pablo" Charlton, Bud Cummins, Todd Graves, Carol Lam, and John "Eddie" McKay; my forever friends and the brothers I never had, Seth Barnes, Kevin McCarthy, Rumaldo Armijo, and my Wrong House buddies; my White House Fellows classmates, in particular Yvonne Campos and Megan Golden; my semper fidelis navy shipmates who are too numerous to count except for Captain Bill Morrison, JAGC, USN, and Rear Admiral Bill Payne, USN; the wonderfully dogged media who refused to let this critically important story die, in particular, Ruben Navarette, Jason Leopold, Paul Kiel, Josh Marshall, Dan Eggen, Marisa Taylor, Tavis Smiley, Tim Russert, Dan Rather, Chris Matthews, Mike Isikoff, Dahlia Lithwick, Phil Casaus, Gene Grant, Jeff Gardner,

Jim Scarantino, and Julia Goldberg; the erudite Professor Jim Eisenstein, who has helped illuminate the history of the U.S. Attorneys; the fabulous professionals at DIILS, Colonel (ret.) John Atkinson, USMC, Walt Munroe, Captain Chris O'Donnell, USMC, Lieutenant Derek Mills, JAGC, USN; my righteous Wheaton supporters, Dr. Duane Litfin, Marilee Melvin, Professor (ret.) Bob and Shirley Bartel, Professor Amy Black, Cindra Stackhouse Taetzsch, Dave Lawrenz, Chet and Diana Stewart, Jeff Hochstetler, Ammon Simon, Matt Farber, and Ryan June; my excellent book agent, Sandy Dijkstra, and her top-notch staff; my new colleagues Chris Kelly, Kurt Stevens, and Cathy Breeze; my brothers-in-arms, Ken Henley, Tom Bearden, Barry Wong, David Palmer, Marty Esquivel, Juan Masini, Henry Narvaez, Don Lobato, Larry Gomez, Tom "Tomas" Gilchrist, James Carroll, Jim Hudson, Bob Tedrow, Patrick Romero, Mikey Weinstein, and Dale Kuehne; Mrs. Victoriana Armijo, who had a special mass held for me, and her wonderful daughter-in-law, Claudia McKay Armijo, and the extended Armijo family; my college classmate Reverend Skip Gilliken, who had his entire church in North Carolina pray for me; my fellow reserve JAG officer, Lieutenant Colonel Derek Hirohata, USAF, whose comrades in Iraq prayed for me; my Wheaton buddy Phil Hull, who kept sending me encouraging e-mails from Yakima, Washington; Judge Stan Whitaker for his wonderfully supportive letters; my kind former bosses, David Campbell, Jerry Walz, and Jim Comey; and finally, the scores of citizens of every political persuasion, race, gender, age, and ethnicity who stopped me in the streets, offices, restaurants, gyms, military bases, churches, and airports across America to express their support. I will be forever grateful.

CHAPTER 1

For Such a Time as This

We have all experienced those moments when a shattering event overtakes and overwhelms us, changing our lives forever. As a nation, we lived through such a time on September 11, 2001, when nineteen men altered the course of history. Before that, you can point to November 22, 1963, when one individual rocked the foundations of our society, assassinating President John F. Kennedy in Dallas, or June 6, 1944, when thousands of Americans gave their lives in the D-Day invasion of Normandy.

I consider it one of the ironies of history that my particular "day that will live in infamy" occurred on December 7, 2006, exactly sixty-five years after the Japanese launched the sneak attack that took us into World War II. Of course, I'm not comparing what happened to me that afternoon to any such epic date with destiny. At the same time, however, I realize that my personal Pearl Harbor Day is not without its own historic resonance. From that moment on, things were not the same, for me or for the country I'd so proudly served. I'd arrived at a point when my history intersected with America's history in a way that would change—and is still changing—both America's justice system and me.

I hadn't the slightest clue of what was about to happen as I walked down a long departure corridor at Baltimore-Washington International Airport to catch a flight home to Albuquerque, New Mexico. It was cold outside. The high windows overlooked the busy tarmac, and a winter sun slanted across the crowds of holiday travelers hurrying to their gates. Bright plastic and tinsel decorations hung overhead. I was feeling a bit of yuletide cheer myself, anticipating my return home, where the sunny Southwestern winter stood in sharp contrast to the dreary drizzle of the East Coast urban hub I was gratefully escaping.

New Mexico is a particularly beautiful place to come home to at that time of year. The snow occasionally blankets the steep ascents of the Sandia Mountains, which rise more than ten thousand feet in magnificent relief right outside my front door. I had spent much of my life in the state, in Gallup, Santa Fe, and, finally, Albuquerque, where I had put down roots, started a family, and launched my career. But even after all those years, New Mexico never fails to live up to its billing as the Land of Enchantment.

Home, of course, was where my wife and four daughters—sixteen-year-old Claudia, fifteen-year-old Amanda, thirteen-year-old Marisa, and the youngest, ten-year-old Sophia—would be gearing up for the family's own seasonal celebration. As Christians, Cyndy and I had always tried to impress on our girls that there was more to the birthday of Jesus Christ than just another opportunity to indulge in conspicuous consumption. But it's hard to deflect any youngster's anticipation of presents under the tree, and I looked forward to sharing their excitement. Although Christmas honors the Advent season, happy kids are what Christmas is all about.

Except, as it turned out, on that particular Christmas. Our holiday that year would be filled with confusion, doubt, and rage, and it would begin right at the moment when I took out my BlackBerry for one last check before I boarded my flight. What immediately caught my eye was a message from my secretary, Lois Golden, the extremely competent assistant whom I'd taken with me through two previous jobs. "Call Mike Battle," was the text, and I stopped as the noisy crowd surged around me. I looked at the words on the glowing screen, wondering exactly what they might mean.

While it was certainly not unprecedented to get a call from Mike Battle, it was nevertheless unusual and just a bit unnerving. Mike had been director of the Executive Office for United States Attorneys (EOUSA) since the summer of 2005, after serving for three years as the U.S. Attorney in the Western District of New York. As the arm of the Justice Department that oversaw the activities and the performance of U.S. Attorneys across the country, the EOUSA served as an intermediary between the field offices and Washington and as a conduit for various policy directives from on high. But neither I nor any other U.S. Attorney reported to Battle. We answered only to the attorney general and the deputy attorney general. As a result, our contacts were minimal with "Main Justice," as we called the DOJ's magisterial headquarters on the corner of Pennsylvania Avenue and 9th Street in the heart of the capital.

I'll never forget the first time I visited that building, which was named after slain attorney general Robert Kennedy. I had come to apply for a position in the Civil Rights Section in 1988—as luck would have it, precisely the same time that the Justice Department announced a hiring freeze. Nevertheless, I was duly impressed with the inspirational aphorisms carved into the building's marble-adorned walls and the stern visages of the men who had spoken those words. They stared down stoically from their commemorative portraits in the offices where more than ten thousand lawyers—an "untouchable" phalanx of world-class prosecutors—work in what the recruitment brochures refer to as the largest law firm in the world. There is a serene and beautiful fountain in the courtyard, which brought to my mind the words of Martin Luther King Jr., when he quoted the biblical book of Amos and called on justice to "flow on like a river."

Thirteen years later, I was helping to channel a small tributary of that river and would visit the magnificent edifice at least once every few months. But the reality was that virtually all U.S. Attorney cases involved activity within our individual districts. Main Justice became interested only when a particular prosecution took on national implications, especially the kinds of organized crime and drug cartel cases on which it had earned a wholly justified reputation for breaking the backs of syndicates and conspiracies. At our level, EOUSA, at the behest of the attorney general, would actively monitor our caseloads and conviction rates, primarily through a database system dubbed LIONS—Legal Information Office Network System—which tracked specifics on defendants, criminal charges, court appearances, and so forth. Otherwise, U.S. Attorneys were pretty much left alone to oversee their districts within priorities established by the administration.

Yet for all the distance maintained between Main Justice and the U.S. Attorneys' far-flung offices, Battle was widely considered to be "one of us." He'd risen through the ranks, beginning in Buffalo, New York, where he'd worked variously as assistant to the state attorney general and as Assistant U.S. Attorney, as well as helping to found the Federal Public Defender's Office in the city. I had previously worked with him preparing testimony for an immigration subcommittee, and I knew that he understood the realities of prosecutorial work in the trenches. Ever since we'd met, I'd considered Mike a straight shooter. After all, he had been on the regional council of the Boy Scouts of America.

I'd seen Mike a few months earlier, back in October in his Washington office on the second floor of Main Justice, where I'd stopped by to say hello and chat about the seemingly endless requests I'd made for more staff and an increased budget. He seemed a bit worried when I walked into his office, and with good reason. By that time, about half of George W. Bush's U.S. Attorneys had left to become federal judges, take other government appointments, or go into lucrative private practice. During our conversation, I could see that Mike was relieved that I wasn't there to tender my resignation. In fact, his face broke into a wide smile when I told him I was planning to stay. I sympathized with his position: he had a tough job trying to keep ninety-three independent-minded U.S. Attorneys happy. The fact is, I'm not certain that Mike enjoyed all that much job security himself: he was the third full-time EOUSA director in six years.

As I look back, it seems clear to me that Mike had no idea what was about to go down a few short months later. It's ironic to think that I had once been offered the position of director of EOUSA. If I'd taken it, I'd have been the one who would have had to make that fateful phone call.

In any case, I wasn't alone in my incessant entreaties for more resources and personnel. At that time, there was a general belt-tightening underway throughout Washington, and I didn't need Mike to tell me that most of the government's resources were going toward maintaining military operations in Iraq and Afghanistan. It was a priority I certainly understood, but, like every other U.S. Attorney, that didn't stop me from regularly registering pleas for more money and staff to do my job. It was, in fact, *part* of my job. Lobbying for the assets I needed was a very direct way of serving my district.

It occurred to me, as I stood back from the airport's holiday rush and dialed Mike's number on my cell phone, that this was perhaps the reason for his call: maybe he'd been able to shake loose a few more lawyers or a couple more dollars for me. On the other hand, I told myself, as the connection went through and I heard the ring on the other end, it could be something else entirely. Yet if there was a still, small voice deep down inside telling me that I was about to get bad news, I wasn't listening. I consider myself an optimistic person. I hoped for the best. I didn't have a chance to prepare for the worst.

"What's up, Mike?" I asked him as soon as his secretary put me through. To Mike's credit, he got right down to business.

"David," he replied, with the slightest trace of his upstate New York accent, "the administration wants to go a different way."

There was a pause, as the static crackled between us. What does that mean? I wondered to myself, then repeated my question out loud.

If Mike hesitated, it was only for a moment. "We would like your resignation," he said, "effective the end of January."

The silence that followed was long and profound, in sharp contrast to the roaring rush of thoughts and emotions that flooded me. The end of January? I remembered thinking, with an involuntary mental calculation. That was seven weeks away. And Christmas was right around the corner.

I felt numb, a hollow sensation that was somewhere between freezing and a fever. I'd been fortunate up to that point in my life not to have ever had a family member or a close friend die, but in that moment I could only too vividly imagine how such a loss might match what I was experiencing. In truth, I felt as if *I* had died, as if some vital, life-sustaining organ had been ripped out of my chest. *I love my job*, I realized in a sudden rush of insight. I'd never appreciated it as much as in that moment. I never understood how much of my identity was bound up with what I did and how much of my self-esteem was tied to doing it well. That might have been a good thing or a bad thing. I wasn't in the position to judge. All I knew was that in a single instant, everything was different.

"Whoa, Mike," I said, after I had managed to catch my breath. "What's going on here?" The silence continued from the far end of the phone. "I've received no warning," I continued, as much to myself as to Mike. I wanted to fill the silence, find an explanation, and somehow turn the clock back. "I was not aware of any problem. If I had been aware of a problem, I would have fixed it." I took another lungful of air, trying desperately to regain my equilibrium.

"Listen," I continued after a long silence on the other end of the line. "I don't think I can line up another job in seven weeks. Is there any way I can get more time?"

"I'll see what I can do," Mike replied, but I could tell from the tone in his voice that it was a forlorn hope.

There was nothing left for me to do but lamely repeat the same plaintive question: "What's going on, Mike?"

When Mike spoke, his voice was barely audible. "I don't know," he said, as I strained to hear him over the noise of the airport. "I don't want to know. All I can tell you, David, is that this came from on high."

So that was that. He didn't have to spell it out. Maybe it was the attorney general. Maybe it was the White House. It didn't really matter. The implications were obvious: there would be no reprieve or appeal.

It was clear—devastatingly clear—from my brief and baffling conversation with Mike Battle that I was not going to get an adequate explanation for the reasons and the rationale behind my precipitous firing, at least not from him. My colleague had made it obvious that much to his own discomfort, he was nothing more than a bearer of bad tidings, a messenger from faceless superiors who had delegated my dismissal as if ordering the trash to be taken out. He was only doing his job.

Which, of course, was exactly the point. We were all just doing our jobs. Comprising an elite corps within the Department of Justice, every incoming U.S. Attorney well understood the premium that had been placed on loyalty to the Bush administration. An implicit qualification of ideological adherence had helped to earn us a chance at our high offices in the first place. No one had ever said as much: with the exception of our positions on the death penalty, we were never subjected to a litmus test to gauge our political purity. It had never been necessary. We were part—a key part—of a major realignment in governmental philosophy and policy, a values-based initiative that depended for its ultimate implementation on team players who understood what they were fighting for and how to win the new war that had started on 9/11.

And it wasn't only the war against terrorism that roused and rallied us. Ever since the Reagan Revolution, the Republican agenda had been steadily gaining traction with the American electorate. The Moral Majority had become Morning in America, which had become the Contract with America, which, at least in principle, had become Compassionate Conservatism. It was up to us, as soldiers for an administration that saw itself occupying a unique historical juncture, to take this extraordinary cultural and political groundswell to its vaunted conclusion: a country reawakened to its founding ethical, moral, and religious principles.

There has been much said about the Machiavellian strategies of Karl Rove and others to implement a permanent Republican majority in America. I can't speak for my fellow U.S. Attorneys, much less for the myriad dedicated career professionals who served in the Department of Justice. All I can say with certainty is that for me, I never felt like a cog in some insidious machinery of political ascendance. It was more personal than that and always had been. I came to the Bush administration with the firm conviction that its values mirrored my values. It was a confidence that naturally commanded loyalty, similar to the feeling I had in the navy, where commitment to core ideals was the bedrock of obedience and the foundation on which the chain of command rested. It had been drilled into me that good leaders always keep as their top priorities the accomplishment of the mission and the safety and the security of the people under their command.

Quite aside from any sense of personal betrayal I might have felt at the dire news that Mike somewhat shamefacedly passed along that afternoon, there was a deeper sense that the link that had been forged between the principles and the practice of my job had been irrevocably severed. I had never questioned the higher purposes to which I had pledged myself or the wisdom of the leaders who articulated the goals I promised to pursue. Yet for reasons I couldn't begin to comprehend, my loyalty was now being called into question. In truly Kafkaesque fashion, I had been tried in an invisible court for a crime I didn't understand and had been handed down a sentence I didn't deserve.

At least, that's the way I felt, as I stood numb and hollow amid the rush of holiday travelers, my BlackBerry now dead and silent in my hand. At that moment, I did what anyone in my position would do if faced with a sudden and complete inversion of a long-settled and comfortable reality: I reached out to the one person in the world whom I trusted completely, whom I knew had my best interests at heart and had shared my every joy and sorrow as if they were her own.

It's an all-too-familiar truism that behind every successful man there is a dedicated woman, but let me just take this opportunity to add my own heartfelt echo to the old saying. There are, I'm convinced, few men in committed marriages for any length of time who, if they're being honest with themselves, will not admit that their wives are the heart, the soul, and the brains behind any achievement for which the world might give them credit. That goes double for my wife, Cyndy. Loyal in the best sense of the word, fiercely determined, and unfailingly supportive, she has made the well-being of her family the primary purpose of her life. It's a single-minded focus that I had a desperate need for that dark winter afternoon.

Unfortunately, I didn't have a way to reach out. I made an immediate call to Cyndy's cell phone and left a voice mail. By then my plane was scheduled to depart. I had to dash down the terminal to make the flight, and when I had finally settled into my seat, I heard the attendant over the intercom instructing us to turn off all electronic devices. I now had four hours to endure without advice, counsel, or solace and what seemed like an eternity to consider the consequences of what had just happened. Instead, I found myself distractedly mulling over the lyrics to one of my favorite 1970s songs, Bob Seger's "Night Moves"—in particular, the line about "working on mysteries without any clues."

Not that I didn't try my best to unravel those clues in the immediate aftermath of Mike Battle's fateful phone call, during the hours of what I can only describe as the plane ride from hell. An experienced traveler, I had long since cultivated the ability to grab a few hours of sleep literally on the fly and often even before the plane left the tarmac. But not that evening. Like a hamster on a wire wheel, my mind raced in a tight, futile circle as I asked myself the same questions over and over again: What happened? What did I do? Whom had I made angry? Why wasn't I warned?

In fact, far from being alerted to any potential problem, I had recently received a glowing report from the DOJ team that was charged with gauging the performance of all U.S. Attorneys. The in-depth inspection, dubbed EARS (Evaluation and Review Staff), and the only metric by which U.S. Attorneys are judged, is conducted by twenty to thirty career prosecutors and DOJ administrators. In both 2003 and early 2006, they descended on my office and, over the course of a week, interviewed everyone who worked for me, along with federal judges and agency heads, and they combed through the files of all prosecutions, upcoming, ongoing, and completed. Members of my staff, as well as law enforcement officers and others in the legal community, were polled as to the effectiveness and the efficiency of my office, and a report was submitted on everything from quality of oral advocacy to workload and productivity to administrative operations. "Competent, professional, and dedicated," was a typical comment from the EARS report on the caliber and the morale of my staff, and even though the evaluation went on to point out how "a steadily growing number of immigration cases is straining criminal resources" in New Mexico, to me that was proof that I had taken to heart the administration's marching orders in my district. In the truest sense of the term, Mike's phone call had come like a bolt out of the blue.

I arrived home late that evening, a Thursday night, and confronted the dismal prospect of a long weekend without answers and with no way to get them. My daughters had long since been tucked into bed, and I wasted no time breaking the bad news to Cyndy as I stood in the living room, my suitcase at my feet. I remember looking out through the patio doors to the backyard, where we would be putting in a hot tub. It seemed, in that moment, like an unconscionable indulgence.

The fact was, being a U.S. Attorney was the best job I'd ever had. Our home, in a brand new development, was tucked against the spectacular 6,000-foot-high Albuquerque foothills. Fortunately,

Cyndy and I had been able to put aside savings—money that it now seemed likely we would have to live on in the immediate future.

In the hours that followed my homecoming, deep into that cold night, we tried our best to piece together exactly what had happened. Yet we also struggled with a growing sense of shared outrage and injustice. Whoever had decided my fate had let the ax fall a few weeks before Christmas, a move that was as ice cold as the frost on the desert outside. Issues of immediate personal concern—How would we pay the mortgage? What about our daughters' education, starting with the ballet lessons they loved so much? Could I find another job with this conspicuous blot on my résumé?—slowly yielded to even more painful questions. As agonizing as it was for Cyndy to broach the subject, it was just as clear that there was no way for her to avoid it. She asked, Was there something I wasn't telling her? Was I being investigated? Had I taken bribes or embezzled funds? And although I understood why she needed to know and had to hear directly from me that her worst fears were unfounded, I can't say that it didn't hurt to have to deny her suspicions. More than anything, I resented having a shadow of mistrust fall across my marriage.

I also knew that the doubts wouldn't stop there. Sooner, rather than later, I would have to deal with the same disconcerting accusations from the media and my staff. Why exactly *had* I been fired? Since I had no way to answer that question, there was also no way to forestall the rumors and the speculation that would rush in to fill the void. Added to that was the fact that I was deeply embarrassed by being forced out of a job to which I had given my best efforts and had pinned my professional aspirations. The first assumption about my ouster that most of my colleagues would naturally make—the same one that *I* would have made, had I heard of such a precipitous dismissal from so powerful a post—would be incompetence or corruption or some combination of the two. My years as a prosecutor had demonstrated over and over how hard it was to disprove a negative. From my vantage point that dire evening, it seemed as if my career in public service could well be over for good. Not only had a door been closed, it had been welded shut.

While Cyndy's and my faith had taught us that setbacks and disappointments could serve a higher purpose and could strengthen resolve, I can't say that we drew much comfort from such reassurances at the time. Neither of us is given to self-pity or fatalism. Nor did we waste time asking God why bad things happen to good people. Instead, what sustained us in those first dark hours, as we emerged from our initial shock and humiliation, was a palpable sense of anger, even rage. This was wrong, and with that indignation came the determination to make it right. I don't think we realized, just then, what that would entail, where it would take us, and how we would get there.

The truth was that as much as we felt that a real injustice had been done, we gave no immediate thought to the character and the quality of the individuals who were behind this totally unexpected blow or even whether it was wise to continue an association, professional or otherwise, with them. Instead, we felt an urgent need to know whether we had any recourse, a way to get back in the good graces of those who, it seemed, held our future in their hands. More than anything, we wanted to find out whether we could turn this around and salvage our comfortable and rewarding lives.

The answer came all too quickly when, over the next few days, I anxiously awaited further word on my dismissal and the reasons behind it. Cyndy and I had decided, for the time being, to keep the news to ourselves, at least until we could get more information and a clearer picture of the circumstances that led to this calamitous turn of events. When Friday morning arrived, I went to work as usual, although I spent most of the day staring out the windows of my tenth floor corner office at the sweeping Southwestern skyline and asking myself the same two questions over and over: What happened? What do I do now? Like most of us, I had heard of the five steps of grieving, starting with denial and running through anger, bargaining, depression, and, finally, acceptance. I went through them all, stopping just short of the last one. I knew that if it was in my power, I had to try to save my job and with it, in all likelihood, my career and my family's future.

When nothing further was forthcoming from Mike Battle's office or, for that matter, from anyone else at the DOJ, I took it upon myself that morning to contact the one person whom I thought just might have the clout and the inclination to intercede on my behalf.

Johnny Sutton, unquestionably the best-connected, most powerful U.S. Attorney appointed by the Bush administration, served the Western District of Texas from his offices in San Antonio. Widely considered to be a favored protégé of the president, whom he commonly refers to as "my dear friend," Sutton worked on Bush's Texas gubernatorial campaign and later served as criminal justice policy director under Alberto Gonzales, then Bush's general counsel. A coordinator for the Bush-Cheney transition team, again reporting to Gonzales, Sutton was subsequently named associate deputy attorney general before being nominated as a U.S. Attorney. In March 2006, Sutton's role as a key player in the Gonzales Justice Department was consolidated when the attorney general named him the chairman of the Advisory Committee of U.S. Attorneys. It was, all in all, a spectacular career trajectory for an attorney who at the time had just turned forty-one.

Shortly before I called to solicit his support, Sutton had garnered headlines for the controversial conviction of two border agents, Ignacio Ramos and Jose Compean, who had been accused of covering up the shooting of an unarmed drug smuggler and whose resultant sentences had exceeded ten years each. It was later alleged that Sutton, all the while insisting that he had no evidence to prosecute the mule, had granted the smuggler immunity in exchange for his testimony, this despite the fact that the man's van had been found carrying more than eight pounds of marijuana. The case became a cause célèbre for Bush administration opponents, thanks largely to the ruckus raised by

Democratic loose cannon Representative Cynthia McKinney of Georgia. Even conservatives like Glenn Beck of CNN railed about Johnny. One Texas radio station went as far as calling Sutton, "Johnny Satan." The Gonzales Justice Department duly circled the wagons for an old Bush ally, and Sutton weathered the fracas, emerging as a staunch regulator of law and order on the wild Southwest border.

If anyone could make my case in the halls of power, it would be Sutton, whom I had met and worked with on various immigration subcommittees and had even accompanied on official trips to Mexico and Colombia. I knew him to be a committed Christian, a loving father, and, like me, a fan of the writings of C. S. Lewis. I had a lot of respect for him and considered him a friend.

As it turned out, I was in no position to appeal to that friendship. "I've got a sense this is a done deal, David," he flatly told me after listening to my story.

"Based on what?" I asked, swallowing hard. Maybe I should have just hung up then. It was clear from the guarded tone of his voice that he wouldn't, or couldn't, help me.

"Look," he said, in the same matter-of-fact manner. "I've been around a while. This is political. If I were you, I'd just go quietly."

I couldn't believe what I was hearing: a U.S. Attorney all but admitting that a colleague was being hung out to dry for reasons that had nothing to do with performance or misconduct. "How do you know?" was all I could ask.

There was long silence on the other end. "I saw your name," he said at last, in a barely audible voice.

It took a minute for the implications to sink in. "Where?" I finally asked. "You mean, there's some sort of list?"

"I can't speak to that," he answered blandly, and I knew, at that moment, that it was useless to continue. When a lawyer gives you that kind of response, choosing his words that carefully, you might as well begin trying to break through a brick wall with your cranium. These were also, as it turned out, the last words I would hear from Sutton.

But I had learned a few things, I realized as I hung up. One was that in the circles I had been traveling in, loyalty was a flexible concept. But more important was the notion that if, as Sutton had hinted, a list actually existed, maybe that meant I wasn't in this alone.

CHAPTER 2

In the Shadow of the Statue of Liberty

Context is everything. It was a truth I had learned through years of experience as an attorney, where the setting, the situation, and the circumstances surrounding a crime can often make all the difference in the final perception of innocence or guilt. And while I was certainly not the first individual to suddenly and precipitously lose his job or even the first whose career went from fast track to train wreck in the blink of an eye, there was, I believe, a unique context that made my fall from grace all the more agonizing and unprecedented.

It's a context that can ultimately be understood only by comparing who I was, personally and professionally, in the moment before I picked up Lois Golden's message, to whom I would become in the moment afterward. Simply put, as I was walking down the broad airport passageway, I was at the high point of my life. I had, by any measure, racked up some extraordinary accomplishments in the last five and a half years as a U.S. Attorney and had every reason to believe that the best was yet to come. I felt sure of myself, confident in the choices I had made, and justifiably proud of my achievements in the administration of justice for the state of New Mexico.

I was forty-eight years old, with a loving wife and four beautiful, vivacious daughters. My world was anchored to faith and family and a fundamental belief that the work I did was righteous and had made a tangible difference for the citizens of my home state. Yet by the time I had fastened my seatbelt and felt the jet roll away from the gate, I was effectively a pariah, brought low by circumstances I didn't then understand and betrayed by those whom I counted as my friends and allies. As the plane soared into the murky December sky, I felt an echoing lurch in the pit of my stomach. In a matter of a few awful minutes, my world had fallen into pieces.

It was a change all the more profound since, only a few hours earlier, I had been savoring the gratification of a job well done. I had come back East, to the Naval Station in Newport, Rhode Island, to teach a course on border and immigration issues for the Defense Institute of International Legal Studies, better known in acronym-happy government circles as DIILS.

It was as a navy reserve captain and a JAG (judge advocate general), or a military attorney, that I had been summoned for duty to teach at DIILS, and I was proud to do my part. I was also proud to be a part of one of the world's greatest armed services branches and felt privileged to belong to the navy's honorable, and honor-bound, tradition. The service had promised me, as a new junior officer back in 1984, that it would "give me responsibility fast," and it immediately lived up to that recruiting slogan, and then some.

America's border crisis was a subject on which I was an acknowledged expert, and with good reason. Since October 2001, when I had begun to serve as the U.S. Attorney for New Mexico, I represented the legal interests of the federal government in a state where 60 percent of all federal prosecutions are directly related to immigration. Along with Arizona and the districts of Southern California and Western and Southern Texas, New Mexico was on the front line in the intractable battle to secure our homeland. As a result, the five Southwest border districts regularly filed an incredible 30 percent of all federal prosecutions. In short, we were doing a lot of heavy lifting for the Justice Department.

As intensive as it might have been, the work I did was also fascinating, challenging, and extremely gratifying. With a staff of 150, of whom 60 were full-time prosecutors, the office I oversaw from spacious quarters in downtown Albuquerque had a vital role to play in America's highest national security priorities. Keeping terrorists from our borders required bold new preemptive strategies and a vigilance that would prevent another attack; the job demanded more creative effort than merely investigating the attack that had already happened. As a result, a whole new level of deliberation and planning went into the task of securing the border, especially one as porous, for all practical purposes, as that between the United States and its neighbor to the south. Suddenly, U.S. Attorneys in every district that adjoined Mexico had a major role to play in the war on terrorism.

Being the U.S. Attorney for the District of New Mexico had put me front and center in a number of arenas, high profile and otherwise, for which I felt uniquely well suited. Indeed, I like to think that the skill set I applied to the obligations I assumed had, in turn, brought me to the attention of my superiors in the Department of Justice. I had, after all, been named chairman of a specially convened committee that advised then attorney general John Ashcroft on border and immigration issues.

In 2001, I was asked to chair the committee by Paul Warner, the only U.S. Attorney who had been invited to stay on from the Clinton administration, and a former navy JAG himself. I was honored to be asked, knowing, as I did, that Warner had a close relationship with veteran U.S. senator Orrin Hatch, who was then the Republican chairman of the Senate Judiciary Committee. This committee oversaw the confirmation of any presidential nominee to the federal courts and the post of U.S. Attorney. It seemed that my name was circulating in high places.

Directly advising the attorney general on such a pivotal issue as borders and immigration was also a distinct honor. The committee I chaired was one of many under the auspices of the U.S.

attorney general; each committee was charged with the in-depth examination of specific and vital issues in order to make direct policy recommendations to the top executive of the Justice Department. The leaders of these committees were, in turn, selected by an oversight group, the Attorney General's Advisory Committee. The AGAC had in the past produced some exemplary leaders, including Jim Comey, who would go on to become deputy attorney general, and Patrick Fitzgerald, who would subsequently be best known for his successful prosecution of Scooter Libby, the one-time chief of staff for Dick Cheney. As I said, I was moving among a very elite group.

In any event, I had already stepped into the big leagues in New Mexico, a state that had an unusually large federal footprint for its size and status. There were, for example, the sprawling government-funded research facilities at Los Alamos, where the first atomic bomb had been developed, and Sandia National Laboratories in Albuquerque, where any number of top-secret projects were underway. Suffice it to say that at a time when the existence of sleeper cells hidden among us seemed only too real, both installations represented tempting terrorist targets, a fact I had kept uppermost in mind during my tenure.

Then there was the fact that New Mexico is also home to twenty-two Native American tribes, which, according to long-established legal precedent, are considered quasi-sovereign nation-states. One exception to this status is when a felony crime is committed on Indian land involving a Native American suspect or victim, in which case the investigation and the prosecution are federal matters. My ability to deal with the cultural sensitivities of the tribal chiefs was a diplomatic skill that I think was immeasurably enhanced by my own racial and ethnic status. My heritage stretches back to the Kuna, an indigenous people of Panama and Colombia and one of the very few tribes that never surrendered to colonial rule. I like to think that those credentials gave me an edge when dealing with often fiercely independent Native American leaders. I also knew that my own family's struggle to ensure tribal sovereignty helped me to more fully appreciate the intense emphasis the North American tribal leaders put on their own autonomy.

Of course, aside from the aspects that were unique to my responsibilities in that time and place, I was also charged with over-seeing the prosecutions that any other federal attorney's office might be engaged in on a routine basis. These included everything from drug importation to bank robberies, to fraud, public corruption, and other white-collar crimes. Part of my purview also took in the enforcement of federal civil statutes, including the Civil Rights Act. Here, too, cooperation was key. A U.S. Attorney has no in-house investigative staff and must depend on the Customs and Border Protection; the FBI; the Secret Service; the Bureau of Alcohol, Tobacco, Firearms, and Explosives; the Drug Enforcement Agency; Immigration and Customs Enforcement; and other federal agen-cies to do the legwork. We generally functioned well together, and as a result, state prosecutors were anxious to pass important cases on to us. They knew, as did the criminals, that federal penalties were, by and large, more stringent. A sentence handed down by a federal court allowed no time off for good behavior: if a crimi-nal was put behind bars for ten years, that's where he would stay for the duration. Making a federal case was the best way to ensure that the truly bad guys would be taken out of circulation for as long as possible.

It was a power over people's lives that I never forgot or never took for granted. I was well aware that the decisions I made might ultimately deprive individuals of their freedom. However much I enjoyed the work I did, I was always alert to the potential for arrogance, abuse, or even simple human error. It was a sobering responsibility.

But it was also undeniably an exhilarating time in my life. My sense of special purpose, of singular suitability, went much deeper than the daily routines of my job. It extended back to that hor-rific morning five years earlier, when two airplanes slammed into a pair of skyscrapers, killing three thousand of my fellow citizens and reawakening a sense of determination and resolve through-out our nation. I'm certainly not alone in my reaction to 9/11, but unlike so many other Americans struggling with their sense of impotence and outrage, I was given the chance to step up and make a difference, to help ensure that such a tragedy would never happen again.

I distinctly remember in mid-October 2001, mere weeks after the World Trade Center towers fell, when I took the oath as U.S. Attorney for the District of New Mexico. At the time, I was reading the Book of Esther in the Old Testament, the story of a woman whose courage and faith saved her people from destruction. The message of this short, masterfully told tale is simple: because of her obedience, Esther was placed at a critical juncture in the history of the Jewish nation. Its significance is summed up in a single question: "And who knows but that you have come to royal position for such a time as this?" I underlined the phrase and, above it, wrote the date, just days after I had been sworn in as U.S. Attorney.

I'm immensely proud of my heritage, which is part German immigrant and part Kuna Indian, a never-conquered tribe from Central America. There's an extraordinary confluence of cultural diversity and Christian commitment that comprise the key elements of my family saga, and like any good life story, it mixes equal parts adventure and inspiration and offers, in the end, an exemplary object lesson in the virtues of faith and hard work and the opportunities afforded in this nation as nowhere else on Earth. It is, simply, an American story, but it begins far from these shores, on the island of Mulatuppu, in an archipelago tucked into the bent elbow of Panama's Caribbean coast. It was there that my father, Claudio, a full-blooded Kuna, was born in 1923, the youngest of twelve children and an affable, outgoing son of the village medicine man. *Kuna* means, literally, "the People."

My grandfather was reputed to be able to look into the future, and I've often wondered whether that was why he took the radical, culturally unprecedented step of allowing his children to receive Western-style educations. With the help of missionaries,

my uncle Lonnie was sent to America, and in 1936, my father
followed.

It's here that the story of my family takes on the epochal turn
that is common in so many American sagas. My father, with a
young nephew in tow, arrived on Ellis Island, where a missionary official was scheduled to meet them. A mistaken date delayed
the rendezvous for two weeks, while the bewildered boys awaited
admittance at the gateway of a new life, in the shadow of the
Statue of Liberty.

Like so many of my fellow Americans, I have made the pilgrim-
age to Ellis Island and have been deeply moved by that echoing and
awe-inspiring place. My father and his nephew may have been no
more than flotsam on a great human tide, yet they were, in the
end, afforded the same opportunity as everyone else staking a
claim to the great American promise. It was a lesson that I frequently related while telling my family history to newly natural-
ized American citizens in federal court ceremonies, in order to
spark in them an appreciation of the great gift they were about
to receive.

In 1949, my father found himself in Norman, Oklahoma, on
the university campus attending a linguistic program hosted by
Wycliffe Bible translators. Since the early thirties, Wycliffe had
been dispatching great waves of missionaries into the field, armed
with ready language skills, and my father was preparing to join
their numbers and return to the Kuna homeland to preach the
gospel in the native tongue of "the People."

Also attending the study group that summer was a book-
ish daughter of a Presbyterian minister from Minnesota, named
Margaret Geiger. At twenty-six, my mother had already racked
up some impressive credentials in the evangelical arena. A graduate of Wheaton College, she had learned the difficult language
of the Masateco, a tribe from the dangerous Oaxaca hinterlands of
southern Mexico, and had lived for four years among them.
Naturally adventuresome and widely read, with an impressive
gift for the teaching and learning of language, Margaret had a
heart for the missionary life.

It is hard to overestimate the singular mix of idealism, fervor, and determination that motivates and drives young missionaries, who take with supreme seriousness the concept of a "calling" in their lives. That calling, in turn, leads them into the most primitive, remote, and often dangerous locales on Earth, where they are faced with the daunting task of discovering, by arduous trial and error, the social and spiritual keys that may or may not unlock among the people a willingness to hear the missionaries' message.

It was also a calling my parents shared when they met, fell in love, and were married two months later. Before the year was out, the intrepid couple had embarked for the Panamanian hinterlands, a trip that, in my father's case, was a paradoxical return to the unknown. His parents had long since died; his brothers and sisters had grown up and married, and the slow and simple subsistence life of hunting and fishing and planting gardens in the mainland jungle was itself a distant memory. Adding to this extraordinary leap of faith was the fact that my parents, as was common with many young missionary couples, hadn't waited to start a family before embarking on their epic adventure. My oldest sister, Lorie, was born in Panama within one year of their arrival.

Establishing themselves on Mulatuppu, a half mile off the mainland, my parents created the first Kuna alphabet with which to begin the work of transcribing the Bible, a translation my mother would use in the school that she and my father went on to build. In the years that followed, they labored steadily in the Kuna vineyard, pastoring a flock and establishing a medical clinic where my father sutured wounds, delivered babies, and pulled hundreds of teeth. At the same time, they built a family that would include a second daughter, Marina, and, in 1958, a son: David Claudio Iglesias, a most unlikely hybrid, and a long way from the country I would come to call my true home.

I spent almost the first seven years of my life on Mulatuppu, a name that in Kuna means "Buzzard Island." We lived in a small concrete house erected by my father with the help of the villagers, on a point overlooking the dazzling turquoise expanse of the Caribbean. We had no electricity, and my earliest memories were lit only by oil lamps. It was as idyllic a childhood as could be imagined: chasing iguanas, hunting blue crabs in the oozy black jungle mud, family picnics after church in the shade of the rain forest canopy. It was the world, whole and complete, as I understood it.

It was also a world that proliferated with a linguistic babble that mixed and mingled Spanish and English and a particular island dialect of Kuna. There always seemed to be at least three ways to describe anything, and it's hardly surprising that at an early age, I developed a stammer that stayed with me most of my childhood. My young mind simply couldn't find the right word it needed, in the right language, and, as often as not, one sentence would contain snatches of all three. This bramble of sound in time developed into a paralyzing fear of public speaking, and only years later, when I was thrust into a courtroom setting as a defense attorney, was I able to overcome my dread.

But although stuttering might suggest a child who didn't exactly know who he was and where he belonged, in point of fact, my parents were determined to nurture in me distinctly American characteristics. The United States of America represented a kind of Promised Land to which we would someday return, and that certainty lent an odd impermanence to life on Mulatuppu. It was as if we were all shipwrecked survivors who awaited a passing ship flying the Stars and Stripes to rescue us. I may not have known a way of life other than that island paradise, but there was never a time when I wasn't aware that our true home was somewhere else.

Much had changed for my parents during those years. In 1964, my uncle Lonnie, who for so long had been the lodestar of their missionary calling, died, and with him, I suspect, something of my parents' early idealism. It was becoming clear that my sisters could not remain simple island girls forever and that I could not fulfill my life's purpose running barefoot down the beach. My parents had to acknowledge that their children deserved more than what this tiny speck of land could ever provide. And so it was, in 1964, that we pulled up stakes and moved back to the

United States, returning to my parents' point of origin, Oklahoma. My father secured a job as the pastor of a mission church at a boarding school for Native American children, while my mother taught Spanish at the local high school.

Huddled on the edge of that flat and featureless land, far from the sultry embrace of Mulatuppu, the town of Newkirk, Oklahoma, was my first introduction to the country I had heard about my whole life. But as jarring a cultural shock as my transplantation might have been, I adjusted with the immediate and enthusiastic elasticity of all children. In fact, I thrived, taking to the expansive abundance of America as if I had been born to it, which, in a sense, I had. I stepped effortlessly into my new role as a full-fledged American youngster. The truest measure of my immediate and complete immersion was my love affair with football, which began in my grade-school Pee Wee League and continued through my college years. I wouldn't be the first one to point out the quintessentially American characteristics of the gridiron, that combination of brute force and meticulous strategy, team spirit and individual heroics, that seems to sum up our national ethos. To me, it was the embodiment of everything I loved best about my true home.

After a six-year stint in Newkirk, my father took another pastoral position for a small congregation in Gallup, New Mexico. From the first moment I laid eyes on the multihued desert vistas and big-domed sky, I knew that no matter where I'd been or where else I might go, New Mexico would always be where I belonged. It was also around that time that I began to take a keen and lively interest in the law. Even at a young age, while still seeking total assimilation, I felt that the law seemed to be what put us all on a level playing field and opened the way for the pursuit of happiness and the possibility of greatness. I had a deep certainty that I would one day become an attorney.

Then, as quickly as I had discovered my American destiny, it was taken away. My parents peremptorily announced that with my sisters married and starting families of their own, I would be returning with them to Panama, this time to an isolated mission outpost in the middle of the isthmus, where they would resume their work among the Kuna. With the move, I was thrust back into a world I neither remembered nor appreciated. I became morosely convinced that my parents had dragged me into this cruel exile as an exquisite form of torture. But what I considered at the time to be the worst year of my life was instead one of the richest and most instructive. I was a student at Balboa High School in the Panama Canal Zone, and my class consisted of an incredibly diverse array of kids, like Santiago Chin, a Panamanian national of Chinese descent who spoke Spanish and English as fluently as he did Mandarin, and Salomon Btesh, an Asian Indian whose family members were prosperous merchants in Panama City. There were Jamaicans and others hailing from the West Indies, Puerto Ricans, and a rich mix of Central Americans. It was at school that I learned firsthand how diversity both defines and enhances a community, a lesson I have carried with me ever since.

At the same time, the year I spent in Panama as a teenager forged in me an awareness of my own unique Hispanic-Latino identity. I knew, from occasional visits to my mother's family, that I was certainly *not* the same as the pale folks who called themselves my aunts and uncles. Instead, the part of me that was Kuna began to assert itself, and I found myself becoming increasingly interested in the history, the culture, and the traditions, not only of my people, but also of South and Central America as a whole. Which is not to say that I wasn't overjoyed when my father took another job back in the States, this time in Santa Fe, as the chaplain of a Baptist mission church. I was sixteen years old when we left Panama, and I was desperate to get back to what I considered my "real" life in America. If anyone had asked me what tribe I belonged to, I wouldn't have said Kuna. I was purely and simply a "jock." I excelled at football during my senior year in high school and lived the role of local sports hero to the hilt. My favorite sobriquet was being called a "tough kid" by an opposing team's coach.

It was, fittingly enough, football that provided the next important opportunity for me. As a tailback in high school, I had attracted the attention of athletic departments at several colleges. Stanford was my first choice, but I didn't make the cut due to my poor math skills. It was a bitter disappointment, which was alleviated by an offer from Wheaton College.

I had, of course, heard about Wheaton my whole life because it was my mother's alma mater. Frankly, I had my doubts that it was the college for me. I had visions of an arch-fundamentalist campus with lots of rules and little joy. What I discovered instead was a school that put a strong emphasis on equipping its students to make a reasoned defense of their faith. Wheaton encouraged academic excellence and an enlightened Christianity that didn't shy away from engaging with the world. That, too, was a lesson I would carry with me the rest of my life.

I graduated in 1980, with a degree in history and no particular notion of what to do next except go to law school. I briefly considered becoming a history teacher until I got a look at the pay scale. While I was waiting to find out what else the world had to offer, I hung around the school and its environs, becoming in Wheaton's parlance a "cling-on," clinging to my fading college life. I did, however, make the best friends of my life and counted the four years there to be the greatest of my life as a single man.

After a year of cooling my heels, I revived my old ambition to become an attorney and enrolled in the law school of the University of New Mexico. I moved back in with my parents and returned to the life of a student. Although I was serious about my studies, I wouldn't really say that I had buckled down to the business of becoming an adult. I was, in every important sense, still waiting to grow up, to find what would stir my passions, which, until then, had lain dormant and untapped.

In early 1984, my last year of law school, I found myself in Acapulco for spring break with three of my fellow students. As we made the regular rounds in that raucous resort town, we met a group of sailors on liberty from the USS *New Orleans* (LPH-11), an amphibious assault ship that had recently pulled into port. They were confident, easygoing guys, with a palpable sense of camaraderie that carried beyond their crisp uniforms and conveyed a kind of self-confidence that, for the first time, I realized I was entirely lacking.

They asked us whether we wanted to take a tour of the huge helicopter carrier, which had served active duty in Vietnam. This was another impressive, even transforming, experience. I had a chance to talk to the sailors and the officers about their life at sea and in the service of their country, and, as a result, something awoke in me that afternoon. It was a sense of purpose or, rather, a sense of the lack of purpose that had defined my life up to that moment. I realized, in a way that went beyond words, that I was adrift, and that, for all of my education and vague plans of a career in law, I had no idea where I was going or how to get there. I needed, in short, what those sailors had. Four months later, I walked into a navy recruiting office in downtown Albuquerque.

There's an old recruiting slogan that says the navy is more than a job, it's an adventure. For me, it was something else entirely. As my first real experience with good order and discipline, I received a life lesson in honor, courage, and commitment, the navy's core values, along with the challenge of building those qualities into my personal and professional life. I took to it immediately and took away from it everything the service had to offer.

I had passed the bar exam in the summer of 1984, still with only a vague idea of my future ambitions. I knew I didn't want to work for a big law firm, doing what amounted to well-paid grunt work. At age twenty-six, I was still living at home, sponging off my parents, staying up late watching MTV, and taking a few clerking jobs for pocket money.

The navy changed all that. I was accepted at the Naval Justice School in Newport, Rhode Island, where, during my nine weeks of training to become a judge advocate general—the same as the JAGs of TV fame—it was made clear to me that I would be given as much responsibility as I could handle. Far from being a glorified gofer carrying some attorney's briefcase, I was quickly afforded the opportunity to actually try cases, despite my lack of experience and my paralyzing fear of public speaking. The realization quickly dawned on me that if I didn't do a good job, the guilty might go free and the innocent might be punished.

In July 1985, I was ordered to the USS *McInerney* (FFG-8) as part of the "Lawyer at Sea Program," which was designed to give JAGs a taste of real navy life. It was there, while the frigate was on patrol in the Caribbean, that I tried my first case, that of a trouble-making nineteen-year-old seaman who had already been before captain's mast twice and was about to be drummed out of the service for drunken escapades in Spain and Pakistan. I lost the case but knew immediately that I had found my calling. Interviewing witnesses and building my case while standing on the ship's fantail beneath a spectacular tropical sunset was like having the best of both worlds.

Following my apprenticeship on the high seas, I was stationed at the Navy Yard in Washington, D.C., where my primary duty was to represent sailors and marines who had medical issues with Bethesda Naval Hospital. Over the course of the next year, I handled several hundred such disability hearings before being transferred to more general criminal and court-martial work. One of my formative courtroom experiences during this time involved a corpsman charged with sleeping on duty. On cross-examination, I was able to get the primary prosecution witness to admit that she had no way of knowing for certain whether the sailor was actually asleep or just "resting his eyes." He was acquitted, and I remember thinking at the time, This stuff really works. I had created a reasonable doubt, the jury had given due consideration, and the system had functioned as advertised. It was a heady sense of power—and responsibility.

But by far the most notable legal contest I was involved in during those early days of my career occurred in the summer of 1986. I was sent to Guantanamo Naval Base in Cuba to assist in the defense of ten marines who had been accused in the assault of a private first class named Willy Alvarado, in a hazing incident gone terribly wrong. Alvarado, who was considered by his company to be a malingerer and a whiner, nearly suffocated when, after being blindfolded, a sock was stuffed and duct taped into his mouth. The defendants maintained that they were following the orders of a first lieutenant in carrying out what was known in Gitmo leatherneck lingo as a Code Red to teach the intractable marine a lesson he'd never forget.

It was a tough case to make. The military clearly establishes that no one is obliged to carry out an obviously illegal order, a nuance that was apparently lost on these nineteen-year-olds who believed that they were upholding the honor of the corps. They were offered a deal that involved an other-than-honorable discharge, which seven of the ten accepted. Of the remaining three, one was my client, a fresh-faced kid named John Palermo whose only role in the incident had been to turn the barrack lights off and on. In the end, I was able to get Palermo off on a simple count of assault and without a bad-conduct discharge, which, under the highly inflammatory circumstances, felt like an unqualified victory. My two JAG colleagues, Chris Johnson and Don Marcari achieved similar good results for their clients in separate trials.

If the details of the case sound familiar, it's hardly surprising. Among my ten fellow JAGs, each representing one of the accused, was Lieutenant Debbie Sorkin, the sister of writer Aaron Sorkin, who would subsequently base his hit play and the blockbuster 1992 film *A Few Good Men* on the ensuing trial. I always found it slightly ironic that the most famous line of the production, Jack Nicholson's savage "You can't handle the truth!" was never actually uttered in the musty Gitmo courtroom. The Tom Cruise role of LTJG Dan Kaffee was based on a composite of the three of us JAGs assigned to the case. This was the biggest case of my early career, and it helped me in ways that I could not have fathomed as a junior officer.

The case of *A Few Good Men* served as a bookend of sorts to my legal career in the navy. Before being discharged in October 1988, I also represented an infamous rogue operative named Commander Dick Marcinko, who had been accused of kidnapping and water-boarding a security officer in a terrorist training exercise that—typically for this legendary U.S. Navy SEAL—

had gotten way out of hand. Marcinko was the most flamboyant character I'd met in the service, a much-decorated Vietnam veteran who had been involved in the aborted attempt to free the captives in the Iran Hostage Crisis in 1979 and later headed the clandestine Red Cell team, which was charged with testing the navy's antiterrorist capabilities. It was during one of these Red Cell operations that Marcinko stepped over the legal line, although his attitude toward the navy's attempt to rein him in can best be illustrated by his drunken appearance at the Admiral's mast, where I was scheduled to defend him. Marcinko later went on to capitalize on his swashbuckling adventures with a series of best-selling novels and memoirs.

Dick Marcinko and *A Few Good Men* had been highlights in a hugely satisfying stint in the navy, but when the time came for me to either reenlist or leave, the decision, however painful, was foregone. A month after I had returned from Cuba, I found myself in need of a haircut and, looking for something a little more stylish than what the Navy Yard barbers could typically provide, I headed to a small salon called Unicorn down the block from my apartment in Old Town, Alexandria, Virginia. It was there that I met Cyndy Sears, who was working cutting hair while she attended college. She was extremely attractive, extremely personable, and, I assumed, extremely unavailable. It turned out that I was right about the first two and wrong about the last. We courted over the next eighteen months, and on October 1, 1988, within weeks of my being discharged from active duty, we were married.

In retrospect, meeting, falling in love, and committing my life to Cyndy was an inevitable next step in a direction I didn't really know I was heading until it was upon me. That I wanted to start a family, to establish stability and consistency for the future, were vague ideas until she and I began to articulate them together. Along with that new understanding came the realization that of all the places I most wanted to be, New Mexico was at the top of the list. I also came to the conclusion, based on my own rather rootless upbringing, that I wanted my children to have the security of a permanent home and not be raised in an open-ended series of military installations around the world. Yet I knew that to make the next move up as a naval officer, I would have to do at least two tours of active duty at sea, which meant long months of absence from my family-to-be.

The decision was no less painful for being obvious. I loved the navy, the camaraderie, the sense of worldwide mission, all that being in the service had given to me and what I had been privileged to give back. It's hard to speak about my time as a naval officer without using clichés, but the truth is, the navy had taught me to grow up, had shown me the world, and had given me the confidence I needed to make the next important step in my life.

By the end of that momentous year, my new bride and I had moved to Santa Fe, where I'd landed a job in the Special Prosecutions Unit of the State Attorney General's Office. I handled primarily complex white-collar prosecutions such as securities fraud. It was the beginning of a long series of positions that I would hold in law enforcement over the next decade, some boosting me up the career ladder, others more or less lateral moves.

After I spent two years with the state attorney general, and motivated by the imminent arrival of our first daughter, Claudia, who was named after my father, Cyndy and I relocated to Albuquerque. There, I took a better-paying post as a legal representative for the city's police force in the City Attorney's Office. Even more than I'd enjoyed chasing after embezzlers and swindlers, I got a lot of satisfaction from standing up for cops, especially considering the charged tenor of the times. It was immediately after the Rodney King beating in Los Angeles, when it seemed as if everyone was suing the police on the flimsiest of pretenses. During my nearly four years at the job, in which I went on ride-alongs and was present at DWI checkpoints and other routine police activities, I gained a genuine appreciation for what law enforcement really does and what the police put up with from the citizens they serve. My appreciation was not immediately reciprocated, because the reputation of the City Attorney's Office among rank-and-file cops was one of settling cases regardless of their merit. I took it as a matter of principle that these officers deserved a good defense, especially considering that their jobs and reputations were often on the line. In one eighteen-month period during my tenure, I tried eleven separate cases, which I think did a lot to earn the trust of the dedicated men and women on the force.

But it was also true that in the thick of my work, both as a state prosecutor and as a city attorney, I often looked back with real longing to my time in the navy, where concepts of truthfulness and sacrifice and personal responsibility seemed to be taken more seriously than they were in civilian life. Fortunately, I still had a conduit to the military as a reserve officer in the JAG corps and was sent on regular rotation to Pearl Harbor for a variety of legal assignments. This helped to remind me of the wide horizons I had once enjoyed.

The truth is, I wasn't purposely navigating toward much on my own horizon at that time. My work, both in Santa Fe and in Albuquerque, had brought with it a share of rewards: justice was being done, at least some of the time, and I was playing a part in obtaining that result. I had learned the ins and outs of trying civil cases and had good instincts for handling both the political and the professional aspects of my career. Moreover, I was able to adequately provide for my quickly expanding family, which would soon include two more daughters.

I could easily see myself settling in as a career state prosecutor or a city attorney, but I'm not sure either position afforded me the same kind of deep satisfaction I had felt standing on the fantail of the USS *McInerney*, preparing my first case beneath a Caribbean sunset. In the spring of 1993, I was thirty-five years old. I had done well, if not spectacularly well, for myself, but it was hard to shake the feeling that I still hadn't begun to realize my true potential. I considered myself something of a late bloomer, and looking back on the years I had spent trying to find myself, I couldn't help but wonder whether I hadn't been wasting my time instead. For all the busy endeavors that occupied my days, I felt as if I was treading water. More than anything, I was waiting for something to happen.

This "something" happened in the fall of that year, when my boss, the Albuquerque city attorney David Campbell, took me aside one afternoon and suggested that I might want to look into applying for a White House Fellowship. The idea had been suggested to him by his uncle, an editor at *Native Peoples* magazine, for whom I had, as a whim, written music and film reviews and whom the fellowship's administrator had contacted in a search for potential applicants. He'd thought of me and passed the word on to David.

I knew about the fellowship and once had even picked up an application while still in the navy. After one look at the requirements, I had thrown it away. At that point, I just didn't have what it took.

Established by President Lyndon Johnson in 1964, the program was designed to identify future national leaders and to provide them with "firsthand, high-level experience with the workings of the federal government and to increase their sense of participation in national affairs." From its inception, the program expected its fellows to "repay that privilege by continuing to work as private citizens on their public agendas." Among those who had been afforded the privilege were Reagan's national security adviser Robert McFarlane; Bush administration secretary of state Colin Powell; General Wesley Clark; Kansas senator Sam Brownback; CNN medical correspondent Dr. Sanjay Gupta; Garrey Caruthers, the governor of New Mexico; and Paul Gigot, the editor of the *Wall Street Journal*.

The list goes on, and it was, by any measure, rarified company. But that didn't stop me, or many others, from giving it a try. The year I applied, there were more than 1,250 applicants for seventeen positions. The selection process included extensive written essays on subjects ranging from life goals to policy recommendations for the president, all in five hundred words or less, although I wrote what amounted to tens of thousands of words in what must have been the fifty drafts I composed for each topic. During the initial round of vetting, which reduced the applicants to about 130, we were each required to deliver an impromptu speech on a topic drawn from a hat, with mine being "The Greatest Lesson of Your Childhood." After a moment's reflection, I recounted an episode when, as a young boy in Panama, I had taken a notion to blow as hard as I could in my napping dog Frisky's ear. He promptly took a chunk out of me, the lesson being, of course, to let sleeping dogs lie. It's advice that some people might have wished I'd followed more closely in light of subsequent events.

The final interviews of about thirty applicants were held in Annapolis, Maryland, and the diverse panel of judges included athlete Edwin Moses, actress Mary Steenburgen, General Wes Clark, and chief justice of the Navajo Nation Robert Yazzie. It was obvious from the range of people who would make the final decision that being a White House Fellow was about more than an applicant's transcripts and résumé. Whatever it was that set the candidates apart, I apparently had it. In late 1994, I packed up my family and our belongings in a moving truck and made the cross-country trek to the nation's capital; although my new job would pay $65,000 for its one-year duration, moving expenses were not included.

Much like the navy, my tenure as a White House Fellow was a defining experience, not to mention a hefty dose of major league cred. All of my mercurial notions of who I was and what I would do with myself were upgraded in a single stroke. I had been fast-tracked, and my main task moving forward was to try to stay ahead of my rocketing career curve. It was one of the most exciting and gratifying opportunities that any American could be afforded, and I felt exhilarated to be considered in the company of gifted individuals who all shared a common goal: to make our country a better place. I was a long way from the sleepy shores of Mulatuppu and a lot closer to the bright dawn of my future.

My assignment was to serve as a special assistant to the secretary of transportation, Federico Pena, and, just as in the navy, I got a lot of responsibility right away. Along with chairing various departmental meetings, writing speeches, and helping to develop policy, I was also privileged to attend weekly luncheons that were convened especially for the fellows, where such special guests as Bob Woodward, Colin Powell, Tom Brokaw, and Janet Reno regularly made appearances. I traveled with the secretary, who made a point of including me in many high-level meetings. As part of the program, my class was allowed to decide among ourselves which region of the world we would most like to visit as representatives of the U.S. government. We chose East Asia and visited China, Hong Kong, Mongolia, and South Korea as a delegation afforded full VIP treatment. It was a heady experience and one that I think we all could have gotten accustomed to.

Then, as quickly as it had begun, it was over. My fellowship concluded, I returned with my family to Santa Fe, where, in 1995, I became chief counsel with the Risk Management Division of the state government, defending state agencies and employees who were being sued for reasons that ranged from serious to simply silly. Our fourth daughter was born in 1996, which was a quick and precipitous return to the real world and all of the routine that this entailed.

Three years later, in 1998, a job opening finally appeared when the office of New Mexico state attorney general was vacated. My experience as a White House Fellow had taught me that I had at least some of the same qualifications as the political leaders I had encountered in Washington, including being an attorney and having a military background, not to mention the advantage of the White House Fellowship itself.

The decision to throw my hat into the ring for New Mexico state attorney general was a reflection of my newly minted sense of self-confidence. I'm not, by nature, risk adverse, and like Babe Ruth at bat, I had the expectation of either striking out or hitting a home run. I'd never know which would happen unless I stepped up to the plate. My decision to run as a Republican was also in keeping with my personal convictions. Although I had registered as an Independent in 1976, I switched to the GOP in 1989 primarily because of its stand on the so-called values issues, particularly its pro-life position. I had since come to consider the

Republican platform a relatively accurate reflection of my own convictions, although I was less than totally convinced by its free-market, government-is-bad rhetoric. I had been in the trenches of law enforcement long enough to know that America had its share of disenfranchised citizens who needed a helping hand from the government and protection from unfettered capitalism. Yet at the same time, in an era when the best hope for a return to biblical values seemed to lie in coordinated political action, it was clearly the Republicans who offered a way forward.

I had met with then New Mexico Republican Party state chairman John Dendahl over lunch to discuss the possibility of taking a run at the attorney general's office, and although he was encouraging, we both knew it was a long shot. With one exception, no Republican attorney general had won election in the state since 1928. But with a promise of help from the party, I decided to go for it and launched an aggressive campaign for the open seat. I announced my candidacy in January of that midterm election year. Unopposed, I gained the nomination six months later.

State Republican assistance came in the form of campaign staffers, including a full-time manager, along with a phone list of potential contributors. The GOP's stake in my future was clear from the beginning: with a rapidly growing Latino and Hispanic population nationwide, the party had a clear demographic mandate to diversify. In a state in which Spanish speakers and other non-Anglos had become a majority, my appeal was as evident as the color of my skin. My run for elected office was a way for Republicans to test their popularity with a new and hugely influential constituency that was just beginning to flex its political muscle.

I took to politicking with a flair, crisscrossing the state with a stump speech that stressed my crime-fighting credentials, but the chore of fund-raising was, for me, nothing short of torture. There was simply no easy way to make one call after another to ask for money, and I hated the hat-in-hand aspect that inevitably carried with it an implied sense of future obligation. But I swallowed hard and did my job and, in the end, amassed over $300,000, three-quarters of what my opponent Patsy Madrid had collected in an overwhelmingly Democratic state. At that time, it was a record for a Republican attorney general candidate, and it enabled us to have a high profile on television, with a number of spots.

As the campaign progressed, I could feel the momentum gathering to support me. I had a real sense of connecting with the electorate and, even more important, of speaking about issues that truly mattered to them—safety, security, and freedom from fear. My platform included a proposal to form a Death Penalty Task Force for the district attorney's office because I knew how capital cases, with their automatic and enormously expensive appeal processes, could put an intolerable strain on the prosecutorial resources. But aside from such technical policy considerations, it was the opportunity to forge personal connections with ordinary citizens on the campaign trail that made all the difference to me. There is no other way to put it except to say that running for political office felt right to me. I'll never forget a particularly bumpy ride I took in a single-engine Cessna to some remote corner of the state. "This plane won't go down," I told myself with complete confidence. "God has other plans for me."

They were not, however, the plans I had in mind. Although, in nine months of intensive campaigns, I shrank the gap between me and my opponent from 20 percentage points to 2, in the end, my best efforts fell short by an agonizingly close margin of 2 percentage points. The fact that I had succeeded in racking up a hefty crossover count of normally Democratic Latino and Native American voters was cold comfort. By any personal estimation, the election was, to use the common parlance, a heartbreaker, a painful lesson in the old Spanish saying that "*El hombre propone, pero Dios dispone*" (Man proposes and God disposes). Late on that November evening in 1998, as the final tally rolled in, I definitely felt as if God had indeed disposed—of my hopes and dreams.

In the aftermath of my failed bid for state attorney general, having cashed out my savings and retirement for living expenses while I campaigned, I had no choice but to look for another job.

I landed a post as general counsel for the New Mexico Taxation and Revenue Department. Like Moses looking across the Jordan River to the Promised Land, I'd had a tantalizing taste of what could be and had no desire to step backward into the confines of a bureaucracy. After leaving Taxation and Revenue, I worked in the private sector for the first time, where I had the honor of working for the person I considered to be the best all-around lawyer, civil and criminal, I knew—Jerry Walz.

As much as the state Republican Party had thrown its support behind my campaign, I knew that it was not about to give me another shot without a proactive display of loyalty on my part. Pulling my tattered ego together, I accordingly threw myself into the 2000 presidential election, becoming a member in good standing of Lawyers for Bush and recording a number of Spanish-language radio interviews for the campaign. In the back of my mind was the possibility that if my efforts brought me to the attention of the right people, I might have a shot at an appointment in the new administration. After all, I had a good political reputation in state GOP circles. I was presentable and had shown myself to be a team player. Then there was, of course, the ethnic factor, a natural advantage in the rapidly shifting electoral dynamics of the Southwest.

But my enthusiasm and hard work for the Republican slate were not simply opportunistic. I was genuinely excited about the prospect of a Bush presidency. I knew that he was a professing Christian, a politician who understood the border issues that were so vital to my state, and a man whose own family had Hispanic members. I had had the opportunity to meet him briefly during a campaign trip through Albuquerque and was as much impressed by his sincerity as I was by his ability to speak passable kitchen Spanish. I was, simply put, a true believer.

Of course, in the aftermath of the 2000 election, true believers were a dime a dozen on both sides of the party divide. If the resulting high drama of the Florida recount and the standoff at the Supreme Court proved anything, it was that the country was

deeply and bitterly divided. Political considerations notwithstanding, as an American who owed so much to his country, I wanted
to be able to do something to heal that breach, to lend my experience and expertise to reasserting the rule of law that had seemed,
in those parlous days and weeks, to have been deeply shaken.
I had a family to feed. That much was certain. But I also had a
nation to serve, and it was that deeply held conviction that, in the
end, prompted me in December 2000 to log onto the USGOV
.org Web site and download the application form to become a
U.S. Attorney.

CHAPTER 3

The Pleasure of the President

A s the scandal that began on December 7, 2006, continued to metastasize in the months that followed, it became clear to me, from media interviews and conversations with concerned citizens, that the role of the U.S. Attorney is not generally well understood. There were some people, in fact, who had barely heard of the office, or they lumped it into a vague legal concept under the general heading of "the Feds" or "the attorneys." It's usually a surprise to them to learn that the post of U.S. Attorney is one of the oldest in the history of America's justice system and one of the most powerful, with a built-in potential to move an ambitious attorney quickly up the career ladder.

But the post is far more than a public service stepping-stone. "The U.S. Attorneys are not only the field representatives of the Department of Justice," wrote James Eisenstein in *Counsel for the United States*, his pioneering study of the office of U.S. Attorney, "they are the sole instruments through which the federal laws are enforced. . . . The effectiveness of their work materially influences the degree of respect and compliance which the citizenry accords the nation's laws."

Those laws, in turn, protect the citizenry from a wide range of crimes and criminal enterprises, and it is largely the decision of U.S. Attorneys as to which particular cases will be brought to trial. "If no one investigates stock fraud, pollution violations, consumer fraud, or corporate tax evasion," Eisenstein pointed out, "few if any of these cases will be prosecuted. . . . If U.S. Attorneys refuse to prosecute certain types of cases, investigative agencies, such as the FBI, Secret Service, Postal Inspection Service and other federal agencies, will devote little energy to investigating them."

Being a U.S. Attorney is, in short, an enormous responsibility that has a direct effect on the way people live in a society of laws. "'You can't prosecute every violation of the law that is brought to you,'" Eisenstein quoted a U.S. Attorney as explaining. "There are a lot of cheap prosecutions available which can shoot your statistics sky high, but would have no significant impact on things."

Having a significant impact on things is what the job is all about and, naturally, that impact varies from region to region and district to district. In New Mexico, for example, as in other states along our southern border, there was no more important mandate for a U.S. Attorney than to enforce America's immigration laws. I can't think of a better example of what I did while in the office than my work in securing the border. But it extended far beyond simply interdicting and prosecuting illegal aliens. A major aspect of my duties included creating and implementing a coordinated effort to stop the unchecked flow of people across the border. It's a good example of the de facto policy-making powers of a U.S. Attorney.

State prosecutors had no jurisdiction to prosecute illegal immigrants for immigration crimes and had to resort to common-law crimes such as theft, assault, and any other applicable statute on state books. At the federal level, we were primarily targeting a criminal element whose drug and gang connections regularly brought them back and forth across the border. But it wasn't the caliber of the criminal I was charged with prosecuting that made my job so significant. It was the fact that after 9/11, border issues had taken on an entirely new dimension.

What had previously been considered largely a matter for law enforcement had suddenly become a national security issue. We needed to know who was in our country and why. Was an illegal alien there simply to work and send money home, as were the vast majority who were driven north by economic necessity? Or had they violated our borders for a more ominous reason, one that had been emphatically underscored by the catastrophic terrorist attack of 9/11?

As part of my responsibilities as a U.S. Attorney, I made it my business to find out what the reality was on the ground. A couple of days before I got the fateful call on December 7, I had, for example, visited a National Guard Forward Operating Base or "FOB" just south of Deming, New Mexico. The compound was part of a continuing presence of more than six thousand National Guard soldiers stationed in the state for a two-year stint by direct order of President George W. Bush in the summer of 2006. Dubbed "Operation Jump Start," their mission was to bolster the efforts of the Border Patrol to regain control of the no-man's land that stretched across the southern flank of the nation. The deployment had wide support from an American public that was increasingly alarmed by the floodtide of illegal immigrants pouring into the country, and, just as predictably, the Guard's presence provoked the ire of Mexican government officials, who raised the specter of a heavily militarized zone between the two nations.

The FOB itself was a few barracks, dining halls, and offices set in a fenced-in perimeter the size of a football field. Equipped with an array of state-of-the-art surveillance equipment, the Guard's sole duty was to scan the Chihuahuan desert that ran south to the border a few short miles away and report any activity to the Border Patrol. No shooting, no interdiction, no prisoners or patrols: it was clear that the Guard was there solely in a support capacity. I had taught many DIILS students about the tragic 1996 shooting of a seventeen-year-old goat herder near Redford, Texas, by a Marine Corps sniper team sent to assist the Border Patrol. It was reassuring to see the military had learned from this terrible mistake.

But it wasn't quite as simple as it might have appeared to the untrained eye. The presence of the two distinct forces—the Border Patrol and the National Guard—in close proximity to each other was complicated by the overlapping and sometimes contradictory levels of command and control that invariably occur when the military and law enforcement combine for a common objective. Helping to sort out the multiple layers of authority was another aspect of my job, which was unprecedented in its scope in the years immediately following 9/11, when questions of cooperation among all branches of government had become an urgent priority.

It was here that my own military training came into play. Having served in the navy as a JAG, I had gained as firm a grip on military law as on civilian practice, and this proved to be invaluable in bringing good order and a clear chain of command to the joint efforts of the Border Patrol and the National Guard. It was just one example of the kind of extracurricular role that a U.S. Attorney could often find himself or herself called on to fulfill.

A coveted reward for party loyalty and a proving ground for up-and-coming leaders, the job of U.S. Attorney is part of the spoils system that has been a fixture of the American political landscape since the founding of this country. And it was not long after that founding, in 1789, when the federal system itself was established, that the position was first created by a congressional act. It mandated a "person learned in the law to act as attorney for the United States . . . whose duty it shall be to prosecute in each district all delinquents for crimes and offenses cognizable under the authority of the United States and all civil actions in which the United States shall be concerned."

Each U.S. Attorney oversees a district that often consists of an entire state, with such exceptions as California, Texas, and New York, where size and population require division into separate districts—ninety-three in all, including outposts as far-flung as the Mariana Islands. According to the U.S. Attorneys' Mission Statement, each U.S. Attorney "exercises wide discretion in the use of his/her resources . . . [and is] delegated full authority and control in the areas of personnel management, financial management and procurement."

U.S. Attorneys are, in other words, fully invested in their turf and are given the complete confidence and authority of the U.S. government, with all the gravitas that conveys. As I said earlier, I took my job as a U.S. Attorney very seriously, and there wasn't a day that passed when I didn't feel the weight of the responsibilities with which I had been entrusted. That entailed the assumption that I would, under all circumstances, maintain rigorous impartiality. It came with the job and went without saying.

Or did it? "Because U.S. Attorneys must enforce the civil and criminal sanctions that accompany many federal programs," wrote Eisenstein, a professor of political science at Penn State University, "their position provides an excellent vantage point to observe the quality of administration and the impact of these programs." But it doesn't stop there. "In their capacity as legal counsel," Eisenstein continued, "Attorneys sometimes inject themselves into the policy making process . . . to shape the decisions rendered." Simply put, the nature of the job itself carried with it a distinct political dimension, worlds away from the clean and conflict-free divisions that Americans might imagine.

Although there is no question that being a U.S. Attorney confers enormous power and prestige, at its core, a seeming contradiction remains, an inducement to divided loyalties that requires a precarious balance to maintain integrity while doing the job credibly. It's true despite the fact that there has always existed, at least in theory, a sturdy and well-buttressed firewall between the executive and other branches of government. Complete independence is the first requirement for any meaningful post within the Department of Justice, and the history of the relationship between a president and his attorney general is one fraught with examples that test the strength of that independence.

Presumptions of objectivity and disinterest are, it would seem, in stark contrast to the political aspects that are inherent in obtaining the post of U.S. Attorney, and therein lies a curious wrinkle in the founding fathers' quest for equally weighted branches of government. It's a paradox posed by the establishing statute for U.S. Attorneys itself, which states, in the three simple clauses of U.S. Code 28, Section 546, that the president "shall appoint, with the advice and consent of the Senate, a United States Attorney for each judicial district." The term was set at four years, underlining the expectation that U.S. Attorneys would likely come and go with each succeeding administration. This purposeful political link is underscored by the statute's final clause, which peremptorily declares that "each United States Attorney is subject to removal by the President." It is a proviso best summed up with the famous phrase "serving at the pleasure of the President." And therein lies the ambiguity. Detachment and disinterest are ostensible qualifications going in, but it can be challenging to detach yourself from, and maintain disinterest in, the priorities of the party and the politicians who have put you there to begin with. At the same time, U.S. Attorneys were each charged with recognizing a distinct ethical line over which we would not cross for the sake of political expediency: our own or that of anyone else. It wasn't always easy.

Presidential pleasure, of course, has varied with each chief executive and the tenor of his term in office. There have been numerous examples of U.S. Attorneys serving effectively through many administrations, both Republican and Democratic. At the same time, there is just as much precedent for mass firings when a new broom comes in for a clean sweep. The most recent example was at the beginning of the Clinton administration when, under Attorney General Janet Reno, every U.S. Attorney who was left over from the George H. W. Bush's administration was given his or her walking papers, en masse. This was, of course, by and large true for all political appointees in most other federal departments.

One practice, however, has remained relatively constant throughout the history of the job. Once at a post, a U.S. Attorney usually remains for the duration of the administration under which he or she serves. Of course, numerous U.S. Attorneys have themselves resigned before their tenure was up, many of them to take high-paying positions in the private sector or federal judgeships or to eventually seek political office. Despite the luster that this job adds to a person's résumé, finding and keeping qualified personnel is difficult, as it is at most levels of government service.

Yet to a remarkable degree, U.S. Attorneys, once appointed, remain on the job for as long as they can, a fact that reflects the extraordinary power and influence invested in the position. And, of course, any U.S. Attorney lucky enough to be appointed by a two-term president can feel relatively confident, absent some malfeasance, of keeping the job for eight full years. This built-in assumption is helpful for appointees when it comes time to plan a career shift. Reagan was the only president in modern times to break with this precedent, a quarter century ago, when he fired two U.S. Attorneys in the middle of his first term for improper conduct. One of them was J. William Pedro from the Northern District of Ohio, who was subsequently convicted for revealing information about an indictment. It was a cautionary tale that would sound loudly as my own saga continued to unfold.

The application for U.S. Attorney that I printed off the federal government's Web site in December 2000 called for an attorney with at least three years' experience, "a quick analytical ability, good judgment and excellent communication and courtroom skills." A questionnaire asked me to detail, in exact percentages, my trial history, including the number of cases I'd tried for violent crimes, employment discrimination, property crimes, and numerous other categories on both the federal and the state level. I was asked how many briefs I'd filed in appellate court, how many depositions I'd taken, and whether I'd ever presented a matter to a grand jury. Under a section headed "Ethics and Professionalism," my interlocutors wanted to know whether I'd had a bar complaint filed against me or had my conduct referred to the DOJ's Office of Professional Responsibility. There was, the application cover letter stated, a "positive factor" in considering a veteran's preference eligibility, which accorded well with my navy active duty and my continued service in the reserves.

As in my campaign, I was the unquestioned beneficiary of shifting political ground, both nationwide and in New Mexico, where an increasingly enfranchised Latino population was making known its own commitment to family values and its distinctive American identity. The state's Hispanics have traditionally been part of the elite, in some cases stretching back to the rule of the Spanish, but there has also been a surge of fresh energy and activism among a new generation of Latino professionals. Among them, the old-time appeal of the Democratic Party for a disadvantaged minority was fading. There was change in the wind, as my own near miss in the attorney general's race two years earlier had proved.

I put my best foot forward in applying for the U.S. Attorney's job, knowing that all of these elements would give me an edge. Yet no matter how extensive my résumé or how bright my prospects, I also knew that without a high-profile recommendation backing up my bid, none of it much mattered. I needed references, and the single most important name on that list would be Pietro Vichi "Pete" Domenici.

Dubbed "St. Pete" by an irreverent Albuquerque reporter, Senator Domenici first took office in 1973 and went on to serve an unprecedented six terms. He became the longest-seated senator in the state's history. Arguably the most influential politician in New Mexico, he was unquestionably the most powerful Republican in a state that had had a well-entrenched Democratic constituency since the Depression. It was a feat he had accomplished with the federal dollars he assiduously funneled to his constituents, bringing a raft of lucrative government projects to New Mexico. Most of them were worthwhile job-generators, but others were pure pork.

It was hardly surprising that Domenici was revered: he had perfectly positioned himself for delivering government largesse to a state that was experiencing rapid development and growth.

A fierce proponent of nuclear power, he was adept at directing resources to the advanced research labs at the New Mexico facilities in Los Alamos and Sandia. Aside from the active development of nuclear technology, for peaceful means and otherwise, Sandia in particular had benefited greatly from Domenici's influence. The facility became a hothouse of advanced science, specializing in everything from synthetic aperture radar to nuclear waste transport, to the latest breakthroughs in chip technology.

As a ranking member on Senate appropriations and budget committees, as well as having a seat on the Senate Committee on Energy and Natural Resources and on the Senate Committee on Indian Affairs, Domenici understood whom he represented. Over the decades, like the political master he was, he had placed himself where he could be of most benefit. As much as his "St. Pete" sobriquet may have had an ironic edge, Domenici had earned his reputation for doing good, most notably as a tireless champion of the mentally ill. The fact that he was also known as one of the Senate's most environmentally unfriendly members, whose affable public persona contrasted with a terse and even imperious manner, completed the portrait of a commanding politician who was at ease with his power and his ability to wield it.

I had first met Senator Domenici briefly at a 1996 fund-raiser hosted by now state party chairman Allen Weh. The encounter, in fact, was more notable for my wife than it was for me. "He was making the rounds," is the way Cyndy remembers it, "working the room, and he came up to me and introduced himself. He asked me what I did, and I told him I was a mother and a homemaker, at which point our conversation was interrupted. But he made sure to come back, a few minutes later, and reassure me of how important he considered what I was doing, raising a family and standing at David's side. I'll always remember that: his personal touch. It was very impressive."

I was impressed as well when, two years later, Senator Domenici campaigned for me in my run for attorney general. He was hardly out beating the bushes, but he did make a fund-raising video extolling my virtues, and it had the predictable money-raising effect. In the end, Domenici's unqualified support wasn't enough for me to win the day, but I had been duly thankful for his efforts on my behalf. In fact, my gratitude and admiration extended far deeper. Although we were only infrequently in contact after my run for state office, I was hopeful that I could count on his support for my shot at U.S. Attorney. More to the point, I had no hesitation in considering and calling him my mentor. Avuncular, influential, and a legend in those parts, Domenici was a man whose approval and approbation were tremendously important for my goals, both immediate and long range. I naturally felt more than a little awe for a person who could make me or, just as easily, break me.

It was an understanding that I think we both shared when we had lunch together at a cozy Mexican restaurant not far from his spacious office in downtown Albuquerque in February 2001. I had driven the senator to the restaurant in the family minivan, with the kids' toys rattling around in the backseat. I had previously contacted James Fuller, one of Domenici's staffers, to formally request a reference to include with my U.S. Attorney application, but the senator let it be known from the moment we sat down to chips and guacamole that this would be strictly pro forma. We started by chatting amiably about local politics. He next wanted to know whether I'd ever headed a legal office before, and I quickly ran down my qualifications. But the not-so-hidden agenda underneath our chitchat was a kiss-the-ring ceremony that gave me the go-ahead to pursue my ambitions according to Domenici's wisdom and wishes. It was all over in less than an hour, and as I walked into the bright sunshine beneath the vast New Mexico sky, I felt that I had a strong shot at getting the appointment, despite the fact that several other qualified attorneys had also applied for the position. Some were career federal prosecutors, others were prominent private practitioners, and one had been a judge. Yet I felt sure that I had the senator's imprimatur. My ticket had been stamped.

Considering the deep rifts that the 2000 election had so starkly exposed, Domenici, as the powerbroker in such a closely divided state—Gore had taken New Mexico by the incredibly close margin of 366 votes—commanded even more clout. The Republican Party was positioned to make a major push in New Mexico, and Domenici, along with then state chairman John Dendahl, would have a strategic role in marshaling those forces. As one of the senator's anointed, I was poised to move into a key job at a time of significant political realignment on my home turf. To assume that being U.S. Attorney, at that time and in that state, would not come with any political baggage would be like walking right into a minefield.

I was under no such illusions. In the early months of 2001, Americans were struggling to define themselves on one side or the other of a yawning ideological divide. It's hardly surprising that in the circles where I would soon find myself moving, ideological purity was put at a premium. Was I a do-or-die Republican? The answer at the time would have been hard to separate from my political ambitions. But when all was said and done, I liked the agenda that the Republicans had rolled out after the ugly win in Florida, and I was aware that the onus would be on the administration to heal the wounds inflicted in the voting booth. I wanted to be a part of that process because, like most of my fellow citizens, I lamented the partition of my country into red and blue camps. Like many who would take up the reins of governance in the early days of the Bush administration, I felt that we had something to prove.

After posting the requisite curriculum vitae and making sure that Domenici's endorsement ended up on the right desks, I settled back to wait. It was a long one. Not until early summer of that year, months after the Supreme Court had decided Bush versus Gore, did I finally get word from the Department of Justice, inviting me out to Washington.

The initial interview was with Kyle Sampson, who worked in the administration under then White House counsel Alberto Gonzales. Two other officials were present at the meeting. Another very important interview had also been slated to take place during that visit, with Attorney General John Ashcroft and his deputy Larry Thompson. They met with me in the ornate and historic Office of the Attorney General, the place where Bobby Kennedy had launched his crusade against the Mafia and Elliot Richardson had resigned over the Watergate scandal. It was a room that reeked of history, figuratively and, at least in one instance, literally. A staffer laughingly pointed out a stained rug where Bobby Kennedy's dog had once left a calling card.

As an example of how any official in the Justice Department should maintain the delicate balance between politics and justice, one need look no further than the tough and principled John Ashcroft, with whom I would often work during my tenure as chairman of his Border and Immigration Advisory Committee. Though hardly a dissenting voice in the Bush administration's efforts to retool the intelligence community in the wake of 9/11, Ashcroft drew a line in the sand over some of the more controversial aspects of keeping America safe against terrorism. His principled opposition to the patently illegal warrantless wiretap program is sometimes cited as a reason that Alberto Gonzales replaced him after the 2004 election.

"The objective of securing the safety of Americans from crime and terror has been achieved," Ashcroft asserted in a handwritten resignation letter in November 2004, after Gonzales, the then White House council, and chief of staff Andrew Card had famously tried to elicit Ashcroft's signature on Bush's domestic surveillance program while the attorney general lay gravely ill in a Washington hospital bed. Ashcroft's contention that security had been vouchsafed for the United States could be argued, but there's no question that he understood the limits of presidential power and did what an attorney general is supposed to do: defend and uphold the Constitution, even in the face of terrorists threats, real or perceived.

Genial but forthright, with characteristic gravel in his voice, Ashcroft told me point-blank that "politics have no role in the position of United States Attorney. You have to leave that outside the door." The comment was in response to Larry Thompson informing his boss that I had run a close race just three years earlier, and Ashcroft's response left an indelible impression. It was only later that I found out that it was part of his standard speech to every potential U.S. Attorney: playing politics was not an option for any of us. Coming from him, an elected state attorney general, a governor, and a U.S. senator, the warning had that much more weight. Only later did his words take on the echoes of ominous foreshadowing.

I was formally nominated in early August but still had to wait for the U.S. Senate to confirm me. It wasn't until mid-October, after the catastrophe of 9/11, that I was officially offered the job, following a cursory confirmation hearing. Naturally, I was thrilled to be appointed U.S. Attorney—it was a dream come true. The position carried with it tremendous honor and portended a very bright future. I had worked hard to get where I was, but I also knew that my career was really just beginning.

"God works for the good of those who love him," it says in Romans 8:28, "and who have been called according to his purpose." At that point, my life accorded perfectly to the promise of the scripture. I loved God and felt called according to his purpose. Consequently, he was working for my good. I had rarely felt I was in the will of the Almighty more strongly than after my nomination. To me, providence was no vague notion but a living and breathing phenomenon.

Once I got definitive news of my hiring, I began to systematically call as many of my predecessors as I could locate, including Norman Bay, the Clinton appointee whom I would replace. Almost without exception, they told me the same thing: this would be the best job I ever had. The level of responsibility and the freedom to run a sizable office of experienced and dedicated professionals pretty much the way I wanted would be an opportunity I would not soon find again, either in the public or the private sphere. One of them even described it as having my own "fiefdom." What more often went unsaid was what the job could do for an attorney's future job prospects. That much I already knew.

In the first flush of my new position, I may not, however, have known with any precision to what purpose exactly God was calling me. It was a telling sign of the times, in those dwindling days of early September 2001, when the myth of our invincibility was still suffused with unknowing innocence. Or perhaps it was ignorance. Whatever the case, it all changed on September 11, and there suddenly seemed to be a compelling and historic reason for me to be where I was. This reason was made explicit that November, scant weeks after the attacks, when all of the newly appointed U.S. Attorneys and Assistant U.S. Attorneys gathered at the Washington Hilton for our introductory briefing.

I'll never forget the electric atmosphere at the meeting. I felt as if I had taken my place among the best and the brightest in the legal profession, men and women of high ideals and practiced skills who together would help to find a way to navigate America safely through a new and dangerous era, the fiery dawn of which we had all witnessed in real time. As deep as our shared sense of outrage might have been, there was also a palpable sense of excitement. Our morale was soaring. We felt that we had been called to help defend America in her time of crisis. This was our generation's chance to do our part, just as our parents had done in World War II.

The DOJ officials who were charged with bringing us up to speed on our duties and responsibilities were similarly focused. The mandate they passed down to us could not have been clearer: our number-one task was to identify, apprehend, and prosecute terrorists.

They were preaching to the choir. I'm confident that not one of us there didn't understand that the enormous power with which we had each been invested was to be deployed in making safe the *homeland*—a newly minted term that even then seemed to resonate with an ineluctable reordering of society.

Over the course of the afternoon, we were also brought up to speed on the administration's other primary law-enforcement initiative: the ramping up of a program that had originally been conceived by James Comey, a bright and respected former Assistant U.S. Attorney from the district surrounding Richmond, Virginia. Dubbed "Project Exile" under the Clinton administration, it was expanded under the Bush administration, which changed its name to the more descriptive "Project Safe Neighborhoods." Comey, who would subsequently be appointed U.S. Attorney for the Southern District of New York and later deputy attorney general, had fashioned a crime-fighting strategy that was both simple and effective: use stiff federal sentencing guidelines to target felons who were caught possessing firearms. Project Safe Neighborhoods had proved to be an exemplary model of putting resources where they could do the most good, and in Comey's two years as an Assistant U.S. Attorney, he had managed to cut the violent crime rate in the city of Richmond by half. Small wonder that the Justice Department wanted to expand the scope of his work and apply it across the country.

Our other main priority, which was outlined that morning, was loosely defined as "immigration," and here the administration allowed for considerable leeway. Not every state had the same ongoing crisis of hemorrhaging borders as did New Mexico and her neighbors, and I appreciated both the recognition of that fact and the flexibility we were given in addressing the problem on a district-by-district basis.

When I subsequently stepped into the role of U.S. Attorney, I had even more reason to be grateful for the free hand I had been given to deal with the immigration problems that are unique to New Mexico. With an estimated ten to twenty million illegal immigrants in the United States, the five U.S. Attorneys posted on the Southwest border knew firsthand that America's immigration policy had been, for a number of years, broken and beyond repair. To begin with, we had more than our share of such cases, most of them being what we called "ewee's" for Entry Without Inspection. But we also concentrated on those who had already been deported, only to return again, which, in legal parlance, was a "felonized reentry." At the federal level, we were primarily targeting a criminal element whose drug and gang connections regularly brought them from Mexico to the United States and back again.

Yet it wasn't the caliber of criminal I was charged with prosecuting that would make my job so rewarding. It was the fact that after 9/11, border issues had taken on an entirely new dimension. What had previously been considered largely a matter for law enforcement had suddenly become a national security issue. We needed to know who was in our country and why.

The border crisis also played an important part in my ongoing duties for the U.S. Navy Reserve. As part of an agenda to effectively coordinate our antiterrorist efforts, the Department of Defense annually gathered military, judicial, intelligence, and law enforcement representatives from far-flung locales across Eastern Europe, Asia, Africa, and Latin America to bring them up-to-date on our latest theories, technologies, and tactics. As part of the program, I had instructed this diverse group of professionals on subjects ranging from deportation as a civil proceeding to the complexities of halting illegal immigration without interfering with the flow of international business. It was undoubtedly one of the most rewarding reserve duties I had undertaken in my twenty-two years as a navy JAG officer.

My work for the Defense Institute of International Legal Studies (DIILS)—a so-called purple command, funded by the State Department, but functioning as a joint service operation with the Department of Defense—was often as much a learning as a teaching experience. I'll never forget one particularly stimulating exchange between an Israeli military judge and a representative of Panama's Ministry of Justice, which took place right around the time when the controversy over building a wall along the Mexican border was at its most heated. Of course, the United States must build a wall, the Israeli insisted: the massive barrier between Israel and the Palestinian territories had virtually eliminated incursions by suicide bombers. A good fence may not necessarily make good neighbors, but it helps to keep them from killing one another. What worked in Israel would not work in the United States, was the Panamanian official's equally vehement reply. America stands for openness and opportunity. It is a country that welcomes immigrants with open arms, not a fortress shut off from the rest of the world. I listened with rapt attention, moderating a lively give-and-take that underscored not only the complexity of the issue, but the fundamental social values that were at stake.

In New Mexico, as elsewhere along the border, both the complexity and the stakes would increase exponentially, especially after President Bush initiated "Operation Jump Start." This initiative stationed more than six thousand National Guard soldiers on the Southwest border to assist the Border Patrol in staunching the flow of illegals. The experiment was not nearly as simple a solution as it might have seemed.

That priority was one of many set forth on that day when my ninety-two fellow U.S. Attorneys and I gathered in a Washington hotel ballroom for our orientation. Whatever else we had in common, we shared a sense of patriotic fervor that underscored our determination never to let the homeland suffer another such outrage. We had been recruited for one of the most crucial battles in the country's history. It was a war of values, of belief, of civilization itself. We had our marching orders.

CHAPTER 4

The Cut

In the days immediately following the call from Mike Battle, as I struggled to put together what had happened and why, I came to the slow and undeniable realization that my seemingly inexplicable dismissal had not been completely without precedent. Like a lightbulb suddenly being switched on, I recalled a phone call I had gotten back in August of that year from Bud Cummins, a fellow U.S. Attorney and a good friend, who ran the federal prosecutor's office for the Eastern District of Arkansas in the state capital of Little Rock.

Bud and I had something in common, in that we both came from a more overtly political background than many of the other appointees in the 2001 crop of U.S. Attorneys. Bud is a loquacious, witty gentleman who is, as they say, "Southern as a sugar sandwich." But his soft-spoken, country-courthouse mannerisms hide a keen intelligence and a firm grasp on the often-harsh realities of politics. He had made a run for U.S. Congress and, like me, hadn't quite made the cut. Also like me, he had ended up on the Republican Party's short list of future electoral prospects. I had originally met him at the National Advocacy College on the campus of the University of South Carolina in Columbia. The Justice Department had used the school for the training of its prosecutors, and over the years, I had attended many classes there, some mandatory but most voluntary, including a 2005 course in media relations, which was later to come in very handy indeed.

I first encountered Bud at the campus exercise facility, dressed in blue gym shorts and a plain cotton T-shirt. From the very beginning with Bud, what you saw was what you got: no pretense, no airs. By the summer of 2006, we had an even closer personal and professional relationship as we found ourselves working together on a drug case that involved both New Mexico and eastern Arkansas jurisdictions.

I was expecting to discuss the details of that case when I answered the call from Bud on a layover in Las Vegas on my way to an Indian Country Conference in St. George, Utah. As I peremptorily launched into some mundane details of our mutual investigation, Bud gently interjected, telling me that he hoped the case would go well, but that he wouldn't be around to help me bring it to trial.

"What are you talking about, Bud?" I asked, a little mystified.

"I got a call last month, David," he informed me, without the slightest hint of rancor. "I've been asked to step down. I thought you should know."

My mystification turned instantly to shock. To call Bud Cummins an effective and dedicated prosecutor is to far understate the case. And to call him a rock-ribbed Republican hardly does justice to his loyalty to the party and his adherence to its stated ideals. It was a reputation he had earned not simply by, as he termed it, "taking the bullet" in a difficult congressional race where the odds had been stacked against him from the beginning, but also during a stint as legal counsel for Arkansas governor Mike Huckabee, a politician with substantial aspirations of his own and a high-profile public record to go with them.

Huckabee is an ordained Southern Baptist minister with impeccable credentials as a social conservative. He was only the third Republican governor in Arkansas since Reconstruction and hailed from the same small town as another ambitious Razorback politician: Hope, Arkansas, the home of Bill Clinton. Widely considered to be an adept and highly effective governor, Huckabee, prior to his 2008 run for the White House, was perhaps best known on the national stage for having lost more than a hundred pounds, an accomplishment that he used to launch a campaign for increased awareness of healthy living.

But even a slimmed-down Huckabee proved to be a tempting target for his enemies. His campaign for the state House was marred by a relatively minor campaign contribution flap, which nevertheless earned him a fine from the Arkansas Ethics Commission. His statements in support of creationism were more grist for the mill for his Democratic opponents, while support from his base suffered as a result of a tax policy that saw state spending increase more than 60 percent during the first eight years of his term. One result of his tax legislation was an "F" grade from the Libertarian think tank the Cato Institute, as well as widespread accusations from the state's powerful right wing that Huckabee was nothing but a liberal in disguise and a "serial tax increaser."

But all of this paled in comparison to the scorching rebuke that Huckabee suffered for his decision in the case of Wayne Dumond, a convicted rapist who went on to sexually assault and murder a Missouri woman after he was released from prison while Huckabee was governor. A firestorm of criticism followed, sparking a feud with then president Clinton, who was a distant relative of Dumond. Simply put, more than once during his time in office, Huckabee had required the skills of a canny legal operative, and it was Bud Cummins who brilliantly fit that bill. At the same time, Bud himself had gained invaluable experience in the take-no-prisoners world of ideologically galvanized political warfare and had seen firsthand how a principled stand could often come at a high cost.

As a U.S. Attorney, however, Bud, like the rest of us, had also begun to feel that he had reached a safe haven, far removed from the blood sport he had seen played out around Huckabee. Yet at the same time, like myself, he was careful to cultivate his own prospects within the Republican ranks, working tirelessly for the Bush campaign. As a result, he had been tagged to be part of the legal team that went to Florida to keep an eagle eye on the crucial recount after the 2000 election and, as an Arkansas Bush booster, had helped to deliver his home state by an impressive 10-point margin.

All of which gave the call that he had received from Mike Battle in June 2006, asking for his resignation, the crippling force of a blow to the solar plexus. "I considered myself a better-than-average friend of Mike's," Bud later told me. "Of course, I knew this decision had hardly come from him, but it seemed to me indicative of the way the whole situation was handled. Not too long before, he had spent a day in my district and had given me a very positive review."

In point of fact, Cummins's entire tenure as U.S. Attorney for the Eastern District of Arkansas had been characterized by positive reviews. "The EARS team sent a full dozen staffers out to Arkansas, and after they turned the place upside down, we came out with the equivalent of an A plus."

"Look," Bud later added, with typically dry insight, "no one's pretending here that they aren't judging you as much on your political standing as on your case-to-case merits. That just comes with the territory. As much as the Justice Department is charged with impartially upholding the law, it is also expected to implement the priorities of the administration. I didn't have a problem with that. In fact, I wholeheartedly approved of the mandate handed down to us. Who wouldn't? We were fighting terrorism, protecting the homeland in a clash of civilizations. It wasn't hard to get behind that agenda. We were on the right side, one hundred and ten percent."

So why, with precipitous ease, had this staunch supporter of the administration's goals been cut loose with a single phone call? "That's what I wanted to know," Bud confessed wryly. "I asked Mike Battle if I had done something wrong. If there was something I wasn't aware of that maybe I could fix. I tried to stay calm and reasonable. I didn't want to sound like I was pleading, but I really did want to know the reasons and rationale behind this. The simple truth was, I couldn't put it together. I had worked very hard to get where I was and, if I say so myself, my credentials were impeccable. It wasn't just the fact that I'd worked for the Bush campaign or put in my time helping Mike Huckabee out of some tight spots. I'd earned this job, and by taking it away, they were in essence telling me that my years of service counted for squat."

To all of his questions, Bud received the same bland assurances from Battle. "He told me over and over that the Justice Department and the White House were very happy with my work, just as pleased as punch." To the cognitive dissonance that followed on this reply, Battle had another ready answer. "Mike said that the reason I was being let go," Bud explained laconically, "was that they want to give someone else the benefit of the experience of being a U.S. Attorney."

That someone else was John Timothy Griffin, the young and eager acolyte of President George Bush's political "brain," Karl Rove. Griffin had traveled a winding road indeed to land on the doorstep of the U.S. Attorney's office for the Eastern District of Arkansas, which included serving as a U.S. Army Reserve JAG on a posting in Mosul, Iraq.

Raised in the pine forest region of southern Arkansas, Griffin had had his political baptism as an assistant prosecutor in the investigation of Clinton's secretary for housing and urban development, Henry Cisneros, in 1997. He next moved to the powerful but shadowy post of deputy research director of the Republican National Committee, which, in turn, had made him available to the 2000 Bush campaign. Griffin's role in the election effort is unclear, but it's been suggested that his forte was "opposition research," that is, digging up dirt on Democratic opponents.

Whatever his role, he acquitted himself well—well enough to be named to the legal staff of the "Bush-Cheney 2000 Florida Recount Team," where Bud Cummins was also doing his best to nudge the razor-edged margins into the Republican column. After the election was settled in the Supreme Court, Griffin worked briefly in the Justice Department's office of Assistant Attorney General of the Criminal Division for Michael Chertoff, who was later to become the director of Homeland Security. Having since caught the eye of Karl Rove, Griffin was brought directly to the White House in September 2005, assuming the dual title of special assistant to the president and deputy director in the Office of Political Affairs. Almost exactly a year later, he signed on as special assistant to the U.S. Attorney in Arkansas and waited to take the job that Cummins had been forced to vacate, ostensibly to make room for him.

Whether the incremental politicization of the Justice Department was an attack on our basic freedoms or an attempt to safeguard those freedoms depends on your point of view. But there is no question that the White House knew exactly how the wheels of power meshed and how to spin them to its advantage. Griffin's rapid rise to U.S. Attorney was a case in point. In the early spring of 2006, some nine months before Mike Battle called me, Bush had signed into law a package of "Improvements and Reauthorizations" to the 2005 U.S.A. Patriot Act, the centerpiece of his antiterrorist legislative drive. Buried in the surfeit of legal tweaking and tuning was a brief amendment to the same Section 546, of the U.S. Code 28, that, since 1789, had served as the basis for the hiring and the firing of U.S. Attorneys. Under the statute, any interim appointment to the post would expire after 120 days, if the Senate had not confirmed a candidate by that time. The administration's tactic was simple and inspired: suspend the 120-day provision. It was a move that effectively lifted oversight of the U.S. Attorney selection process from Congress and transferred it to the White House. Bush, in short, could select anyone he wanted, for whatever reasons, and hold it as an interim appointment for as long as his pleasure was served.

There was abundant irony in this change of the Patriot Act, beginning with the fact that prior to the legislation being introduced, every U.S. Attorney had been directed to contact his or her congressional delegation to determine whether, and to what degree, the representatives supported the act as it stood. That, in itself, was a break from the customary practice of prohibiting U.S. Attorneys from lobbying on behalf of the administration. But Main Justice cleared the ethical hurdles without a backward glance when we were further instructed to let Congress know just how useful, not to mention strictly constitutional, the Patriot Act would be as a tool in our antiterrorist efforts. At a single stroke, we had become pitchmen for administration policy. In fact, the last time I would see President Bush, in January 2006, was when I had been selected as one of a handful of U.S. Attorneys specially designated to meet with him on the provisions of the Patriot Act and to later participate in a joint press conference outside the West Wing.

The proposed change to Section 546 seemed, at the time, no more than a rather inconsequential step in an ongoing effort to concentrate terror-fighting resources in the White House. As an improvement on the government's ability to safeguard the homeland, the change might have been a dubious proposition. As a way of ensuring the continuing party loyalty of U.S. Attorneys, it was nothing short of a masterstroke, giving the president wide room for an end run around the Senate confirmation of U.S. Attorneys. Griffin's tenure as Arkansas U.S. Attorney would remain an interim appointment for the duration, one of the first under the Patriot Act's altered Section 546.

Barely two weeks after I had received my Pearl Harbor Day phone call, Cummins was out and Griffin was in, a tidy game of musical chairs that left only the lingering sense that something unconstitutional had just transpired. It was a mark not only of our friendship, but of our shared sense of outrage over the way we were being manhandled that I was the first U.S. Attorney to whom Bud had revealed his extraordinary news. In turn, he would be the first U.S. Attorney I told about my own forced resignation, with the phone cradled on my shoulder as I washed dishes at the kitchen sink. What I most wanted to know was how long Main Justice had given him to resign. For Bud, it was six months. For me, it was seven weeks. "Misery loves company," was all Bud could say in response.

"No one promised me a job for four years," Bud admitted, "and I was certainly not given an eight-year, two-term, guarantee.

But there was a very strong unspoken understanding that there was at least a modicum of job security and that one needed a very compelling reason for that precedent to be broken. In the modern history of the office, the notion of serving at the pleasure of the president almost automatically entailed a four-year commitment. And even then, if a guy was doing a good job, he had a shot of carrying on through a change in successive administrations, Republican or Democratic. Suddenly all that tradition counted for nothing."

It was a way of doing business that Bud characterized to me as "inexperienced, arrogant, and calibrated for disaster." "I was offended, and I think with good reason, that they chose to handle it the way they did." He paused for a moment. "Maybe 'chose' is the wrong word," he added at length. "I got the definite feeling that no one was really calling the shots in this whole process. There was an element of common courtesy involved that had nothing to do with my hurt feelings. For example, it would have been helpful to the administration, politically speaking, to have notified the state's senators beforehand of their decision to replace me. It would have given the local people the feeling, for whatever it was worth, that they were in the loop on choices that directly affected their constituencies. But they didn't deem that important enough to follow through."

Bud didn't need to even get into the uncomfortable situation created by the fact that Tim Griffin was planted in his office for the better part of three months. It must have been a little like having a vulture perched over your shoulder, waiting for you to die. Not to mention the question of authority that was left hanging. Both Tim and Bud knew where the situation was heading. So who was in charge? Was Cummins supposed to be making significant decisions in cases that Griffin would be taking over in the near term? Of course, it's always difficult to handle a transition, and I'm sure they both did the best they could. But I got the impression that they were both in the dark as to what the will and wish of the big boys in Washington might be. Indeed, Bud's best one-sentence summary of the circumstances surrounding his firing was that it was "a bad plan poorly executed."

That was an impression underscored by the fact that Bud had received absolutely no instruction on how to handle the public-relations aspect of his "resignation." "Tim did not tell me, nor did anyone else, how to spin this with the press," Bud recounted. "That was left entirely up to me. I could tell the truth—that I was being replaced because Karl Rove had someone else in mind for the job, or I could tell everyone I needed to 'spend more time with my family,' or whatever. They didn't seem to care one way or the other."

But for Bud, the cavalier treatment that he had received at the hands of the administration and the indifference of administration officials as to how it would be perceived would have a much greater impact than the purely public perception. "I really wasn't sure how to move forward," he admitted. "Part of that uncertainty came from not knowing just how far off the Republican reservation I had strayed. Maybe, if I played my cards right, I could find my way back on, if you'll pardon the mixed metaphor. But I wasn't even sure what the game was anymore. I knew from the minute I first sat behind that desk, that my time as a U.S. Attorney was limited. But I also had the confidence that I would be able to anticipate my departure and plan for the next step in my career. I had hoped to be considered for a federal judgeship. Was that even possible anymore? And to whom could I go to ask the question?

"I was in a difficult position. I kept trying to sell the story that I had voluntarily resigned until I was on the verge of telling outright lies. I still believe that the reason I had been given for being let go was legitimate as far as it went: they wanted their guy in my job. And I had done that job well. No one had dared dispute that. There was never a hint of incompetence or impropriety. I was a team player, even when they made it clear they didn't want me on the team anymore. But it was hard to ignore the way I had been treated. Look, I know that politics can be a bruising contact sport. It's just that this demonstrated a lack of understanding of the most basic rules of the game: don't make enemies of your friends; leave everyone you can with as much of their dignity intact as possible. But I never heard another word from them. Just a dead silence."

It was at that point, in February 2007, when Bud came to the conclusion, as he put it, "that my colleagues had been thrown under a bus. It was no longer a question of what was expedient for my career or my future in the party. It was a question of what was right and what was wrong." Earlier that month, he had received a request from the *Washington Post* for an interview, with the subject certain to be the political dimension of his firing. "I talked it over with my wife," he told me. "She confirmed what I was feeling. We both knew that if the roles were reversed and the false allegation of deficient performance was being leveled at me, my colleagues would hang with me and help me fight against the lies. Jody and I both knew that I wouldn't be able to live with myself if I simply took Paul McNulty's explanation for my case and walked away from what was happening to my colleagues. It wasn't just that I hadn't been treated fairly. It was that they had brought this on themselves and didn't seem to care. To us, that didn't bode well for their ability to govern. I needed to step forward, to tell what had happened, regardless of the consequences. At that point, I knew where my loyalties lay—with my conscience and my country. I did what I did because I would have felt too guilty not doing it."

I had no way of knowing, after my abrupt termination, how much the fate of Bud Cummins served as a grim harbinger of all that was to follow. As a very private man, he had kept the full scope of his situation pretty much to himself, and beyond the vague awareness that my friend had come to a career crossroads, I had no clear idea of the dilemma he found himself in or the terribly tough choices he had been forced into facing.

But as much as he had suffered under the callous and clumsy disregard of the administration, his firing was not the first true gauge of the size and the scope of the gathering scandal or even the most egregious. The fact that Bud and I had a close and abiding friendship naturally drew my attention to his plight as I tried in those early days to make sense of my own fate. Yet in reality, the cautionary tale of yet another victim of the administration within the Justice Department had even more relevance to what had happened, and was about to happen, to me.

As the U.S. Attorney for the Western District of Missouri, Todd Graves brought with him an impressive curriculum vitae. Immediately after graduating from law school at the University of Virginia in 1991, the engaging and gifted Tarkio, Missouri, native was named assistant attorney general for his home state, serving at the same time on the Governor's Commission on Crime. In 1994, after a stint in private practice, he was elected prosecuting attorney for Platte County, with the distinction at the time of being the youngest full-time prosecutor statewide. Reelected in 1998, he was subsequently tapped by the incoming Bush administration for the U.S. Attorney spot and was confirmed by the Senate in October 2001.

Four and a half years later, he was suddenly ordered to resign. When asked to speculate on the reasons for this removal, he recalled an early job interview in which he had been requested to single out the attribute that best described who he was and what he stood for. "I said independent," Graves recalled, before he added without blinking, "Apparently, that was the wrong attribute."

Under the circumstances, the remark had all the resonance of a classic understatement. In March 2006, the month that Graves's resignation had become effective, the country was in the early throes of a convulsive midterm election, in which the entire Bush agenda and, by extension, the sweeping Republican mandate that had brought him to power, would be tested and found woefully wanting. One of the battlegrounds for that historic struggle was Missouri, where Republican incumbent Jim Talent was in a pitched senatorial race with Democratic contender Claire McCaskill. The election would, in fact, prove to be one of the closest of the 2006 midterms.

Part of the GOP's strategy for winning the state was to aggressively push a lawsuit that required the removal of questionable registrations from Missouri voter rolls. The reputed purpose was twofold: to discredit the newly elected Missouri secretary of state,

Democrat Robin Carnahan, and, in a more sinister interpretation, to disenfranchise those voters who might not have fully understood the electoral process, such as recent immigrants and the poor, who were de facto assumed to be in the Democratic column. It was a ploy that Graves saw through immediately and forthrightly refused to pursue. "I didn't have an objection with the concept of ensuring clean voter roles," Graves explains. "My objection was bringing a suit that I thought would not succeed. It was slipshod and rushed, and there seemed to be little interest in the technical aspects of winning a lawsuit."

Whether his principled stand against a bogus and politically motivated legal maneuver contributed to his precipitous departure, the fact that Graves was replaced by Bradley Schlozman, a DOJ attorney who had made a name for himself by digging up convenient voter fraud cases, real or imagined, appears to speak, loudly and clearly, for itself.

One can find the obvious implications in the expertise that Schlozman brought to the job. The Kansas native had served in judicial clerkships in his home state before relocating to Washington, D.C., in 1999, where he eventually joined the Justice Department as deputy assistant attorney general, supervising, among other things, the Voting Litigation Section of the Civil Rights Department. Under Bush, the Justice Department had a far different approach to the concept of protecting voter rights than previous administrations had. While the emphasis had formerly been on safeguarding the franchise for disadvantaged citizens of every description, the new emphasis was on using federal power to expunge from the rolls those who, for whatever reason, were judged not to belong there.

"Democrats are always looking for people who've been denied their voting rights," is the way Bud Cummins put it, "and Republicans are always looking for people who shouldn't be voting. It was pretty much business as usual, with the only difference being the aggressiveness with which the Bush people pursued their ends."

It was clear that Schlozman was focused on those ends with laserlike precision. Although he had absolutely no experience as a prosecutor prior to his appointment as U.S. Attorney for Missouri's

Western District, this graduate of George Washington University had plenty of practice in the political leveraging of the ballot box.

While in the Justice Department, Schlozman overruled virtually the entire staff of the Civil Rights Division when they recommended against approving a newly enacted Georgia state law that required all voters to show photo identifications at the polls and to eliminate, in the process, all previously accepted forms of ID, including birth certificates and Social Security cards. According to the Voting Rights Act of 1965, Georgia was required to prove that any change in its law would not have an adverse impact on minority voters, given its history of rampant discrimination—a history that Schlozman willfully ignored in allowing the new statute to go unchallenged. He even wrote an editorial in the *Atlanta Journal-Constitution* supporting his position. I knew Schlozman. I'd participated in a human trafficking news conference in Albuquerque with him. He was fiercely partisan and had a penchant for calling his friends and allies "good Americans." I later figured out that he was talking about Republicans when he used that phrase. Brad was young and full of political enthusiasm, untempered by real-world prosecutorial experience.

But it didn't stop there. When, in 2003, House kingpin Tom "the Hammer" DeLay launched an ambitious and legally dubious redistricting plan for Texas, Justice Department attorneys vigorously opposed it for, once again, failing to protect minority voter rights. And once again, Schlozman joined other political appointees in overruling the finding and allowed the blatant gerrymandering to go forward until a major part of DeLay's proposal was struck down in the Supreme Court.

It was, in fact, Schlozman who was also the driving force in a lawsuit that Todd Graves considered of doubtful merit, a decision that many in Missouri politics felt to be the primary cause of Graves's dismissal. Schlozman's gambit focused on the voter registration organization ACORN—Association of Community Organizations for Reform Now—which had ostensibly allowed fraudulent registration forms to be filled out in Kansas City.

Five days before the 2006 elections, Schlozman announced indictments against four former ACORN workers, who had been paid $8 an hour to sign up unqualified voters in poor neighborhoods. ACORN had already fired the employees and informed election officials of their fraudulent actions. Not that it mattered to Schlozman regarding his master plan for Missouri, which conveniently ignored the long-standing policy of waiting until after an election to bring any federal indictment that might affect the outcome of the vote. In the words of Joe Rich, a thirty-five-year veteran of the Justice Department and for six years the head of its Voting Rights Section, "The timing of the Missouri indictments could not have made the administration's aims more transparent."

As it turned out, Schlozman's efforts were in vain: Jim Talent lost his Senate seat and, with no further need to occupy the U.S. Attorney post in Western Missouri, Schlozman resigned less than a year after taking the job. His next assignment: working with Mike Battle at the Executive Office for U.S. Attorneys. He didn't stay long at that office; he resigned in August 2007, a casualty of the scandal he had helped to set in motion.

It was Battle who, early in 2006, had informed Todd Graves that his services would no longer be required. This was a message that Battle had become accustomed to, if not entirely comfortable with, delivering by the time he'd worked through Bud Cummins and on to me. "One key aspect of my particular situation was that I was planning to leave anyway, and within a matter of months before I was asked to resign," Todd told me. "What's remarkable in light of later events is that Mike Battle used almost exactly the same script on me that he did with the other U.S. Attorneys. It was almost down to the same words. If I had to guess, I would say that my response emboldened them. I just took the phone call, listened to what Mike had to say, and finished my sandwich. It was very low-key. I'm convinced they thought, 'Hey, that was easy. Let's do it again.'

"Of course," Todd added after a moment, "I could have done without the humiliation. I'd never gotten a call like that in my life, and I hope to never get another one again. But the fact that I already had one foot out the door took the sting out of it a little."

Graves's experience made clear early on the means and the methods that the administration had adopted to deal with obstreperous or uncooperative or simply inconvenient Justice Department personnel. First would come spurious allegations of voter fraud, then unvarnished legal manipulations to sway elections, followed by a rigorous insistence on absolute and unquestioning obedience, and, finally, a phone call from out of the blue. It was all part of a pattern that was only just beginning to emerge. What I had no way of knowing was the part I would soon play in turning over the rocks where the truth lay hidden.

CHAPTER 5

Caged

B y the end of that first week after I had been told to resign,
I found myself going over and over the shreds of information I had been able to piece together. As a decidedly sur-
real Christmas approached, the understanding was slowly sinking
in that far from being some terrible mistake, my firing had been
all too deliberate. And, as far as I could tell, the dead silence from
Washington was deliberate, too, along with the message that it
implied: don't ask questions; go away quietly; get on with your life.

All of which was easier said than done, although no one was
actually saying that either, or anything else, for that matter. After not
hearing back from Mike Battle for several days about my request for
an extension of one month to look for another job, I put a call in to
Paul McNulty, the deputy attorney general and a Justice Department
veteran with whom I had previously had contact on an advisory committee for John Ashcroft.

McNulty, a former U.S. Attorney for the Eastern District
of Virginia and a Pittsburgh native, had begun his Washington
career in the House of Representatives. First, he was a lawyer in
the minority leader's office, and he subsequently became chief

counsel for the House Subcommittee on Crime, where he drafted a number of important statutes dealing with everything from firearms to fraud. He had assisted John Ashcroft during Ashcroft's tumultuous confirmation hearings and, in the immediate aftermath of 9/11, had spearheaded the prosecution of terrorist suspects Zacarias Moussaoui, Omar Abu Ali, and "American Taliban" John Walker Lindh. In a short and terse phone conversation, McNulty promised vaguely to look into my request for more time. I didn't bother asking him the question that was uppermost in my mind: why had I been fired? I figured that even if he knew, he wouldn't tell me. He was on the other side of the cone of silence that had descended around me.

But I couldn't afford to be silent. For one thing, I had my staff to think about. The direction and the oversight of ongoing investigations and prosecutions, some historic, needed to be addressed. It was important to me that the dedicated professionals in my office understood that my firing had nothing to do with their performance. Morale had been good and productivity high, and I wanted, as much as possible, to keep it that way for whoever would take my place. I was also painfully aware that despite the Justice Department's apparent desire to keep my firing as clandestine as possible, word would eventually leak out and questions would arise: the same questions I'd been obsessively asking myself. To the degree that the news of my departure would stir interest, at least in New Mexico, it was both surprising and distressing that like Bud Cummins before me, I had gotten absolutely no advice or counsel from Washington on how I was to handle the media when the story broke. Maybe Todd Graves's estimation was right: since he had moved on without a whisper of protest and with a lucrative job in the private sector waiting for him, it was expected that I, too, would go away quietly.

It didn't work out that way. On December 19, I composed an e-mail to every employee under my supervision with the subject line "A Time for Everything."

"As was written thousands of years ago," I began by citing the book of Ecclesiastes, "'There is a time for everything. There is a time to plant and a time to uproot . . . a time to search and a time to give up.' Those of you old enough to remember the Byrds' classic song 'Turn, Turn, Turn' recall the words of this eternal truth."

After informing my staff of my impending resignation, I went on to let them know as emphatically as I could that their "devotion to duty and commitment to justice has been awe-inspiring. . . . We have accomplished much in these past five years. We have zealously defended the government in difficult civil cases, we have cared for victims and their family members and we put behind bars dangerous criminals who have committed terrible crimes against our fellow citizens and innocent children. We have made New Mexico history by successfully prosecuting historic political corruption cases. We have made a difference and we have made New Mexico a better and safer place. But our job is not yet done. Many of you who are career public servants will have the honor of continuing the struggle for justice for many years to come." I signed off, "Semper fidelis, semper paratus." Always faithful, always ready.

I meant everything that I said, and even now I'm stirred when I consider the extraordinary men and women I had the privilege of leading during my time as U.S. Attorney. I knew, of course, that they could and would carry on without me, and as much as I tried to convey my admiration for them, I believe I also wanted to express how transformative those five years in office had been for me, personally. Whatever else being a U.S. Attorney might have meant for my future career prospects, I had been able to put into practice the idealism, even altruism, that I had felt as an American citizen. I was proud of my service and honored to have been called.

As it turned out, I was barely able to get the word to my colleagues ahead of the press. That same day, the *Albuquerque Journal* ran a front-page story headlined "U.S. Attorney Plans to Resign." My hand had been forced. More than one person had contacted a pair of investigative reporters in Albuquerque, Larry Barker of Channel 13 and Mike Gallagher of the *Albuquerque Journal*, and told them that I'd been asked to resign. I had intended to try to exit gracefully, but there were others who wanted to make sure that didn't happen.

I think I must have read the article with as much interest as anyone else in town, hoping that between the lines, Gallagher, the investigative reporter, might have uncovered the facts that, as far as I could tell, were being deliberately kept under wraps. The story blithely asserted that I had had "discussions with officials in Washington, D.C."

But there were other, more troubling aspects to Gallagher's story than simply reflexive spin doctoring. "Rumors that Iglesias was in trouble with his superiors at the Department of Justice," the article continued, "had been circulating for months. The criticism of Iglesias has been that he had not provided enough resources for public corruption investigations. Some of that criticism has come from the political arena and some from the FBI, which had made political corruption its No. 2 priority behind terrorism." Gallagher should have dug further, because the rumors came from the right wing of the state Republican party not from the Justice Department.

Gallagher, who had previously treated the office and me fairly, had obviously not done his homework on this story. No one at Main Justice had ever contacted me about any problem, real or perceived. By the same token, the FBI historically stays out of politics and for good reason: its job is law enforcement and not partisan infighting. The FBI would lose all credibility if it entered into the political mosh pit.

Gallagher's allegations were news to me, although, to be fair, I knew that there were people, especially within the state Republican Party, who were less than happy with my performance, especially as it related to the outcome of a high-profile corruption case in 2005 against state treasurer Robert Vigil, a Democrat. As the result of a two-year investigation by the FBI, dubbed Operation Midas Touch and conducted in coordination with my office, Vigil, along with his predecessor Michael Montoya, had been indicted on twenty-four counts of extortion, money laundering, and racketeering. In a complicated kickback scheme, Vigil and Montoya, bankrolled by nearly

$3 million in bond money that had been allotted to the Treasurer's Office for annual state improvements, used independent advisers to find brokers who were willing to pay the highest interest rates for the funds. The advisers would garner a commission, from which the accused demanded a cut, sometimes as high as 30 percent, which could translate to $50,000 per transaction.

We were confident going into trial, with solid evidence that included a color video of Vigil taking a $10,000 payoff in cash. We would subsequently gain the cooperation of Montoya, who gave testimony in our case against his successor in exchange for a guilty plea. He ended up with a forty-month sentence.

The result of the Vigil prosecution was, however, less than what we had hoped for. After the first trial ended in a hung jury, with eleven jurors voting to convict on many of the charges, a second trial produced, over four weeks, a conviction on one of the twenty-four counts. Even though Vigil would eventually receive a sentence of thirty-seven months, the longest sentence ever given to a sitting elected official in state history, there were nonetheless whispers among state Republicans that I had dropped the ball, whispers loud enough to eventually reach my ears.

Although I didn't exactly brush the criticism off, I also tried not to let it get to me. Winning some cases and losing others was not what the job was about; it was about whether justice had been served. All things considered, my office had achieved a just outcome. Eliciting Montoya's cooperation, for example, had saved the people a good deal of time and money, and even a single conviction in the Vigil case had served to take the crooked official out of circulation. But at the same time, I had to acknowledge that the result didn't sit well with some people whose interest in the case was primarily to discredit Democrats at a time when corruption in high places was both a law enforcement priority and a hot button public concern.

The simmering discontent went even deeper, though, as did its purely political roots, which extended far beyond the borders of New Mexico to the highest levels of the Bush administration.

The national trauma of the 2000 elections had convinced Republicans that as far as it was in their power, there would never again be a presidential race so close and contested. That the very nature of the electoral process carries with it the potential for squeakers and close calls of every variety was apparently not considered in their tactical plans. If the future of the Republican agenda was to be decided at the ballot box, then it was at the ballot box that the problem of a secure party plurality was to be resolved forthwith.

Accordingly, in the late summer of 2002, less than a year after I had stepped into my new job, the Justice Department sent an e-mail to every U.S. Attorney in the country, suggesting, in no uncertain terms, that we should all immediately begin to work closely with election officials at the state and local levels to offer whatever assistance we could in investigating and prosecuting voter fraud cases. The e-mail imperatives came again in 2004 and 2006, by which time I had learned that far from being standard operating procedure for the Justice Department, the emphasis on voter irregularities was unique to the Bush administration.

It was a fact that former U.S. Attorney Todd Graves, who had fended off bogus voter fraud cases in Missouri before being replaced by Bradley Schlozman, knew only too well. The administration had put its shoulder to the wheel, relentlessly pushing a more stringent Voter ID system. This issue played into the fears of a country inundated by illegal immigrants who, without proper identification, could flood polling stations and ostensibly throw elections. That these unauthorized voters would vote for Democrats went without saying.

But there was a more sinister reading to such urgent calls for reform, not to mention the Justice Department's strident insistence on harvesting a bumper crop of voter fraud prosecutions. That implication is summed up in a single word: *caging*. It's alleged that in the 2004 election, an estimated quarter million voters were turned away at the polls for lack of proper identification. Many of them had been first-time registrants who had joined the rolls as a result of intense registration drives that year.

New Mexico had been the focus of one such drive, with notable success: voter counts in Bernalillo County alone had increased by sixty-five thousand in the months prior to the 2004 election, mostly due to the grassroots efforts of ACORN, the same Association of Community Organizations for Reform Now that would face Schlozman's attack-dog methods two years later in Kansas City during the midterm elections.

Citizens who were subsequently refused the ballot were overwhelmingly students, the elderly, and minorities who, for a variety of reasons, did not possess adequate proof of identity, address, or registration. But those in whose interest it was to suppress turnout among such constituencies were not content with whatever challenges they could mount based on simple carelessness, ignorance, or lack of experience. Instead, the nefarious practice of "caging," it has been widely assumed, was used to deny the franchise to these voters.

The technique is simple, effective, and reprehensible. Voter registration applications would, for example, be sent to a predominantly black college during the summer months. When absent students failed to fill out the forms and these were returned as undeliverable, effective challenges to residency could be mounted. But caging didn't stop there. In one alleged incident at a military base in Jacksonville, Florida, entire units that were scheduled for tours of duty in Iraq were targeted. Young GIs, fighting a war thousands of miles from home, received mail addressed to their stateside bases late or not at all. As a result, they forfeited the opportunity to decide the fate of the very politicians who had sent them into harm's way in the first place.

Using the ballot box as a political weapon is nothing new. As Bud Cummins pointed out, Democrats chronically complain about access, while Republicans carp about fraud. And Bud knew this firsthand: his replacement as Arkansas U.S. Attorney, Tim Griffin, was, it has also been alleged, an old hand at caging. But the fact was, not only did the administration stoop to such seamy expedients to press its agenda in 2004, it had the full might and authority of the federal government and its prosecutorial powers to accomplish its ends.

At the time when I received my first exhortatory e-mail in 2002, it appeared clear to me, from looking at the lack of credible cases in the state, that there was no reason to expend valuable time and manpower in pursuit of electoral infractions. Two years later, with the election heating up, the situation had changed considerably. That's not to say that there was a sudden flurry of plausible voter fraud cases, only that the pressure to find them had been ratcheted up by an order of magnitude. Just as the Bush-Kerry contest began to gather steam, a group of New Mexico Republicans, led by Bernalillo County sheriff Darren White, the chair of the local Bush-Cheney campaign committee, appeared at the county clerk's office, demanding to know whether there were any "problem registrations" on file.

White was very much a shoot-from-the-hip kind of lawman and later claimed that I would only prosecute cases that were "wrapped in a pretty bow." After the tragic shooting of one of his deputies, White tried to lay blame on my office for failing to investigate the case, even though it was strictly a state, not a federal, matter. He knew better, but as a loyal Bushie, he was trying to discredit me for speaking out about his mentor, Senator Pete Domenici. Not surprisingly, White announced he would run for Congress when Heather Wilson stated she would run for Domenici's Senate seat.

The county clerk, Mary Herrera, referred White and his posse to approximately three thousand forms that were either incompletely or incorrectly filled out. Spurred on by this revelation, the concerned citizens next held a press conference in which they accused a variety of registration groups, most notably ACORN, of submitting fraudulent forms. The purported examples that were then produced included a woman who had correctly filled out two different registrations with slightly different signatures and another in which a husband, with his wife's permission, had signed her name to the form. It was demanded that I take action against what was perceived as rampant abuse of the system.

I had no choice but to respond. My decision wasn't based so much on legal concerns—I still hadn't been handed a voter fraud case that I thought I could win—but on the growing public perception that with all the smoke being generated around the issue, there must be a fire somewhere. The media were busy with investigations of their own, none of which, naturally, bore the same burden of proof that I was obliged to meet. With the benefit of hindsight, it would perhaps have been wiser to wait for such proof to surface, but in that super-saturated political atmosphere of a divisive White House race, I decided that it was prudent to determine for myself the merits of the issue in my district, once and for all. As much as my job was about upholding the law, the inevitable public-relations aspects of being a U.S. Attorney could not be overlooked.

New Mexico Republicans had, in the meantime, filed a civil lawsuit seeking wide-ranging changes in the state's voter ID statutes. With the election fast approaching, the possibility that hundreds of legitimate voters would be disenfranchised by a sudden change in the rules was all too real. The case was duly dismissed, which only served to stoke the fires of the voter fraud frenzy.

On the same day that the court decision was handed down, I called a press conference and announced the formation of an Election Fraud Task Force and launched a joint investigation with the New Mexico secretary of state, the state police, the FBI, and the Department of Justice. "Mischief was afoot," was the quote that picked up the most ink, along with, "There are questions lurking in the shadows." It was an action that I took as a calculated political risk. I knew that the clamor had grown so loud that, sooner or later, a scapegoat would have to be selected, and I was the obvious candidate. At the same time, I had logically deduced that if we looked hard enough, we might very well come up with something. It had been back in 1992 when the New Mexico U.S. Attorney's office had last prosecuted a voter fraud case, and I assumed that with the ground lying fallow for so long, abuses would have had ample opportunity to take root.

Was I caving to pressure from the Republican power base that had done so much to support my bid to become a U.S. Attorney in the first place? That's a judgment I'll leave to others, except to say that at the time, Sheriff White had referred a case to me that, on its face, seemed to have more merit than mismatched signatures or a married couple's honest mistake.

Late that summer, Kevin Stout, the thirteen-year-old son of an Albuquerque policeman, received a voter registration card in the mail. His father brought the matter to the sheriff, and when the card was traced back to ACORN, it appeared as if the youngster's signature and date of birth had been forged. The name of the canvasser on the application was an ACORN worker who had been paid on a per-registration basis and had been fired by the organization three months earlier for altering other forms to get remuneration for work she hadn't done.

"We have proof," declared Republican state representative Joe Thompson, making his voice heard above the uproar that followed. From my perspective, he might well have been right. The Stout case looked, on the face of it, suspicious, and, along with several other ACORN-related irregularities, I concluded that a task force was indeed warranted. Voter fraud accusations had, in fact, been leveled against the organization in several states, including Florida, Michigan, and Colorado, during the final month of the 2004 elections, and the organization had long been in the administration's crosshairs. On a Fox News interview during this period, Karl Rove referred to "a bunch of workers from ACORN . . . a highly partisan group, carrying a bunch of prisoner ballots out of the prison illegally and attempting to vote them."

I was determined to get to the bottom of the matter in my jurisdiction, but my announcement of a dedicated task force notwithstanding, the firebrands were still not placated. Following my press briefing, during which I had assured the public that I was "ready to investigate all legitimate referrals," I got an angry e-mail from Mickey Barnett, an attorney who, like me, had worked on the Bush-Cheney campaign in 2000 and who berated me for "appointing a task force to investigate voter fraud instead of bringing charges against suspects." Republican state party chairman Allen Weh was also vociferous in his displeasure. "If I saw a felony taking place," he told the *New York Times*, "and reported it to the police, I would be mad if they didn't do anything." He went on to relate to the newspaper a phone conversation that he had had with me during which he insisted, "There were well-known instances of voter fraud and people expect them to be prosecuted." What Weh did not know, is that I was in close contact with the investigating FBI agent and with veteran career election fraud lawyer Craig Donsanto of Main Justice's Public Integrity unit. In addition, I had assigned the whole matter to my most trusted prosecutor and my close friend Rumaldo Armijo. We had tried civil and criminal cases together as young lawyers and I knew him to be relentless. I held my ground, systematically investigating the allegations of fraud against the worker, along with more than a hundred other incidents. In the end, Main Justice, the local FBI, and I agreed that there were no prosecutable cases. Being close doesn't count in prosecutions where the government has to prove its case beyond a reasonable doubt. This very high standard was intentional and a necessary check of government power against an individual. The main problem was that the government had to prove beyond a reasonable doubt that the worker intended to affect the outcome of the election. The facts did not support what the law required.

The election came and went, with New Mexico going to George W. Bush by the narrowest of margins, and by January 2005, I was ready to announce the results of the four-month probe. There was insufficient evidence to prosecute any of the alleged voter fraud cases. "Most of the complaints were completely without basis," I told media outlets at the time. "At the end of the day, we decided that we did not have any cases we could prove beyond a reasonable doubt . . . we cannot prosecute rumor and innuendo."

It was not an assertion that was universally shared. With the benefit of hindsight, I can see that this decision, based on cut-and-dried legal considerations, convinced my one-time Republican patrons, on both a state and a national level, that I lacked the fire in the belly to effectively implement their partisan agenda. I think the Vigil case may, to their minds, have been an aberration in my status as a loyal operative. It would, in any case, have been hard to argue that I was lax in my prosecutorial zeal of the state treasurer. My conclusions in the voter fraud flap, on the other hand, smacked of nothing less than an unwillingness to wield the power of my office for purely political purposes. It was in the aftermath of the announcement that I would not bring any charges of voter fraud in New Mexico and that, by implication, the entire firestorm had been little more than a gust of hot air that I began to hear the rumblings of a whispering campaign among Republican operatives giving voice to their discontent.

In one of the enduring ironies brought to light by subsequent events, I was chosen almost a year later as one of two U.S. Attorneys to teach what was called a "voting integrity symposium" sponsored by the Justice Department, which was held in Washington and attended by more than a hundred prosecutors from around the country. Along with Steven Biskupic, the U.S. Attorney for the Eastern District of Wisconsin, I had been selected because we were the only ones who had actually formed task forces to actively investigate voter fraud allegations during the 2004 election. The seminar was probably the only one where rock-and-roll group Guns 'n Roses was ever quoted in a DOJ setting, when I cited its song "Welcome to the Jungle." The luncheon speaker during the two-day event was Attorney General Alberto Gonzales.

As I said, it was a twist to the tale that is evident only in hindsight. All that I was aware of, in the early days of 2005, were vague rumblings of discontent over my handling of the ACORN case and others. In January, a longtime colleague had turned a friendly lunch into an occasion to warn me of my quickly eroding support within the party. Republicans had wanted splashy headlines trumpeting voter fraud indictments, he told me, and when they didn't get what they wanted, they were only too ready to assign blame. From my perch as one of the party's anointed, with all of the enhanced political possibilities that came with it, I was systematically being knocked down to the status of a persona non grata.

I did what I could to mend fences, but the truth was, even then I had a growing sense of ambivalence about my suddenly precarious position. I had taken this job because of my love for the law and my belief that I could help in the cause of justice. I was, perhaps naively, stubborn in my response to the political pressures I faced. After an exhaustive examination of the facts, I felt that I had dispelled the phantoms of voter fraud in New Mexico. But some people had wanted a different result, whether or not it was warranted by the facts. What *was* wavering was my own sense of loyalty and solidarity, as if I was suddenly on the outside looking in. It was a feeling I did my best to ignore.

That task was made more difficult as my office became embroiled in another high-profile case that had charged political implications. In 1998, the New Mexico legislature, in a special session, approved a $46.5 million bond issue to finance construction of a new, state-of-the-art Bernalillo County Courthouse in downtown Albuquerque. The project had been relentlessly promoted during the previous two years by court administrator Toby Martinez, and it was under the Senate president pro tempore Manny Aragon that the funding was finally approved.

Among the most flamboyant politicians in the state, Aragon had been elected to represent Albuquerque's South Valley district in 1974. He was a liberal Democrat known for taking good care of his constituents, and his career at the state House was marked by conflict-of-interest allegations and the outsized influence he exerted on the Democratic state machine.

Manny, who would later be named president of New Mexico Highlands University, had a fondness for lavish and expensive gestures. His district home was a literal castle, complete with crenellated turrets, a drawbridge, and bathrooms of Tuscan marble. But as work on the courthouse commenced in 1999, it became clear to those close to the project that the senator's interest extended into areas other than architectural splendor.

Allegedly conspiring with Martinez and his wife, along with an array of local architects, lobbyists, contractors, consultants, and even a former Albuquerque mayor, Aragon oversaw an elaborate kickback scheme that involved dummy invoices, cash payments, and a robust money-laundering operation, bilking large sums of bond revenue that were earmarked for the expansive construction project. It was an indication of just how deeply Aragon and his cohorts had their hands in the state's pockets that a good percentage of their take came from inflated contracts for the courthouse's audio-visual equipment.

Hints of what in legal parlance is termed a "jointly undertaken criminal activity" first came to my attention in late 2003, and after looking at the available evidence, I turned the case over to the FBI. The Bureau launched an investigation that continued over the course of the next year and right into the 2004 election season.

It was, of course, virtually impossible to keep word of such a high-profile probe a secret, and as months went by, rumors and word of mouth spread that an indictment of Aragon and his co-conspirators was in the works. In point of fact, the good case was taking shape, thanks in large part to plea agreements we had obtained from one of the principle architects, a subcontractor, and the former mayor Ken Schultz, who were facing some hefty charges of their own for their part in the long-running scam.

It's always been my contention that like a fine wine, no indictment should be served before its time, when every piece of the prosecution is in place, and the case has been examined from every possible angle and is ready to be presented in a cogent and coherent fashion. It was a rule of thumb all the more applicable to white-collar cases, which typically involve complex and often confusing paper trails and the likelihood that the defendant can afford the very best in legal representation. These cases are, simply put, hard to prove, but I felt confident that we were moving in that direction on the Aragon case, and the last thing I wanted to do was jeopardize the outcome by rushing it into court. I guess, after the less-than-perfect outcome of the state treasurer's prosecution, I felt that I had something to prove, and I was determined that when the time came, we would make the charges stick.

Which is not to say that I wasn't aware of the stakes involved in dragging Manny Aragon, a tainted but still formidable player in

New Mexico politics, into court on federal conspiracy charges. I had no idea how much of a liability he had become to state Democrats, but I knew one thing for certain: New Mexico Republicans were salivating at the possibility of an Aragon indictment. He had been in their target sights for decades but always managed to escape unscathed.

The primary beneficiary of such a headline-grabbing case would be Heather Wilson, who in 2006 was facing a stiff challenge for New Mexico's 1st Congressional District seat against Patricia Madrid, my opponent for the attorney general's office eight years earlier. A graduate of the Air Force Academy and a Rhodes scholar, Wilson had earned a doctorate in international relations from Oxford University and had worked at the National Security Council before becoming secretary of New Mexico's Department of Children, Youth, and Family. My old office, state risk management, had represented her on numerous occasions when she or her employees were sued. I had also campaigned with her in 1998 when I ran for state attorney general. When she was elected to Congress in 1998, she was the first female representative from the state since the 1940s and had since gone on to become something of a star in the Republican Party. She was given the Hero of the Taxpayer Award a year after taking office and making a name for herself, in the words of the *Albuquerque Tribune*, "as a loyal, dependable vote for the official Republican Party on the overwhelming majority of issues."

Wilson came to national attention when, at a Federal Communications Commission hearing, she denounced Janet Jackson's infamous Super Bowl halftime "wardrobe malfunction" and showed herself to be a staunch defender of the uranium and lumber interests. The latter put her on the League of Conservation Voters' "Dirty Dozen" list of environmental offenders, which is a virtual badge of honor among the state's mining and forestry interests. Smart and engaged, Wilson was a formidable campaigner and won reelection in 2000, 2002, and 2004 by narrow margins, on both occasions with the help of large cash infusions from the Republican National Committee.

In 2006, with the nation's mood souring over the Iraq War, it was a different story. From almost the beginning of the congressional campaign, Wilson was shown trailing Madrid in polls, sometimes by as much as 9 percentage points; at other times, the polls showed a dead heat. Madrid was the first woman to be elected in New Mexico as a district court judge and was a fierce campaigner in her own right—a fact to which I can personally attest. She had also launched task forces to deal with violence against women and Internet crimes against children, as well as a victims' services unit. She was savvy and ambitious and, as much as the 2006 election may have served as a vote of no confidence on Republican scandals and war policy, Madrid also presented a real alternative to Wilson's strict party line.

On the other hand, Madrid pulled a hare-brained stunt that is probably without precedent in state legal history—she indicted in state court the cooperating witnesses in the federal retrial case of Robert Vigil. Her evidence: the transcripts of the first Vigil trial. Our key witness promptly refused to testify again in federal court since his words could be used in a future state trial against him. I wanted to blast Madrid in the media but quickly reconsidered when I realized that it would have political ramifications in her campaign against Wilson. I publicly criticized Madrid only after the election, calling her move "a form of legalized obstruction of justice."

As the election got closer and grew tighter, the tension in the New Mexico Republican camp was almost palpable. Wilson was a darling of the party—a favored position that I had, up until recently, been very familiar with myself. As the GOP saw the midterm handwriting on the wall, it became even more imperative to hang onto the seats it had. The prospect of an upset in New Mexico was all the more unsettling as the party saw a state where it had made real progress in recent years slipping away.

It was against that backdrop that I traveled to Washington, D.C., during the week of October 16, for what would prove to be my last visit to the capital in my official capacity as U.S. Attorney. I was there for meetings both on the border and immigration issues and on an innovative information-sharing program that was developed by my colleague and close friend John McKay, the U.S. Attorney for the Western District of Washington State. Standing at the registration desk in my hotel, I picked up a message on my cell phone: Heather Wilson had called. I remember thinking how odd it seemed and wondering what the congresswoman wanted. Our paths rarely crossed and only in occasional official settings. I had made a point of staying above the fray of the election as much as possible, which meant limiting my contact with candidates and incumbents. Something must be up.

Something was. After a moment of polite chitchat, in which I told her I was in Washington, and she expressed her condolences, Wilson got to the point. She had heard that there were sealed indictments that had recently been filed. What could I tell her about that?

Alarm bells went off in my head even before she finished asking. I can't say that I was surprised that she had heard about the indictments. Someone had specifically leaked the news to her in a muddled attempt to get me to move up the timetable on the Aragon prosecution. Of course, there were a lot of rumors swirling around regarding the massive courthouse swindle, and, like most rumors, this one was only partially true. Since the case was not ready to go to trial, I was negotiating the pleas of the cooperating witnesses, who would later be charged with one federal count apiece, and then my office would seal their pleas, while I prepared to move forward against Aragon. It was an unusual move but not unprecedented, especially if a prosecutor can show sufficient cause to keep his witnesses under wraps. Heather must have heard an incorrect version of the matter and believed I had already sealed the pleas when she called me in October. In fact, they were not sealed until well after the election, but Heather did not know that. Even had she been right about the sealed pleas, she did not have a right to know this privileged information—she could have written me a letter on her official letterhead naming the constituent and asking me about the proposed indictment, and it would have still been highly improper.

I was shocked that Wilson was asking me to disclose privileged information on an ongoing case. Sealed indictments are sealed for a reason, and there are stringent rules, as stated in the Federal Rules of Criminal Procedure, that forbid federal prosecutors from even revealing information about their existence. It was, in fact, New Mexico senator Carl Hatch who had codified the prohibition in 1939 in the act that bears his name. This act forbids federal employees from engaging in partisan politics. The law's official title: An Act to Prevent Pernicious Political Activities. By the same token, legislative rules forbid a member of Congress from contacting a prosecutor about an active case except when the congressperson might have information that would help the investigation. Anything less is construed, quite rightly, as potential interference, especially when the one doing the asking is running in the race of her life against a standing attorney general. Wilson knew all this. Why was she compromising both of us by prodding me for details?

That answer was as plain as day. I could almost have written the TV spot myself, complete with a sonorous voiceover. "Has Heather Wilson's opponent been asleep at the wheel? As attorney general, Patricia Madrid looked the other way while corrupt officials got rich off the County Courthouse boondoggle. Now the feds have had to step in. [Pregnant pause.] And do-nothing Patricia Madrid wants to be *your* member of Congress?"

As much as anything, I was irritated with Wilson. I didn't know whether she assumed that I was simply too stupid to make the political connection to her query, and I didn't really care. I was more upset that someone in her position could presume on the U.S. Attorney's office to provide her with information that could very well influence the outcome of an election. In retrospect, my reaction might rather have been one of considerably more outrage. As annoyed as I was and as evasive in my responses as I became, the fact remained that Wilson had stepped over the line, and I would have been well within my rights to report her to the House Ethics Committee. I was sure that Wilson was desperate for anything that might give her an edge in the race, and I was just as certain that she wasn't going to get it from me. "Sometimes we request sealed indictments in juvenile cases," I replied vaguely. "And sometimes for national security cases." A long pause ensued, as if she was giving me the opportunity to add corrupt Democrats to that list.

"I see," she said, after it was apparent that nothing more would be forthcoming. Then she added cryptically, "I'll have to take your word for it."

I hung up genuinely puzzled and more than a little put out. I knew well enough that the line between a simple question and subtle pressure could be blurred or even erased in my line of work. The whole concept of pressure as it applies to politics and the law is, in fact, malleable and subjective, as asserted by Jim Eisenstein in his groundbreaking study of U.S. Attorneys. "The role pressure plays . . . defies complete analysis," he wrote in *Counsel for the United States.* "Whether a communication received . . . assumes the status of 'pressure' depends on the recipient's reaction to the message."

In other words, it's in the eye of the beholder. Knowing how the system worked, I wasn't sure what blowing the whistle on Wilson would accomplish, especially considering my own precarious position with the party. Suffice it to say, the nagging unease that I felt from Wilson's highly inappropriate and even illegal phone call would take on a whole other dimension a couple of weeks later.

On a sunny morning in the waning days of October, I sat in a red recliner in my bedroom when the phone suddenly rang. On the other end of the line was Steve Bell, Senator Pete Domenici's chief of staff. "We've been hearing a lot of complaints about you," he announced peremptorily. "Here's the Senator." A moment later, Domenici himself got on.

"St. Pete" was my mentor and the man who, with a nod of his head, had given the go-ahead for me to step into a respected and high-profile job that had immeasurably enhanced my future prospects. I owed this man a lot, and to receive a call at home from so significant a national figure, not to mention a veritable legend in the governance of my state, was not only unprecedented; it was unnerving. I remember feeling an immediate and vertiginous flutter when I realized whom I was talking to. At the same time, there was a sudden rush of blood to my brain while I ran through the ramifications of his call, trying earnestly to get ahead of whatever curve I was about to head into. It wasn't a good feeling. There was no reason, especially on the heels of Bell's brusque introduction, for it to be otherwise. This was all too far out of the blue to bode well.

As Domenici dispensed with pat pleasantries, I cast back to the last time I had seen the senator. Aside from the few courtesy visits we had extended to each other over the years—convenient enough, since our offices were in the same downtown building— nothing really stood out. Except, that is, for one such casual meeting earlier in 2006 when, without blinking, he had asked me to get him up to speed on another corruption investigation I was supposedly conducting at the time. The target had, according to media accounts, allegedly received hefty contributions from a local bank to a nonprofit organization that he headed, and he had intervened on an insurance claim for a family member after an auto accident. Domenici may not have blinked, but I did. I could tell from the questions he had asked then that he wanted to gauge how strong a case we had built against the target, and I counted myself lucky when I was able to tell him honestly that I did not know anything about the alleged investigation since the FBI hadn't briefed me. He dropped the subject, leaving me with a sense of being both relieved and puzzled, as if I had dodged a bullet but with no idea why it had been fired in the first place.

Such mixed emotions are hardly unique within the delicate and deliberately indistinct relationship between U.S. Attorneys and their home-state senators. What was true in my case had been true for the vast majority of U.S. Attorneys who had come before me: without a senatorial nod, it's difficult, if not impossible, to land the plum position. "The custom of 'senatorial courtesy,'" wrote Jim Eisenstein, referring to a long-established tradition of deferring to senators in the selection of U.S. Attorneys, "has transformed the procedural requirements of Senate confirmation into a potent resource for senators of the president's party. In fact, some students of senatorial courtesy believe that senators actually control the nomination of federal officers such as U.S. Attorneys."

By this very precedent, I was, of course, acutely aware of being beholden to Domenici, which made me all the more determined, as I settled into my office, not to seek favors or influence from him. On the occasions that he asked me whether I had everything I needed, I was diligent in assuring him that I did, even though I occasionally mentioned our need for more immigration prosecutors to handle our caseload. But even then, I tried to keep it general and low-key. I had seen directly what happened to U.S. Attorneys who used their sway with senators to get the vital manpower and funding they chronically lacked. Paul Charlton, the U.S. Attorney for Arizona and a first-rate prosecutor and friend with whom I'd worked closely on various Southwestern issues, had run into a lot of flak from the Justice Department after prevailing on Arizona senator Jon Kyl to secure approval for eleven new staff attorneys. In the noisy turf battle that ensued, it was made clear that Main Justice did not look kindly on interference in its funding and staffing procedures, regardless of who was making the request. My scruples even extended to not visiting New Mexico senators when I was in Washington. I just never felt comfortable "dropping by," so I did not.

Domenici seemed to have no such compunctions, at least in regard to a surprise phone call on my day off. But worries of being called on the carpet for my deteriorating relationship with state Republicans were quickly dispelled. The senator had other things on his mind.

"I've been reading about these corruption matters," he said, quickly cutting to the chase.

I think I actually felt the short hairs rising on the back of my neck. I knew exactly what he was talking about: Manny Aragon and the courthouse case. It was the only "corruption matter" that the local press had been covering, for months on end at that point. The fact that Domenici was being clever—too clever by half—in keeping it vague, served only to make his probing that much more unsettling. It suggested, in no uncertain terms, that he knew that what he was asking was patently improper and could get us both into a great deal of trouble if it was ever revealed. He was asking me, in a roundabout but utterly unmistakable way, to be a party with him in an unethical leak of highly sensitive and privileged information. It was also information that, with the election only weeks away, had explosive political ramifications. An indictment of Aragon was, by extension, an indictment of Patricia Madrid and her tenure as attorney general. I knew it, Domenici knew it, and between us, that understanding hung in the humming static of the phone line.

But in case I had any doubts as to where all this was heading, Domenici's next question dispelled them completely. As I muttered something noncommittal, trying desperately to think my way out of the corner into which I had been painted, the senator interrupted me to lay it all, and in no uncertain terms, on the line.

"Are these going to be filed before November?" he asked with a bluntness that was as shocking as the substance and the implication of his question. "These" clearly meant the indictments.

I swallowed hard. There was no way that I was going to wiggle out of this. Senator Peter Domenici, in all his gravitas, wanted an answer, and he wanted it then and there. "I don't . . . think so," I stammered. After I'd let that much go—when, by the standards of my office, I shouldn't have said anything at all—it was hard to stop. I felt an acute desire to give him what he wanted, while, at the same time, I fought a rising sense of panic. I forced myself to stop talking, knowing that I was a hairbreadth away from fatally compromising my office, my career, and myself. On the other end was a brief but pregnant pause.

"I'm very sorry to hear that," Domenici said at last. And with that, the line went dead. I was left with a dial tone in my ear and a sick feeling in the pit of my stomach.

CHAPTER 6

The Link

I n the wake of my firing on December 7, 2006, all manner of
milestones, crossroads, and points of no return became retro-
spectively apparent. But there was none more singular than
the call I received from Pete Domenici on that crisp October
morning. I knew by my deep-seated feeling of distress, as I sat
there with the mute phone in my hand, that something ominous
had just occurred, for me, for my family, and for the office of U.S.
Attorney in the District of New Mexico.

It was an instinctive realization that was confirmed over and
over in the scandal that would subsequently engulf me, not least
in the considered opinions of both my critics and my allies, who
parsed out my response to Domenici's unwarranted inquiries that
morning. There were those who pointed out that for all the innuendo that made the conversation so fraught, the senator never
once actually said the name of Manny Aragon or made any specific mention of the courthouse case. By the same token, any
assumption I might make as to the import of his call was just that.
Maybe I was, after all, just being paranoid.

My response to that is simple: I wasn't born yesterday. I knew what Domenici wanted, and he knew what he wanted, and it was on the basis of that unspoken understanding that rank was pulled, pressure brought to bear, and accommodation sought with a wink and a nudge. The senator was too canny a politician to come right out and say what he wanted, and, in his way, he was giving me credit for being smart enough to figure out what he was after. But it wasn't rocket science, and I certainly didn't need it spelled out for me.

Others, including a former U.S. Attorney who stated this on national television, said that my proper response should have been to tell the honorable senator to "go to hell." Maybe so. And if Domenici hadn't been a beneficent mentor, a powerful public figure, and a man for whom I had great admiration—and to whom I owed a great obligation—that would certainly have been an option. But he was, and it wasn't. Yet it went even further than purely professional considerations. Pete Domenici was old enough to be my father, and I had been taught to honor and defer to my elders. Given my military background, it was likewise inevitable that I would come to view him as a de facto five-star admiral on the ship of state where I was serving as an executive officer. Old habits of hierarchy, obedience, and duty are not easily set aside. It's simple enough to summon courage and even righteous indignation in the abstract but considerably harder when sitting in your bedroom on a bright morning with your whole professional life suddenly hanging in the balance. I make no excuses. My own moment of truth and redemption—many of them, as a matter of fact—would be coming soon enough.

On that morning, though, I was still a long way from realizing what exactly had transpired. Hanging up the phone, I looked across the room to where Cyndy was standing just a few feet away. She had overheard my end of the conversation, and the look on her face must have mirrored the one on my own.

"Who was that?" she asked, her voice barely above a whisper.

"It was Pete Domenici," I replied, looking down at the receiver and wondering if, by some chance, we had been disconnected and he hadn't been as abrupt and discourteous as he had seemed. Only later did I learn that the senator had a reputation for cutting short any conversations that displeased him, on the phone by hanging up abruptly. I briefly considered calling him back. Perhaps it had just been a technical glitch, but even as the thought occurred to me, I dismissed it. Domenici's demand had been as clear as his response when the request wasn't fulfilled forthwith.

"What did he want?" Cyndy asked me, still rooted to her spot on the carpet. We traded a look, and I could see the fear that I couldn't hide reflected in her eyes. Something bad had just happened, and, in the way of husbands and wives, that reality flashed wordlessly between us.

"He wanted to know when I was going to file the corruption case," I told her. It was easy to see from her startled reaction that my wife understood the implications of the call, although, in point of fact, all that she knew about the Aragon case was what she, along with everyone else, was reading in the newspapers. Spouses of U.S. Attorneys are certainly not included in the need-to-know circle of an ongoing federal investigation, and Cyndy had long since learned what not to ask. But she hardly had to be an insider to grasp the precarious position in which we suddenly found ourselves. She knew only too well what Domenici represented, both politically and personally, and what it meant to get on his bad side. It was as if, in that moment, we both shared some burden akin to a guilty secret, as well as the unspoken hope that the whole incident would simply fade away like a bad dream.

But as profound as that hope might have been, I was also aware that Domenici's call could very well have an effect on the Aragon investigation itself. It was important that someone in the upper echelons of my office be made aware of the political pressure being brought to bear on the developing case. That someone was my first assistant, Larry Gomez, a twenty-seven-year veteran of the New Mexico U.S. Attorney's office and, among other things, a top-notch narcotics prosecutor. Although Larry wasn't directly handling the Aragon case, as first assistant he had an oversight function in all the operations of the office and had been briefed by the FBI on its progress. Like me, Larry knew that we were close to filing indictments on the suspects in the courthouse swindle but were certainly not close enough to predict a date. He was naturally shocked when I told him about the call from Domenici.

What I think we both avoided addressing as we discussed what had happened was what should be done about it. I was still struggling with a misplaced sense of loyalty to the senator and, much more so than with Heather Wilson, was reluctant to even consider reporting the incident. At that stage, the last thing I wanted was to further stir this seamy political stew, much less bring it to a boil.

But as time passed, the implications that I tried to ignore or avoid began to crowd in on me. It wasn't just that I was waiting for the other shoe to drop. It was clear enough that crossing Domenici would have consequences considerably more dire than the fallout from telling Heather Wilson, in so many words, to mind her own business. I simply didn't believe that she had the clout to do me any real harm. The senator was another matter entirely, and all I could do was wait uneasily for how he might choose to express his disappointment.

What instead captured my attention in the days immediately following Domenici's phone call were the first faint glimmerings of a web of connections among these events, the upcoming election, and the overarching ambitions of the Republican Party to rescue its dream of permanent political hegemony. As it faced a restive and disgruntled electorate in that crucial midterm election, a kind of panic had descended on the party and, with it, a determination to cut corners and bend rules to hang onto power. It was that panic, I was convinced, that had prompted Wilson and Domenici to ratchet up the stakes on the Aragon investigation. The wagons were circled. You were either for them or against them, and for the first time in my political life, I felt the stinging sensation of ostracism.

Then came December 7, and the sting became a deep wound. In the aftermath, Cyndy and I spent hours in the hot tub that we could no longer afford, trying to piece together some feasible reason for my firing. I knew from the years I had served that there are only two legitimate reasons a U.S. Attorney is taken out: the first is, obviously, misconduct; the second, performance. But it was hard to square either of those with the consistently high ratings my office had gotten, including numerous votes of confidence from Attorney General Alberto Gonzales. During visits to my office, most recently in the summer of that year, the attorney general seemed to be making a point of letting me know what a great job I was doing. There was no mention of problems or any suggestion that my job was in jeopardy, not during our face-to-face or later, when we had dinner together.

Like many Hispanics, I felt a lot of pride when, in 2005, Gonzales was confirmed as the successor to John Ashcroft and became the eightieth attorney general of the United States. I had followed his career with some interest, especially since we shared a similar background: his Mexican grandparents, his working-class upbringing. These were origin stories I could relate to. Our paths crossed occasionally at various U.S. Attorney conferences, and in the summer of 2005, I invited him to New Mexico to attend a border conference I was hosting. After staying a day, he rushed back to Washington, D.C., as news of the London terrorist bombings broke, while, as recently as August 2006, he had made an official visit to New Mexico. At his side on that occasion was his chief of staff, Kyle Sampson.

But my first encounter with Gonzales was back when he was the White House counsel in 2001. It was a few months after I'd become a U.S. Attorney, and I had asked for a few minutes of his time to introduce myself. Those few minutes turned into an hour as we got to know each other. He even asked me who my hero was, and I told him that it was my father. But it was something else he said that had really stuck in my mind. "This is a tough town," he told me. "They are out to destroy the president, and it is my job to protect him."

From all the evidence that followed in the disastrous wake of his tenure, it was a conviction he carried with him into the Department of Justice. And it explains completely, at least to me, why he did what he did or, rather, failed to do. Simply put, Alberto Gonzales lost his way. He chose loyalty to Bush over fealty to the Constitution and his sworn duty to uphold it. To Gonzales, duty meant not standing up against improper political hirings and firings or speaking out against warrentless wiretaps or telling Karl Rove and his operatives in Main Justice to go pound sand. But that's not what happened, and we are where we are as the direct result of one of the most acute leadership crises in the history of the Justice Department.

I'm getting ahead of myself, though. Back in December 2006, I could only stare up at the starry sky from a steaming spa with no clear picture of what had happened, much less why it had happened. I was confident in my record as a U.S. Attorney. As best I could, I had scrupulously avoided even the appearance of wrongdoing. Was there something I was missing, some infraction I had inadvertently committed? I turned the question over and over in my mind but could find no crime to fit the punishment. Equally unlikely, it seemed, was any shortfall in my job performance. It wasn't only the statistics: the increases in arrest and conviction rates; the intense focus on the border issues that struck so close to home in my state. Stats are never as hard to achieve as the intangibles that make a law enforcement operation successful: morale, teamwork, commitment. I had worked hard to build these among members of my staff.

That left only one last, but very distinct, possibility: pure politics, or maybe that should be impure politics.

It was a conclusion that I was hardly surprised to have arrived at. It was all but unavoidable. I'm trained to examine evidence and to weigh facts. Politics was the only explanation that fit what I knew. It was a classic criminal formula: motive, means, and opportunity. There was, I began to realize, a wealth of motives: the decision I had made not to pursue voter fraud cases at just the moment when they could have done the most damage to Democrats or the shortfall on the Vigil case. And, of course, the timing, or lack thereof, in the Aragon indictments. Both Wilson's and Domenici's calls had been about seeking the same information. It seemed reasonable to assume that once the congresswoman couldn't get what she wanted, she handed it off to the senator.

It was an assumption underscored by the troubling news I heard the week after December 7, when a close friend advised me that Wilson was calling around to Republican attorneys asking whether they were interested in being interviewed as my replacement. The story of my resignation had not yet been made public, and it seemed decidedly inappropriate that a member of the House, which does not confirm U.S. Attorneys, would be making such calls. The timing made sense in light of an email that was produced several months later to Congress. In it, Steve Bell crows that they were "not waiting for his body to cool." Another email describes Bell as "happy as a clam" that I had been asked to resign.

This had been a concerted effort, a political strategy that was aimed at the removal of an obstreperous underling guilty of—what? Insufficient zeal? Disloyalty? Treachery? Maybe all of the above.

The question of means seemed equally obvious and underhanded. It was clear enough that whoever wanted me unceremoniously dumped had the power to make it happen. Naturally, I wondered who it might be: one individual or a mysterious cabal? Were some of them my friends? My coworkers? Those I trusted and whom I thought trusted me? Or maybe it was just some faceless bureaucrat with a rubber stamp in an office deep in the bowels of the Justice Department. Again, perhaps all of the above.

As to opportunity, the time line seemed unambiguous enough. The midterm elections had been a disaster. The Republicans had gotten what President George W. Bush jocularly referred to as a "whuppin'," and the party had been rocked repeatedly by lurid scandals. When the going gets tough, the politicians get antsy, and there were a lot of rattled nerves in the waning days of 2006. It was time to clean house, sort out your friends, and call in your favors. Maybe I was just collateral damage in the general rush to the lifeboats, with all the vindictiveness and the acrimony and the suspicion that make up the dark side of the democratic process.

Maybe, after all, not knowing was better than knowing. Somebody out there wanted to get me, someone powerful and connected. Did I really need to find out who it was? What would I do about it if I could? "All things work together for good to those who love God and are called according to His purposes." I remembered believing that. Did I still believe it?

All of these thoughts came to me, one by one and in a rush, as my hot tub sessions which became political analysis time for Cyndy and me got longer and longer. More than anything, even more than the anger and the embarrassment, I remember how lonely I felt, after Cyndy had gone to bed and the neighborhood lights were low, under that big New Mexico sky. The Belt of Orion moved ever so slowly and silently above. I felt so completely alone, cut off, and isolated. It turned out that I wasn't. Not by a long shot.

As was customary, the office closed for the holidays. Facing the prospect of a bleak Christmas, I was reluctant to close the door behind me at the end of our last full workday. There was also, undeniably, a palpable sense of sorrow, of a promise left unfulfilled and a mission cut short just before completion. All of my predecessors, the ones I'd talked to after my nomination, had been right: being a U.S. Attorney was the best job I'd ever have. I would miss the extraordinary people I worked with and the sense of mission that we all shared.

But most of all, I regretted the way it had ended: not with the satisfaction of a job well done but in the humiliation of a forced resignation. It was a disappointment made deeper by the nagging thought that I somehow had only myself to blame. Should I have seen this coming? Could I have done something to avert it? I had tried my best to stay above the fray of politics. I couldn't help but wonder whether I shouldn't have learned instead to be a more accomplished player in the game of ambition and influence, to circle a few of my own wagons and call in some of my own favors. The problem was, I had no one to call. The one powerful political broker who could have helped me had already called *me*, and it seemed increasingly likely that this had been the beginning of the end.

It was then, just before I turned out the lights and headed home, that I checked my e-mail one more time. There was a message from John McKay, the U.S. Attorney from the Western District of Washington State. Its subject line was "Resignation."

I had always considered John McKay the first among equals in the community of U.S. Attorneys and have been honored to call him a friend. He is, by any measure, an extraordinary individual: clear-eyed but passionate, hard-nosed but idealistic, and, like me, a man who wanted to do some good.

And he had done a lot of it during his five years as a U.S. Attorney. Appointed by President Bush in October 2001, McKay brought with him a wealth of hands-on history, both legal and political. The fifth of twelve children in the sprawling McKay brood, he was the scion of an established Republican dynasty in the Northwest, a clan often referred to as the "the Kennedys of Washington State." His older brother Mike had been a U.S. Attorney before him. John had served a stint as an aide to Congressman Joel Pritchard before becoming a litigation partner in a prestigious Seattle law firm. John had been a White House Fellow under George H. W. Bush and had served as a special assistant to the FBI director. Once he was confirmed as U.S. Attorney, he got off to a quick start. He did his part for the war on terror by overseeing a four-year investigation of "Millennium Bomber" Ahmed Ressam, which resulted in this man's successful prosecution and conviction in 2005.

But John McKay was about a lot more than putting together headline-grabbing cases. His real work went on far from the limelight as he labored tirelessly and with great effect to improve the capabilities of law enforcement across a broad spectrum. He is an exceptional public servant, relentlessly focused on upholding the law and creative in his approach to improving the odds in the pursuit of justice.

And nothing improved those odds better than the Law Enforcement Information Exchange (LInX), a powerful criminal data–sharing network pioneered by McKay and without question the most important innovation I had seen in my time as a U.S. Attorney. Challenged by entrenched law enforcement bureaucracies that were clinging stubbornly to their turf, McKay confronted an interagency stranglehold on information with a nimble solution that allowed individual jurisdictions to retain control of their databases while still offering their criminal-identification services to others, up and down the chain of command. In the wake of 9/11, at a time when intelligence and law enforcement communities were struggling to break down institutional barriers in the name of national security, McKay made an end around prickly territorial disputes with LInX, which allowed a free information exchange without forcing any agency or department to relinquish control of its files. McKay not only understood that information was power, but he knew that information resided in many different pockets of power. Instead of engaging in a fruitless struggle to centralize that power and information, McKay let technology create virtual portals that authorities could plug into and out of as necessary.

McKay's implementation of LInX may have had a national impact, but his reasons for tirelessly promoting the system were distinctly local, as is true of any U.S. Attorney who is attending to the needs of his district. "We were facing an almost free flow of marijuana across the border from Canada and a returning tide of guns and cocaine from America," McKay explained. "These were full-blown criminal conspiracies, and I needed to know the names of those behind them, names I knew existed elsewhere, in some database nationally and internationally. Trying to get that information was sometimes as difficult as actually catching the criminals."

LInX, developed in conjunction with the Naval Criminal Investigation Service (NCIS), changed all of that. John had put together an unprecedented partnership between the Department of Justice and the Defense Department to bring LInX into wider use. As soon as the system's capacities were demonstrated to me, on a trip to Seattle in 2004, I knew I had to have it for New Mexico, despite the fact that there were no naval jurisdictions to speak of in my landlocked state. Ironically, it was on a trip to Washington two years later to push for LInX in my district when I received my phone call from Heather Wilson.

LInX had created tremendous excitement among U.S. Attorneys, and McKay was lauded for his vision and determination, especially in the face of some rumored foot dragging from certain individuals within Main Justice. But McKay, who radiates an aura of intense energy and conviction, had prevailed in a pilot program, and the system was just beginning to show impressive results. It was only then, on December 7, that he received his own phone call from Mike Battle.

"Being a U.S. Attorney was not the best job I ever had," John wrote wryly in the resignation e-mail that he forwarded to every U.S. Attorney later that month. "The best job I ever had was being a paper boy for the *Seattle Times*. I loved getting the tips." He concluded with a fond farewell and announced that he would be stepping down, effective the end of January 2007.

I was stunned. John McKay might have distinguished himself in any career he chose, but it seemed that as U.S. Attorney, the man had been matched perfectly to the mission. It's a small wonder that he had been interviewed for a federal judgeship by White House counsel Harriet Miers. He had the singular ability to somehow utilize both the political and the legal dimensions of the job to get things—important things—done. He brilliantly worked the angles without for a moment losing his integrity, his idealism, or his focus. McKay was a rock star among U.S. Attorneys. His resignation simply made no sense. Nor did the fact that he hadn't announced in his e-mail where he was going once he left his post. It was totally out of character for him not to have a well-established game plan well in advance, especially when it entailed leaving his U.S. Attorney office before his term expired.

Unless, like me, he was being forced out. I had a lot of mixed emotions as I sat at my computer in the empty office, looking at his words on the screen. A sense of anger arose, similar to what I'd felt about my own firing. Maybe there were "reasons" for getting rid of me. But John McKay? What kind of value did Main Justice put on excellence to let someone of his caliber go? Yet at the same time, I also experienced a rush of relief. Suddenly, I wasn't alone in all of this anymore. In fact, it was possible that I was in very good company. I needed to know for sure but didn't want to ask directly. For the moment, I had determined to keep the news of my being forced out to myself, at least until I had a chance to figure out why. If McKay hadn't been fired as well, I didn't want to tip my hand before I was ready.

"Hey Buddy," I replied in a deliberately oblique return e-mail to John. "Did you get the same phone call that I did?"

Within minutes, his answer bounced back. "I sure did," he wrote. "And I'm not the only one."

Mike Battle, the director of the Executive Office for U.S. Attorneys, had been very busy on December 7, 2006. He hadn't given only me the bad news but was, in fact, the official bearer of bad tidings for a total of seven U.S. Attorneys. It was, in the bloodiest political sense of the word, a massacre. It was also unprecedented. Aside from the periodic clean sweep that often accompanies a change of administration, the simultaneous firings of seven U.S. Attorneys had never before happened in U.S. history. We all understood that we served at the pleasure of the president. What we didn't understand was how the president's pleasure could have turned against so many of us, all at the same time. No president in America's history had ever forced out so many of his own U.S. Attorneys.

The fact that one official—and, at that, an inappropriate one in the hiring and firing protocol of the Justice Department—had been left to do the dirty work is a sad chapter in the annals of the unfolding scandal. In the small, tight fraternity of U.S. Attorneys, current and former, Battle was "one of us." His position as director of the Executive Office, I think, counted for less among his colleagues than did his three years as the U.S. Attorney in the

Western District of New York. He'd been in the trenches like the rest of us, not only fighting crime but sometimes fighting the bureaucracy as well. None of us, I think, held it against him that he was now on the other side of the desk, carrying out the priorities of Main Justice. Quite the contrary: it helped to know that a real U.S. Attorney was overseeing the Executive Office in Washington.

That had not always been the case. Yet at the same time, it was well understood that overseeing the EOUSA was one step removed from the real action. It was for that very reason that I had turned down an offer in 2005 to become director of the office myself. I have more than once reflected that if my decision had been different, it would have been me who was called upon to make those painful calls.

Would I have done so? I like to think I might have drawn some line in the sand at that point, offered up my own resignation or, at the very least, demanded to know the reason that seven of my fellow U.S. Attorneys were getting the sack. There is no way to know for sure what would have transpired if I had been in Battle's shoes. But I wasn't, and it's Mike who has to bear whatever psychic scars might have been inflicted that day, on him and on us. In the end, I share the sentiment of John McKay, who, after receiving his Battle call on December 7, e-mailed Battle back to say that he was glad the bad news had been delivered by a good friend.

As a friend, I feel bad about the position Battle was put in, and I understand his reluctance to speak about it. "I can't say it was anything other than distasteful," he told NPR reporter Ari Shapiro in his only interview on the subject, and when asked whether he remembered what he had told each of us, Battle replied, "I don't know that I'll ever forget it."

In point of fact, Mike might as well have been reading from a prepared script on December 7. He revealed in his interview with Shapiro that just a month earlier, he had been called into a meeting with the attorney general's chief of staff, Kyle Sampson, to discuss how the firing process would go down. Early on, Sampson told the gathering that "Everybody here knows the purpose of the meeting except Battle," although there was no discussion of *why* they were taking us all down, just how to control the process.

In that respect, Battle wasn't kept in the dark for long. By the end, he remembered, "It was very clear that I was going to be the one to make those calls." But the clarifications didn't stop there. He was further instructed to not, under any circumstances, answer any questions and to say, in fact, as little as possible outside of a set of pre-prepared remarks, to us or anyone else.

In retrospect, the entire procedure was laid out with the kind of reckless disregard of a choreographed train wreck, with Battle's foot stuck in the tracks. A few weeks earlier, in mid-November, Sampson had sent a document to key DOJ and White House officials titled "Plan for Replacing Certain United States Attorneys." In it, the December 7 strategy was detailed, beginning with an insistence that Battle's calls to seven U.S. Attorneys would be made simultaneously with the White House's official contacting of Republican home-state senators or "Bush political leads." The fait accompli strategy was obvious: those senators and politicians who had been instrumental in securing our jobs would be informed of our dismissals precisely at the hour that we were told. No recourse was to be allowed, no objection to be noted.

Battle's marching orders were similarly draconian. "Battle informs U.S. Attorneys as follows:" the memo's bullet-pointed to-do list continued:

- What are your plans with regard to continued service as U.S. Attorney?
- The Administration is grateful for your service as U.S. Attorney but has determined to give someone else the opportunity in your district . . . for the final two years of the Administration.
- We will work with you to make sure there is a smooth transition, but intend to have a new Acting or Interim U.S. Attorney in place by January 31, 2007.

I have no idea in what order my call appeared in Battle's phone log that day. Maybe by the time he finally got to me, assurances of gratitude and a smooth transition just rang too hollow to repeat. I know I didn't hear them and later learned that Battle had been called on the carpet for being "too abrupt" and unclear about whether we were "permitted to resign or instead were being fired."

I've tried on occasion to put myself in Battle's shoes on that day: one call would have been difficult; two agonizing, but by the time he got to five, six, and seven, had he simply gone numb? "Distasteful" is certainly one way to describe what must have been a personal and professional ordeal.

Whatever Battle's behavior was expected to be, Sampson's plan did its best to anticipate what direction *our* responses would take and how best to stonewall us along the way. In a section titled "Prepare to Withstand Political Upheaval," the memo had predicted, "U.S. Attorneys desiring to save their jobs (aided by their allies in the political arena as well as the Justice Department community), likely will make efforts to preserve themselves in office. We should expect these efforts to be strenuous." Appeals, Sampson continued, were certain to be made to a number of key individuals, including the attorney general and his chief of staff, as well as to Battle directly. Also included on the list was the same Johnny Sutton I had called immediately after my firing for advice and assistance. It was a moment of prescience for the engineers of our removal.

"Recipients of such 'appeals' *must* respond identically," the memo demanded.

- What? U.S. Attorneys serve at the pleasure of the President (there is no right, nor should there be any expectation, that U.S. Attorneys would be entitled to serve beyond their four-year term).
- Who Decided? The Administration made the determination to seek the resignations (not any specific person at the White House or the Department of Justice).
- Why Me? The Administration is grateful for your service, but wants to give someone else the chance to serve in your district.
- I need more time! The decision is to have a new Acting or Interim U.S. Attorney in place by January 31, 2007.

Months later, when I, along with millions of other Americans, was finally able to read this document, after the administration was required by Congress to make public all relevant material on the scandal, I couldn't help but admire the way that Sutton had bottom-lined the whole thing. "This is political," was how he put it to me. "If I were you, I'd just go quietly."

In the lonely aftermath of December 7, it seemed like sensible advice. The isolation I felt had brought with it a kind of paralysis, which was also, it turned out, exactly according to specifications. Three days earlier, on December 4, Kyle Sampson had sent an e-mail to deputy White House counsel William Kelley, putting the final touches on their preparations. He noted that on December 6, all U.S. Attorneys would be in Washington for a conference on an administration initiative to curb Internet predators, called Project Safe Childhood. Though mandatory, I chose not to attend in favor of taking a trip to the Mexican border, where National Guards soldiers were even then being deployed as part of the beefed-up patrols of Operation Jump Start. John McKay, among others, was in attendance at the conference, however, and had the opportunity to hear Deputy Attorney General Paul McNulty praise all of them as being the best class of U.S. Attorneys with whom he'd ever worked. That was one day before seven of us were summarily dismissed.

In the ramp-up to December 7, Sampson had instructed, in a parenthetical aside in his e-mail to Kelley, that "We want to wait until they are back home and dispersed to reduce chatter." It was a concern echoed in Sampson's explicit guidelines to Battle. Under no circumstances, Battle later recounted, was he to let any one of the targeted U.S. Attorneys know that there were others on the forced resignation list. We were, if at all possible, to be kept in the dark about the scope and the specifics of our common fate. The last thing the White House and the Department of Justice wanted was a show of solidarity.

It was the fatal flaw in an already ill-conceived and clumsily executed political hit. The notion that we would simply slink into our respective corners to lick our wounds was more than a dangerously naive miscalculation of the nature of the professional relationships among U.S. Attorneys; it was a cynical underestimation of our friendships. The administration's strategies of divide and conquer, of humiliate and intimidate, could only prevail for so long. The fact that it took upward of two weeks for us to begin to make the connections proves only how badly shaken we were. But that was all about to change. We were trained to be the legal world's equivalents of gladiators, and the time was fast approaching when we would be entering the Colosseum.

CHAPTER 7

A Few More Good Men, and Women

Within a half hour of getting John McKay's response to my e-mail, we were in a deep phone conversation, a mutual data dump that did wonders for my morale and, I think, his as well. There was more to it than simply misery loving company. For me, it was the confirmation of what I had come to strongly suspect: that we had been caught in a political ambush. There was more than a little satisfaction in having that confirmed by what John was telling me. I no longer needed to blame myself for what had happened. This wasn't just about me anymore.

There were others, McKay assured me, more than only him and me, although at that time, just as most of our offices nation-wide were getting ready to close for the holidays, it was hard to get an exact count. But he knew of three more for sure: Paul Charlton, the U.S. Attorney for the District of Arizona; Daniel Bogden, the U.S. Attorney for the District of Nevada; and Carol Lam, the U.S. Attorney for the Southern District of California.

As with almost every other aspect of the scandal that would soon erupt, I had a complex and paradoxical mix of emotions when John told me that Paul, Dan, and Carol had joined the ranks of the soon to be unemployed. It was, by an order of three, as shocking as the news that McKay himself had been fired. These were some of the best U.S. Attorneys in the country, with consistently high EARS performance evaluations to prove it. In a culture like the Justice Department, where your value is constantly being measured by the exacting metrics of caseloads and convictions, Charlton, Bogden, and Lam were at the head of their class.

That wasn't only my opinion. As the scandal continued to unfold in the fall of 2007, I vividly remember another former Bush U.S. Attorney, Matt Orwig of the Eastern District of Texas, who had come in with us as part of the class of 2001, telling a room of former U.S. Attorneys in a conference that those who had been fired were "the superstars." "It's as if they deliberately took out the leaders," he continued, "as if they were trying to send a message to the rest of us." The waste of talent and experience that the administration was willing to tolerate by removing such exemplary public servants did indeed send a message—one of fear and intimidation.

Yet at the same time, I have to confess to a feeling at least slightly akin to elation. Not only was I no longer alone. Not only was I in good company. Now, I was in the *best* company. I couldn't think of four people I would rather be sacked with on the same day, and that thought brought with it a surge of new courage. Alone, we were at the mercy of mercurial forces more powerful than any of us. Together, we could fight back.

The sense of solidarity that would come from standing with these four colleagues was underscored by the tremendous mutual respect we all shared. Paul Charlton and I, for example, had worked very closely over the years on vital issues that affected our adjacent states, most conspicuously, the flood of illegal aliens across our borders. But we had also worked on a death penalty case for which we had joint jurisdiction; it involved a team of hit men from an organized criminal group in Phoenix who had executed a father and a son in New Mexico—in cold blood. The case went through numerous federal judges, one of whom, I'm convinced, was scared off the case. It became the largest federal criminal prosecution in New Mexico history.

Paul and I also shared a common interest in maintaining good relationships with tribal leaders in Indian Country, including the sprawling Navajo Nation, which straddled Arizona and New Mexico. For example, Paul created a Four Corners amnesty plan for archaeological artifacts that were found in Indian Country. Charlton knew that enforcing ARPA (the Archaeological Resources Protection Act) and NAGPRA (the Native American Graves Repatriation Act) was next to impossible, so he asked me and the Utah U.S. Attorney to grant amnesty for ninety days if the person in possession of illegal artifacts turned these items in, no questions asked. As a result, we were able to recover many priceless artifacts, such as ancient pottery, headdresses, and even Native American skeletons. It was Charlton at his creative best, and I was honored to be part of his team.

Of course, Paul had, on his own, also made extraordinary contributions to law enforcement in Arizona, throughout the Southwest, and indeed across the country. Along the way, he had racked up an unmatched record of achievement.

In late 2006, on the eve of Charlton's firing, Main Justice had singled out his office for its "model program" in the protection of crime victims, a program initiated and overseen by Paul. He and his motivated and effective Phoenix staff consistently ranked in the top three, usually number one, nationwide for their number and quality of prosecutions and convictions, and they scored especially high in successful immigration, drugs, and weapons cases, with a fourfold increase in the latter over a four-year period of Paul's leadership. He had established the pioneering Anti-Terrorism Advisory Council (ATAC), specifically to improve communication and coordination between various agencies, an innovation that, in its way, was as significant as McKay's LInX program. A native Arizonan, a former career prosecutor, and married with two children, Charlton had mastered beautiful continental Spanish during a stint in Spain, and in honor of his bilingual skills, I had taken to calling him "Pablo" as we traveled to Mexico and Colombia together on official trips.

As had been the case with both McKay and me, Pablo was shocked and dismayed to receive his December 7 call from Mike

Battle. "More than anything, I wanted to know the reason," Charlton recounted. "If there was something I could fix, I wanted to fix it. I never had a job that I loved more than being a U.S. Attorney or, for that matter, worked harder at. There was no advance warning of a problem that would justify a firing. And it simply never occurred to me that my removal could have been politically motivated. I had a fifteen-year career at the U.S. Attorney's office, working my way up through the ranks, and had made it a point, as much as possible, to stay out of partisan infighting. From the time I was a line assistant, I'd never had a 'D' or an 'R' after my name. Perhaps in retrospect, it was naive to assume that I could stay above the fray. But that's what I truly believed was one of the first requirements of the position. Later I came to believe that politics may have played a role I my firing."

Charlton was, however, hardly naive in the immediate action he took to save his job. "I put in a call to McCain and Kyl," he continued, referring to, respectively, the senior and junior senators from Arizona. Jon Kyl, who had held his seat since 1994 and was a member of the Judiciary Committee, seemed particularly troubled by Paul's forced resignation and promised to do what he could to get an accounting from the Justice Department. "He called Paul McNulty," Charlton explained, "and got the deputy attorney general to agree to reconsider the decision to let me go." He paused, before adding with sigh, "But you know, by that time, I had reconsidered myself. I felt I had done a good job. If, for whatever reason, Main Justice didn't share that opinion, maybe it was time for me to move on. I seriously questioned how effective I could be without the confidence and support of Washington and, in the end, it seemed that our views were so disparate that I did not want to work under this Attorney General."

Dan Bogden, the U.S. Attorney for the District of Nevada, shared Paul Charlton's initial skepticism that his firing could have been politically inspired. "It never occurred to me," said the soft-spoken former U.S. Air Force JAG, who had first joined the Nevada U.S.

Attorney's office in 1990. Suffused with quiet authority and a sincerely selfless dedication to the work at which he excelled, Dan was another colleague with whom I was often in contact, again mostly in regard to the law enforcement concerns of Indian Country, which extended over large swatches of both Nevada and New Mexico. Perhaps more than most others on the December 7 hit list, Bogden had a difficult time ascribing his call from Battle to unvarnished political expediency.

"I immediately asked Mike who I could call," Dan recalled. "He was reluctant to say anything, but he finally suggested I try McNulty. The first thing I asked Paul was whether my dismissal was performance-related. 'It's not your performance,' he said, but that's all he would say. It was very cryptic and very frustrating not to know and not to be told.

"I still can't put my finger on why it happened," Dan insisted, almost a year after the fact. "It was all the more painful since, just a few days earlier, I had been with both Paul McNulty and Mike Battle in Washington, where we all attended the Project Safe Childhood conference. Nobody said a word. It was all very cordial. Since then, I've gone over and over the facts, and it still doesn't make any sense. It's been an agonizing period in my life."

On the face of it, I would have to agree: there is nothing in Dan Bogden's tenure as U.S. Attorney that would provide an adequate explanation for his sudden dismissal. True, he had had his share of setbacks: we all had. A major case against the Hell's Angels had unraveled in late 2006, while a case alleging that false Medicare claims had been submitted by a politically active Las Vegas physician was also dismissed. But Bogden also had his share of successful prosecutions, most conspicuously proving his mettle in a sweeping Las Vegas corruption case in 2003, dubbed "Operation G-String." In a joint investigation with the FBI, Bogden had uncovered bribes amounting to nearly $400,000 taken by county commissioners in exchange for the favored treatment of a strip club entrepreneur named Michael Galardi. Intent on crushing his competition and thwarting new rules that regulated illicit sexual activities in his clubs, Galardi had enticed Clark

County officials with everything from election campaign funding to tuition for an Olympic ski school.

Operation G-String was a high-profile case that underscored Bogden's determination to make Nevada a family-friendly environment that would maintain its status as one of the fastest-growing states in the country. But it was hardly his only accomplishment. He had also done important work in his district on drugs and weapons prosecutions and put dozens of violent gang members behind bars, as well as making terrorism a top priority, in accordance with the administration's express wishes.

But showing appreciation for Dan's accomplishments was not precisely what concerned the Department of Justice. Instead, an appallingly slipshod and cynical criterion was applied that made Dan Bogden's dismissal, among all of us, one of the most egregious.

"I'm a little skittish about Bogden," McNulty wrote in an e-mail two days before Battle's scheduled phone call barrage. "He had been with the DOJ since 1990 and, at age 50, has never had a job outside of government."

The deputy attorney general's "skittishness" was reportedly based on his belief that Bogden would have a hard time finding another job with which to support his family. Shortly afterward, a meeting was convened in the office of Kyle Sampson, the chief of staff for Alberto Gonzales, to address McNulty's last-minute qualms. Among those in attendance was a thirty-three-year-old senior counsel to the attorney general named Monica Goodling, who assured McNulty that he need not be overly distressed about Bodgen's future prospects. Dan wasn't married, she told him. He had no family. The total elapsed time for a meeting that would decide the fate of this dedicated public servant with fifteen years of service and an impressive record of upholding justice: ninety seconds.

But Dan's dismissal was not exactly the smooth procedure its instigators had envisioned. Like Paul Charlton, Bogden received vocal senatorial support, specifically from Nevada senator John Ensign, who had originally nominated him back in September 2001. "I can't even tell you how upset I am at the Justice Department,"

Ensign fumed when news of the firings began to spread. "I'm calling on the president of the United States and the attorney general to restore Dan Bogden's reputation. . . . I believe a good man was wronged and a process was flawed." Although partisan motives may have come into play, even Nevada's liberal Democratic senator Harry Reid weighed in, asserting through a spokesman that "Dan Bogden had been given a raw deal."

The senatorial concern must have caused Alberto Gonzales to call Bogden three times after his dismissal. Gonzales offered to help Bogden find another job, but Dan just wanted his old job back. Gonzales demurred. Of all of us, I could never figure out why Bogden had been taken out so unceremoniously. I heard many months later one theory that made sense; Kyle Sampson was stymied at being appointed U.S. Attorney in Utah, so he persuaded the administration to let him have the neighboring state of Nevada. If true, it was as if these presidential appointments were being treated as cavalierly as a game of Risk, except in the real world, U.S. Attorneys don't win a board game, they are empowered to take away your life, liberty and property.

That much was evident in the treatment of each of us, although the vindictive political nature of the "deal" was perhaps less apparent in Dan's circumstances than in the others whose names John McKay had given me during our phone conversation in late December. Unlike my own situation, with both the voter fraud controversy and the courthouse corruption cases having taken on ominous partisan dimensions, one look at Bogden's record as U.S. Attorney revealed a notable dearth of politically charged prosecutions. His firing was, on the face of it, utterly incomprehensible.

It was, on the other hand, all too comprehensible in the case of Carol Lam, the U.S. Attorney for the Southern District of California. At the time that she had received her fateful phone call from Battle, Carol, a brilliant, principled, and extraordinarily experienced attorney and judge, was hip deep in a scandal that stands as one of the most blatant and brazen ever to involve public officials in her district or, for that matter, the nation. And Carol was every bit equal to the challenge.

As with Paul Charlton and Dan Bogden, my path crossed that of Carol Lam's on many occasions, particularly as they led us into immigration realms. Both New Mexico and California have extensive and hard-to-patrol borders with Mexico, and our common concerns ranged from interdiction to internment, to infrastructures strained by the influx of illegals and beyond. As tough as conditions for effective enforcement might have been for me, they were even more difficult for Carol, who had one of the busiest jurisdictions in the nation and a workload exacerbated by chronic understaffing and lack of resources. The Southern California U.S. Attorney's office was also a battleground for the state's intractable political infighting, and Carol's eventual confirmation had come only after a pitched battle between Democratic senators Boxer and Feinstein and Republican congressmen Randy "Duke" Cunningham, Darrell Issa, and Duncan Hunter. Carol Lam was not confirmed, in fact, for several months after her nomination, and when she was, it marked the first time that the district had had a presidentially appointed, Senate-confirmed U.S. Attorney in five years.

Carol was quick to dispel the cloud under which she had assumed office. For fourteen years as an assistant U.S. Attorney and the head of the district's Major Fraud Section, she was subsequently appointed a Superior Court judge, somehow finding the time to raise four children in the midst of it all. A respected expert on white-collar crime, she moved quickly on a number of complex cases, including the bank fraud prosecution of the software firm Peregrine Systems and an alleged Medicare kickback scheme by Tenet Heathcare. Aside from everything else, Carol, who as a young prosecutor had earned the Attorney General's Award for Distinguished Service, was also a leading authority on health-care fraud, having written a hefty textbook on the subject. A graduate from both Harvard and Stanford, Carol was without question a formidable opponent, but she was also lively and engaging, with a great sense of humor and a lilting, infectious giggle.

She found nothing funny about December 7, however, when she received a call from Mike Battle. "It was a complete surprise," she told *Stanford Lawyer*, the journal of her alma mater, in what had become a familiar litany among the fired U.S. Attorneys. "There was no hint of what was coming, nothing in the air. . . . It wasn't until later that I realized I wasn't the only one and the reason I didn't say anything publicly for several weeks after I was asked to resign was that I knew the plan to keep it quiet wasn't going to work. Who in his right mind could think you could fire seven U.S. Attorneys on the same day and that nobody was going to notice? It was just headbangingly frustrating."

Carol knew a thing or two about banging heads. She had stood up against some of the most entrenched special interests in her region in a lurid corruption scandal that revolved around the combative archconservative congressman Randy "Duke" Cunningham. The case had broken in the summer of 2005, when an enterprising local journalist reported that Cunningham, a Vietnam-era navy flying ace and a member of the Defense Appropriations Subcommittee, had sold his home in the swank San Diego suburb of Del Mar to a defense contractor named Michael Wade for $100,000 more than market value. Shortly afterward, Wade's company, Athena Innovative Solutions, began to receive tens of millions of dollars in defense and intelligence contracts from the government. It was later alleged that along with the inflated house purchase, Wade bought Cunningham's considerable influence on the subcommittee with nearly $750,000, along with a lavish yacht dubbed the *Duke Stir* on which the congressman entertained a series of young women in rapid rotation while in Washington.

As Lam's office and the FBI launched an investigation, the plot thickened. Another defense contractor, Michael Wilkes, was shown to have made more than $1 million in real estate loans to Cunningham, one of which was paid off by Wade. Cunningham obliged by pushing the Pentagon for the purchase of a $20 million document-digitizing system developed by Wilkes's company, ADCS Inc.

Carol's case was ironclad by the time she brought an indictment against Cunningham in late 2005. The prosecution's evidence was so overwhelming, in fact, that the congressman's attorney later said that he had no choice but to recommend a guilty plea. In exchange for Cunningham's cooperation, he was sentenced to more than eight years in prison.

But the saga didn't stop there. In March 2006, the press reported that an internal investigation had been opened on the activities of the CIA's third-ranking official, Kyle "Dusty" Foggo, in connection with the Cunningham corruption case. Foggo, it was alleged, had steered agency contracts to his best friend, Michael Wilkes, including a deal to supply water to CIA agents during the Iraq invasion. Early in 2007, an indictment against Foggo was handed down, then was superseded and expanded three months later with new charges of fraud, conspiracy, and money laundering.

Carol Lam had, in no uncertain terms, opened a can of worms in the Cunningham investigation and, in the process, brought down one of the most reliable votes for the administration's agenda in Congress. It was hardly a stretch to imagine that she had earned the ire of more than a few Bush loyalists along the way. Yet while it was one thing to take out a loose cannon like Duke Cunningham— who had once called gay servicemen "homos" on the floor of the House of Representatives—it was quite another to pursue an investigation that was veering towards other Republicans, such as a canny and polished politician like Republican congressman Jerry Lewis, the influential chairman of the House Appropriations Committee. Yet rumors of just such an investigation, which was conducted by the U.S. Attorney's office in the neighboring Central District of California, had been circulating for months within the Beltway, based primarily on allegations that millions of dollars in Appropriations Committee funds had been earmarked for Lewis's friends and family in exchange for reelection campaign contributions. Somehow, Lam was linked with the Lewis investigation even though it was being pursued by U.S. Attorney Deb Yang in Los Angeles. The prospect of yet another Republican stalwart being targeted by the US Attorney's office must also have served to raise more than a few hackles.

While typically keeping her own views close to the vest, Carol was certainly aware of the charged atmosphere that she was working in. It was, simply put, the price of doing business as a U.S. Attorney in a district where a culture of corruption, fed by federal dollars, was deeply rooted. The professional blow that her forced resignation represented was, I think, assuaged somewhat by the fact that she quickly landed a prestigious position as a Senior Vice President for the San Diego–based communications giant Qualcomm. But she never lost sight of the larger implications of what had happened to her and six of her colleagues, telling *Stanford Lawyer* that the events following December 7 were "a reminder of how tenuous the balance is between political pressures and the responsibility of the DOJ to do the right thing at all times." Carol had warned a Justice Department official not to force her to resign, in light of the ongoing corruption investigations, since it smelled of retaliation. The official, in one of the more memorable miscalculations of the scandal, dismissed her well-founded concerns by saying that it "would be a one-day story."

The right thing, in Carol's view, had less to do with the off-handed and insensitive manner of our dismissals than with what the whole catastrophic chain of events had to say about leadership within the department. "The language that was used with me was something along the lines of 'we want to take your office in a new direction,'" she continued. "But my dissatisfaction with the way this was handled doesn't have anything to do with Mike Battle's bedside manner. It had to do with the decisions made by people higher in the department that an appropriate way to deal with such a monumental decision would be to have somebody make calls, give people no substantive information, and expect that we were just going to accept the decision. . . . It was a very immature way to handle it."

Once I had gotten the preliminary list of names from John McKay, I quickly put in calls to Paul, Dan, and Carol to confirm what I had been told. As we shared our individual experiences and additional information, it became clear that the bloodletting hadn't stopped with us. I learned that Paul, John, and Carol had been in contact and that they were reaching out to Dan. I had already been in touch with Bud Cummins, so it was natural to put us all together. There had been two more targets on December 7, both of whom would assume lower-profile roles in the drama that was about to unfold.

As the U.S. Attorney for the Western District of Michigan, Margaret Chiara oversaw a largely rural area that, with its widely dispersed demographics and solidly Dutch Reform values, could hardly be described as a hotbed of crime and conspiracy. Nonetheless, the area had its share of community-based challenges that Margaret went far, as a U.S. Attorney, to address. With large Arab and Muslim populations in and around Lansing and Grand Rapids, she established increased communication links to the Islamic citizens with programs that became a model for the nation.

As Michigan's first female U.S. Attorney, Margaret, who had once studied to be a nun, targeted drug trafficking organizations and medical fraud during her tenure. A former teacher and educational administrator, she had served two terms as the prosecutor for Cass County in southwest Michigan before being recruited to the staff of the chief justice of the state Supreme Court. Appointed U.S. Attorney in 2001, she brought to the job the same steady hand and sober judgment that had marked her tenure at the county level. She was perfectly suited to the specific requirements of a region that was intent on maintaining the status quo.

Yet her low-key approach belied a prosecutor who knew her duty and vigorously fulfilled it. Although personally opposed to capital punishment, she successfully prosecuted Michigan's first death penalty case since 1938, involving a drug-related murder. She had targeted a pair of companies for the hiring of illegal aliens, putting the state's business community on notice in the process, and she spearheaded the investigation of Barton Watson, a Grand Rapids computer entrepreneur who had defrauded investors of millions of dollars. Despite the relative lack of criminal activity at the federal level, Margaret, a woman whose personal warmth outshone her natural reserve, had managed to increase felony prosecutions and convictions in her district by 15 percent before her abrupt dismissal. She developed a much-admired attorney training and mentoring program, and we often had occasion to work together when she became the chairwoman of the Native American Issues Subcommittee, of which Paul Charlton, Dan Bogden, and I were members. She worked tirelessly to insure tribal rights to hunt, fish, and engage in other traditional activities on land ceded to them by treaty.

When news of the firings began to spread like wildfire in early 2007, the inclusion on the list of Margaret Chiara presented journalists and commentators with a persistent puzzle. "We are left with little clear explanation of why this particular U.S. Attorney was dismissed," wrote pseudonymous blogger Rayne Today. "What remains is a black hole–like object, definable by the outline around it but not by any readily distinguishable characteristics."

I'm not sure Margaret would agree with that description, but it's certainly an accurate metaphor for the puzzlement and the dismay that greeted the rest of us when we got word of Chiara's firing. Leave it to Margaret herself, with a typical forthrightness, to sum up her estimation of the machinations behind the Pearl Harbor Day massacre. "To say it was about politics may not be pleasant," she remarked in one of her few public utterances on the subject, "but at least it is truthful."

The truth was not, however, quite so cut-and-dried in the waning days of December, when we first began to put together the implicit intent and scope of the Justice Department's fait accompli. What slowly emerged was a virtual graph of potential political causality: at one end of the scale were U.S. Attorneys like Dan Bogden and Margaret Chiara, for whom there was no rational basis to a politically motivated dismissal. At the other end were Carol Lam and myself, for whom there seemed to be abundant political cause, however unethical and unjustified. The case of Kevin Ryan, the U.S. Attorney for California's Northern District, however, fell somewhere outside the grid entirely.

Ryan, a native San Franciscan and the son of immigrant parents, began his career in the Alameda County DA's office, where he prosecuted a number of homicides and was a member of the

Violent Gang Suppression Unit. In 1996, he was appointed as a Municipal Court judge and was later elected to the San Francisco Superior Court before being nominated to be a U.S. Attorney.

I didn't know Kevin nearly as well as I did some other U.S. Attorneys, but I did know that he was fiercely loyal to the president and that he had inherited a district that had more than its share of morale and performance problems. In that congenitally liberal atmosphere, it was difficult to make drug cases stick, and drugs, of course, contributed to much of the criminal activity in Northern California, from Mendocino pot farms to international smuggling through the busy ports of Oakland and San Francisco. I doubt that anyone could have turned around his troubled office.

I have no idea what the actual challenges were that Ryan faced as a U.S. Attorney, and I am in no position to pass judgment on the work he did. This is especially true given the fact that once we had all connected and begun an active and ongoing exchange, both on the phone and through voluminous e-mails, we extended an invitation to Kevin to join our extemporaneous correspondence. He wanted to move on with his life, however, and did not become part of our group.

David Iglesias. John McKay. Paul Charlton. Dan Bogden. Carol Lam. Margaret Chiara. Kevin Ryan. The list of those taken out simultaneously on December 7 was complete. But as I pondered the names on that list and wondered about the possible reasons that each of us had been put there, I couldn't help but recall the phone conversation I'd had back in August, when I was living in what seemed in retrospect to be a state of blissful ignorance. That ignorance, I realized with a start, had begun to erode the day I'd heard that Bud Cummins had been asked to resign. Had his ouster, and perhaps even the removal of Todd Graves before him, been a warm-up for what was to come? Had the body count actually risen from seven to nine? "If you need a place to live when they run you out of New Mexico," Bud had joked when I called him to compare notes, "why don't you come on down to

Arkansas? We have a great witness protection program. There's lots of hunting here, and you're even allowed to carry a weapon."

The only weapon I really needed was the truth, the proverbial double-edged sword, to parse the purpose of what had happened to us, individually and collectively. The removal of Graves in the Western District of Missouri had occurred against the backdrop of a heated voter fraud controversy in the midst of a closely fought election. That certainly sounded familiar. But Bud Cummins had staunchly maintained that his resignation had been demanded simply to make room for Karl Rove's protégé Tim Griffin. Regardless of how awkwardly it was handled, that was well within the purview of the president's pleasure.

I accepted the explanation as far as it went, but in the hypervigilant aftermath of December 7, I couldn't help but wonder whether it went far enough. I knew that after the Missouri U.S. Attorneys had recused themselves to avoid a conflict of interest, Bud had been recruited to investigate an alleged public corruption case that potentially could have implicated Missouri governor Matt Blunt. Bud simply didn't see a connection. "I have never been concerned personally that there's a connection between the Blunt case and my case," he later told *Truthout* reporter Jason Leopold. "I don't have evidence that there's any connection."

It was a position I completely understood. An experienced attorney, Bud was not about to jump to conclusions he couldn't substantiate. The challenge facing my fellow fired U.S. Attorneys and me in the fading days of 2006 was, however, not in simply avoiding unfounded leaps, but in following up the peculiarly coincidental connections that existed between us, the work we each did, and the obstacles we had each encountered. Was what we were trying to unravel nothing more than a chain of circumstantial evidence? There was no question about it. First, there was the fact that the individual circumstances leading up to our dismissals were widely varied. We all fell out in different places along that imaginary chart of possible political motivation, and it would be hard to prove that Carol Lam and Margaret Chiara had been let go for anything like the same reasons.

On the other hand, what were we to make of the fact that voter fraud had been the focus of major criticism for both John McKay and me? It was a question that, in turn, raised another intriguing aspect of our firing: how much could we, or any U.S. Attorney, for that matter, actually affect the outcome of an election through the threat or the actual implementation of a voter fraud investigation? The answer, of course, depends entirely on the margin by which the vote was won or lost. A huge plurality would be safe, no matter what sort of tampering had occurred on the margins, but in a close contest, such as those in New Mexico and Washington, a few hundred votes could well decide the outcome. If a fraud investigation, for example, turned up evidence of such time-honored tricks as voting under the names of the deceased, knowingly registering minors or felons, or, as the old saying goes, voting early and often, it was possible that a U.S. Attorney could very well turn the results of an election around or at least cast a lingering pall over the results. By the same token, a U.S. Attorney with a partisan agenda could tie up otherwise settled election results with all manner of investigations, indictments, and prosecutions, no matter what the merits of the case. In short, U.S. Attorneys wielded the power to wreak havoc on the electoral process if they so intended.

That was not our intent, and as the scandal developed, it seemed that we were paying the price for refusing to prosecute spurious and potentially disruptive voter fraud cases. My assorted run-ins with people in New Mexico who were convinced that the 2000 election had been stolen had done much to shake the confidence I'd held up to that point in the Republican powerbrokers in my district. It was a falling out that was virtually identical to that experienced by John McKay in the 2004 Washington gubernatorial race, when Democrat Chris Gregoire beat Republican Dino Rossi by 129 votes in what can only be called the ultimate squeaker. The race was so close, in fact, that it was decided after three recounts, the first two of which went to Rossi, while the third and final one gave the razor-thin majority to Gregoire.

McKay had already generated a good deal of ambivalence, if not outright resistance, from the administration and, in particular, from Paul McNulty for his impassioned advocacy of LInX, the information-sharing technology that he had virtually willed into existence by wrangling unprecedented interagency cooperation. In October 2006, at a meeting convened by McNulty and the U.S. Attorneys who had seen the obvious advantages of the system for their jurisdictions, including me, the deputy attorney general became so agitated at what he apparently construed as an encroachment on his decision-making authority that he stormed out of the room. I was sitting closest to McNulty and could not believe his childish behavior. His agitation was in response to a remark by a U.S. Attorney who is now a federal judge and who simply stated that "this is an opportunity for leadership we shouldn't turn away from." Later, at dinner, we all looked around the table and said to one another, "What just happened?"

McKay's leadership had, in fact, been consistently undermined in the rampant acrimony and the endemic partisanship that followed the Gregoire-Rossi results. "I believe to this day that the Governor's race was the reason I was fired," John asserted. "It was seen as a stolen election by Republican groups in the state and eventually throughout the nation, since right-wing bloggers and talk show radio hosts complained to anyone who would listen. One of them even gave out my e-mail address, so I was aware firsthand of not just what was being said about me but of the fact that some of it was being cc'd directly to the AG." Eventually, the Evergreen Freedom Foundation, a group of conservative Republicans, lodged a formal complaint with Attorney General Gonzales, charging McKay with lax oversight of the election, and a civil lawsuit was later filed to try to overturn the results.

"Look," McKay continued, "it never bothered me that there was a political dimension to these accusations, for which I could find absolutely no evidence. Quite the opposite: I relished the opportunity to make a principled decision, regardless of the partisan reaction. This was a straight-up legal question. There are facts, the law, procedure, and outcome. Everything else is just noise, and I had no trouble tuning it out. That's what you're supposed to do when you're a U.S. Attorney. And what the Justice Department is supposed to do is watch your back. Instead, I would get called to task because of the wild allegations of fringe groups with an ax to grind. They had blogged themselves into believing that it was my duty to roll out indictments that would either deliver the election to the Republicans or punish the Democrats so badly that they would end up in jail. In the midst of it all, I had the opportunity to confront one of my critics and ask him directly, 'Who should go to jail? The election director? The supervisor? The little old lady at the polling station?' I never got a straight answer."

It wasn't for lack of trying. McKay had been in close contact with the FBI, which had duly assigned a case agent to look into the fraud charges. "We had several joint agency meetings, which included representatives from the DOJ's Public Integrity section, to review the facts," McKay recounted, "and I'll never forget the conference where I first laid out the so-called evidence that had been presented to me. One of the agents laughed out loud. It was that flimsy."

John had also taken the trouble to reach out both to the DOJ's Civil Rights Section and to Steven Biskupic, the U.S. Attorney for the Eastern District of Wisconsin. Biskupic had had experience with a legitimate case of voter fraud and would subsequently play a walk-on role in the mushrooming scandal of our dismissals. "I wanted to get a sense of what the framework for an actual election fraud prosecution might look like," McKay explained. His quest would eventually lead him into the upper echelons of Main Justice, but the direction and the advice he received from Washington were, in the end, so contradictory that he was forced to rely on his own best judgment. "I was looking for a benchmark. The impression I got was that I should make it up as I went along. The preference, at least as it was expressed by the attorney general's office, was simply to file as many such cases as possible. I wasn't willing to do that, certainly not in the gubernatorial race.

I understood, of course, that with a margin of 129 votes, there are sure to be certain irregularities that will appear. But was there a conspiracy to steal the election? Absolutely not."

Election fraud, real or imagined, may have seemed like a tenuous link on which to hang our suspicions of political influence in the mass firings. But other clues were beginning to emerge, together creating a patchwork pattern that seemed to suggest that we had all been under close observation by the same jaundiced eye.

In the weeks immediately following the election, John received a call from Ed Cassidy, the chief of staff for Republican congressman Doc Hastings, from the conservative 4th District in the center of the state. "He asked me if I was going to pursue an investigation of voter fraud in the governor's race," McKay later recalled under oath. "I stopped him and I told him that I was sure that he wasn't asking me on behalf of his boss to reveal information about an ongoing investigation or lobby me on one, because we both knew that would be improper. He agreed, and we ended the conversation in a most expeditious fashion."

This highly improper call was eerily reminiscent of Pete Domenici's and Heather Wilson's inappropriate calls. The notion of dialing for data on an ongoing investigation was clearly de rigueur in some quarters of the Republican Party, and there was a clear methodology emerging. Another example of the not-so-subtle political pressure being brought to bear on U.S. Attorneys was in the case that Paul Charlton was handling at the time of his forced resignation, involving allegations of a complex land-swap scheme that implicated Arizona Republican congressman Rick Renzi in 2005. The deal allegedly included an unreported $200,000 payment funneled through the legislator's family wine business by James Sandlin, a former business partner. In exchange, Renzi introduced a bill in the House that would trade federal land for undeveloped real estate owned by Sandlin, which would serve to substantially increase the value of, among other parcels, an alfalfa field. In late October 2006, less than six weeks before Paul's dismissal, an Associated Press story reported that the U.S. Attorney's office had opened an investigation into the matter, and the leak received wide coverage in both the state and the national media.

Remarkably, the Justice Department leaped into the breach but not in support of Paul or his investigation of a congressman who, among other administration-approved moves, had enthusiastically voted for the reauthorization of the Patriot Act. Instead, in an unprecedented display of backpedaling, Main Justice officials contacted media outlets to warn them that the Renzi case was "not a well-developed investigation by any means." The press was further cautioned "not to chop this guy's head off" and that, in the case of two newspapers, there were "chunks of stuff in their stories [that were] wrong."

The *Arizona Republic* was quick to ask the obvious question, reporting on October 26, 2006, that the spokesperson "would not discuss whether the Justice Department was being manipulated for political purposes. However, the official said that it is unusual for the department to publicly acknowledge concerns about the accuracy of media reports."

That was putting it mildly. In point of fact, Main Justice had been dragging its feet on the Renzi matter at every juncture, stalling on approvals for search warrants, subpoenas, and wiretaps, in some cases for the better part of a year. From every appearance, what the department was attempting to do was cut Paul's investigation off at the knees, beginning by second-guessing him in the press. It was hardly surprising, under the circumstances, that two weeks after his phone call from Mike Battle, Charlton contacted Main Justice to say that the media wanted to know "if I was asked to resign over . . . the Congressman Renzi investigation." He never received a reply. Ironically, in 2007, Renzi announced he would not seek re-election. In early 2008, he was indicted on thirty-five counts.

But in the early days after the case had become public, other people were only too anxious to reach out to Pablo. "My press secretary Wyn Hornbuckle got a call from Brian Murray, who was a top Rick Renzi aide," Paul recounted. "He was fishing for information about the case."

Like the call that John McKay received from congressman
Doc Hastings's office, the significance of the improper contact
that Charlton had been subjected to was clearly of a different
order than the ones I had received from two elected officials.
"Rick Renzi was not my mentor," Pablo pointed out. "I knew
the drill and made it clear that I could reveal nothing about an
ongoing investigation. Their attempt to elicit information was, at
the very least, poor judgment." Paul shrugged. "I guess I could
understand their position. The news of the investigation had just
gone public. They were nervous. Maybe they figured it was worth
a shot." At the same time, he also well understood the improper
implications of Murray's inquiries and duly reported the call to
Main Justice, something that I should have done when Wilson
and Domenici phoned me. The DOJ, in turn, never bothered
to inform Congress about the glaring ethical lapse of one of its
members.

CHAPTER 8

Fallout

In the first days of 2007, there was an abiding sense of uncertainty among the seven of us who had been so peremptorily singled out and set aside for apparently inexplicable reasons. Through our initial e-mail contacts and phone calls, we had established a few discreet channels of communication that quickly formed into a single and very busy chat room, as we discussed with one another the circumstances of our individual situations, advanced theories that ranged from the purely coincidental to the conspiratorially paranoid, and offered one another advice, encouragement, and condolences. Within a matter of weeks, my computer in-box was stuffed with nearly a thousand messages, which were supplemented with numerous conference calls.

There was, almost from the beginning, a consensus that we would all simply move on and try to put our careers back on track, while at the same time trying to draw as little press and public attention as possible to what was, after all, an unprecedented occurrence in the history of the Justice Department. There was no question that we had been fired without cause, but the persistent question in the first weeks of January was what, exactly, would be the advantage in pointing out the injustice and the impropriety of our dismissal? It was an inclination deeply influenced, I think, by the sense of embarrassment that we shared. In the fish-bowl environment of the federal legal community, the events of December 7 were becoming common knowledge.

Common also was the assumption that there must have been a good reason for letting us go. It was simply impossible to believe that seven good men and women, among whom were some of the most accomplished U.S. Attorneys in the country, would be cut loose without a compelling cause. Of course, along with such speculation came the unspoken intimation that the firings themselves may have been intended as a none-too-subtle warning to our remaining colleagues, all of whom would be left to work out for themselves the implications on both their careers and the conduct of their jobs.

In the meantime, we had our own job concerns. Some of us, like Carol in San Diego and even, much earlier, Todd Graves in Missouri, had seamlessly transitioned into the private sector. I don't think we had any real doubts that we would all land on our feet sooner or later. But that didn't make our present predicament any easier to tolerate. Without question, we had each been knocked down a considerable notch, and it was hard to gauge what impact there might be on our future employability. That was especially true since, in the weeks after we were simultaneously shown the door, Main Justice had stayed entirely silent as to any plausible reason for letting us go. Into that vacuum rushed all manner of conjecture and crosstalk. It seemed inevitable that one way or another, an explanation would have to be proffered, and it was John McKay who best expressed the attitude most of us shared as to that eventuality. "If they even hint that any of this was performance-related," he said, "I'm going to go public."

Even though I harbored the strongest suspicion that our dismissals had been politically prompted, I wasn't quite ready to go as far as John's thinly veiled warning. I had a family to support, and, at least for the moment, it was in light of that primary concern that I wanted to keep confrontation to a minimum. In a very real sense,

I still needed to be in the good graces of the Justice Department, which explains why, on January 10, I contacted the attorney general's chief of staff, Kyle Sampson, to ask him whether I could use Alberto Gonzales as a reference. "You can list the AG as a reference," Sampson wrote cheerfully. "Not a problem. Good luck!"

Even though Deputy Attorney General Paul McNulty had finally come through with a response to my request for an extension of time until my resignation became effective, essentially giving me until the end of February to vacate the office, I knew it would never be too early to start looking for another job. With that sense of urgency came the realization that I would have to engage in some rigorous damage control to keep my dismissal from affecting my employment prospects. I felt a little like tainted goods, and it was important to stave off that impression, for myself and others, as much as possible as I began my search for work.

But the truth was, my heart just wasn't in it. Added to the severe blow that my ego had sustained was the fact that I had been on a nonstop career trajectory for the last two decades. What other U.S. Attorneys had told me when I was first appointed had proved only too true: it was the best job I'd ever have. Now it was over, and with it, a whole chapter of my life had abruptly closed. As much as I needed a paycheck, I felt as if it was time to step back and take stock. For the moment, I wanted to focus on my family, even as I watched the story of the firings take on a life of its own, assuming proportions that could quite possibly affect the well-being of my wife and daughters.

In mid-December, I began to get the first calls from curious local journalists, fishing for the truth among the rampant rumors about my dismissal. From my time as a U.S. Attorney, with the post's strong public-relations component, I had developed a sense of how a news story built and broke and wondered whether I would now be in the middle of a major scoop. It was on the eighteenth of the month that I was contacted by a local TV reporter asking for comments on persistent accounts he'd heard that newly elected representative Heather Wilson had been calling potential candidates for my job before my resignation was made public.

"What's going on, David?" he wanted to know. I had no choice, no Plan B from Main Justice. I confirmed my resignation, set now for January 31, but refused to speculate on the reasons for it.

The reporter promised that he would get back to me, and I didn't have long to wait. The story broke on December 18 on a local television station. I knew it would be reported more widely on December 19, and the timing could not have been worse—the eighteenth was two days before Cyndy's birthday and also marked the twenty-second anniversary of my navy commissioning. I called home immediately to let Cyndy know, and that night, we sat Claudia, Amanda, Marisa, and Sophia down and tried to explain to our daughters what was about to happen. Of course, we weren't really sure ourselves, which made a difficult parenting task that much more challenging. Eventually, in the way that only children can manage, the girls took it in stride, but on that cold evening, there were tears and fearful questions.

"They had two concerns," is the way Cyndy remembered it. "The first was: are we moving? The second was: why would President Bush want to fire Daddy? For them, it was all very black and white. My reaction was a little different."

From the moment I had arrived home bearing the bad news on December 7, Cyndy had struggled with powerful emotions. "When we got the phone call from Senator Domenici," she recalled, "more than anything I felt like we had made our father mad. I was afraid of what he might do to retaliate. Then, when I heard that Heather Wilson was out looking for a replacement before the body was even cold, I got angry myself. I stayed angry for a long time."

Cyndy and I, in fact, had very different reactions to the chain of events that we had been caught up in. "David just wanted to move on," Cyndy reflected, "and I certainly didn't blame him. It was painful, and he wanted to put it behind him. I couldn't do that. It became almost obsessive for me: to know why, to get answers, an accounting. We both instinctively understood the political nature of what had happened, but I needed more: names and dates and places. Someone who would admit responsibility."

At the moment, none of that was forthcoming. "For about three weeks we just hibernated as a family," Cyndy continued. "The kids were on Christmas vacation, and we kept all the normal bustle of the season at arm's length. But I think that whole time I was dealing with rage and grief, and when I heard that the story was about to be broadcast on the evening news, I just lost it."

When I arrived home that evening, I found Cyndy curled up on the floor of our bedroom closet with the door shut. "I didn't want the girls to see me in that condition," she explained. "I had to be alone and, through all the tears, somehow pull myself together. I think after that night, things began to turn around for me. I could see past the embarrassment of the whole world knowing that my husband had been fired. It was becoming clear to others, David included, what I had felt from the beginning. This was wrong. It needed to be made right, regardless of the personal costs."

By the time the girls returned to school that January, my name and face were appearing regularly on front pages and TV screens. Far from being mortified, my daughters demonstrated a characteristic aplomb. "I kind of like it," Amanda had quipped when I asked her how she felt about my sudden notoriety. Her teacher had brought up the subject in class, and Amanda was enjoying the attention. Of course, all four of my girls were still too young to pose the question Cyndy had asked when I told her I had been fired: was I hiding something? No shadows of suspicion had fallen across my daughters, and that's something I'll always be grateful to God for. The family bond held strong.

In retrospect, I think it was an impressive achievement that as a group, my fired colleagues and I held our tongues for as long as we did. It probably helped that Battle's phone calls had come, perhaps purposely, on the cusp of the season when the last thing any American wants to think about is a brewing political scandal. Holiday cheer took the story off the front burner, although within the close-knit community of which we had so lately been a part, it was increasingly more difficult to tamp down the buzz. It didn't help that some of us were being provoked—or perhaps strong-armed is a better way to describe it.

Shortly before my story broke on Albuquerque television stations, John McKay got a call from Michael Elston, the chief of staff for Deputy Attorney General Paul McNulty. As a former Assistant U.S. Attorney in the Eastern District of Virginia, again under McNulty, Elston, a much-admired courtroom attorney, had participated in the prosecution of Zacarias Moussaoui and John Walker Lindh. He was also adept at carrying out the wishes of his boss. Elston's message from Main Justice was succinct. As was later reported in *Newsweek*, "Elston suggested to McKay that in exchange for his silence, the Justice Department would not make public specific reasons for his firing. "He was offering me a deal," John said. "You stay silent and the attorney general won't say anything bad about you."

It was a sharp escalation in the scare tactics that the administration had heretofore only obliquely applied. According to subsequent testimony, McKay considered Elston's tone too "sinister and that he was prepared to threaten me further if he concluded I did not continue to remain silent about my dismissal." Elston was, in John's estimation, trying to "buy my silence by promising that the attorney general would not demean me."

In a textbook example of the law of unintended consequences, threatening McKay was like lighting a match to gasoline. "I greatly resented the call," John said with ominous understatement.

Borrowing a page from Mike Battle's phone log, Elston made three more calls in quick succession, all with the same blunt attempt at intimidation. "It was a quid pro quo agreement," was Paul Charlton's frank appraisal of his conversation with Elston: "my silence in exchange for the attorney general's."

"Michael Elston erroneously accused me of 'leaking' my dismissal to the press," Carol Lam asserted, in an account echoed by Bud Cummins. "He criticized me for talking to other dismissed U.S Attorneys." Carol had the best response to these thuggish phone calls from Elston when she e-mailed us saying, "What's next, horse's heads in our beds?" This was an allusion to the graphic scene from the movie *The Godfather* where a severed horse head was put in the bed of an enemy. It was a tragic-comic comment but one that served to underscore how the highest levels of the Justice Department were acting like organized crime figures.

It was at that point that I began to see the dimensions of what we were actually dealing with. It is facile to ascribe every scandal that exposes corruption or ethical lapses in the upper reaches of government to calculated conspiracies undertaken with knowledge or malicious aforethought. They are just as often the result of what John McKay would come to describe as "incompetence combined with arrogance." The whole notion that seven U.S. Attorneys who had all been dismissed on the same day with the same dismal lack of common decency or even common sense would somehow *not* talk to one another—at length and in detail—conveys either an appalling lack of experience or the sheer hubris to believe that everything, including our pride and self-respect, could be manipulated.

Equally disingenuous, not to mention patently absurd, were the wide-eyed disavowals that Elston was forced to make once news of his browbeating methods became public. He was, he professed, "shocked and baffled" that Bud Cummins would misconstrue the amicable intent of his friendly call and said that he "certainly had no intention," of leaving Paul Charlton with the impression that he was being bullied.

Of course, back in late December 2006, nobody was disavowing anything. Quite the contrary: by leaning on John, Carol, Paul, and Bud, the inexperienced and the arrogant had made the first move in a damage-control campaign that would, in time, prove more disastrous than the firings themselves. All of this went to prove the old adage that the cover-up is always worse than the crime. In a very real sense, Elton's clumsy coercion marked a turning point. As foolish as it was to suppose that the seven of us would somehow forget to talk to one another, it was exponentially more boneheaded to believe that pressure tactics to keep us silent would have cowed any of us.

I can't say whether it was simply anger at Elston's call or the fact that I had more or less opened the door by acknowledging publicly, at least in the New Mexico press, that I had been asked to resign, but it turned out that Bud was right behind me. On December 20, the day after stories of my firing had appeared on television and in the *Albuquerque Journal* and I had e-mailed my resignation to my staff, Bud let it be known that he had been asked to leave as well. As much as anything, the announcement was a calculated rebuke to Elston and whoever had put him up to the task. I was proud of my friend Bud for telling the truth exactly when it needed most to be heard, across the country and through the halls of power.

Bud, it was later revealed, was very much on the minds of those in Main Justice whose mission was to fire us and hire our replacements. At the same time that the news of my forced resignation was airing in New Mexico, Kyle Sampson was suggesting to his boss, Alberto Gonzales, that Bud be used as a de facto guinea pig for the administration's newly minted power to name U.S. Attorneys. Simply put, they wanted to test the open-ended interim appointment provision in the just-passed Patriot Act reauthorization package. "If we don't ever exercise it," Sampson wrote to the attorney general in an e-mail, "then what's the point of having it?"

At least one of the points was to name Tim Griffin as U.S. Attorney for the Arkansas district. But Sampson seemed to be hedging his bets about the new U.S. Attorney when, in a parenthetical aside, he advised the Judge—as Gonzales was known throughout the DOJ—that he wasn't "100% sure that Tim was the guy on which to test drive this new authority. . . . But know getting him appointed was important to Harriet, Karl, etc."

By the time this correspondence became public knowledge, of course, it had long been a matter of furious debate whether former White House counsel Harriet Miers, Bush's political master strategist Karl Rove, and whoever else was alluded to under the catch-all of "etc." were in fact behind what amounted to a takeover of the Department of Justice. Like the rest of the nation, I had no way of knowing. My personal contacts with both Miers and Rove had been glancing. I had met the president's political adviser only once, at a Domenici fund-raiser in 2002 when Rove took the trouble to seek me out and introduce himself. I was surprised that he even knew who I was, since I was there in my law enforcement capacity as the Secret Service's on-scene legal adviser.

As far as Miers was concerned, it was John McKay who had more direct contact with the president's chief legal counsel. Miers had interviewed him when he was being considered for a federal judgeship, and the first question she asked was what he had done to get Washington State Republicans so angry with him. Miers would, of course, become something of a symbol of the political hubris of the White House, after a disastrous attempt to shoehorn her into the Supreme Court went down in flames. Those who saw it as an attempt to pack the judicial branch of government with partisan loyalists already had as a precedent the firing of eight U.S. Attorneys for nakedly political reasons.

Back in the first days of January 2007, few of us could have guessed that there was no place for the growing scandal to go except straight up the chain of command. The situation was shrouded in mystery, all the more so since it seemed utterly irrational to have let so many top prosecutors go in the first place. There must, so the conventional wisdom went, have been a valid reason to do so.

California senator Dianne Feinstein, along with Vermont senator Patrick Leahy and Arkansas senator Mark Pryor, all Democrats, thought they had a pretty good idea of what that reason might be.

Of all those interested in the news of our firings, Senator Feinstein had the most invested in finding out the facts. California had, after all, lost two of its four U.S. Attorneys, and political repercussions within the state would be inevitable. This was especially true considering that the U.S. Attorneys in both the southern and the northern district had had more than their share of controversy.

Feinstein, a powerful voice on the Senate Judiciary Committee, had earlier been one of a number of California politicians who had

expressed concerns about how it was that seemingly so few border prosecutions were coming from Carol and her office. It was
a concern that the senator shared with conservative Republican
congressman Darrell Issa from San Diego. A vociferous critic of
Lam's border policy almost from the day of Carol's appointment,
Issa had recruited eighteen other GOP lawmakers to sign a letter
in October 2005 addressed to the attorney general. "Many illegal
aliens," they complained, "who deserve jail time, fall instead into
the current practice of 'catch and release.' . . . Your Department's
lack of action aggravates rather than remedies this problem."
Among the signatories was Duke Cunningham, who, less than a
month later, would plead guilty to the bribery charges Lam had
lodged against him.

Contrary to accusations against her of incompetence and lax
oversight, Carol knew exactly what she was doing. "When you
bring one indictment against ten people you only get one statistic," she pointed out in the *Stanford Lawyer.* "If you prosecute
a border guard who is letting through hundreds of aliens, you
only get one statistic. If you're not looking at the significance of
the prosecution . . . you're taking a one-dimensional view of law
enforcement." It was, she asserted, "a numbers game," and the
message from Justice under Gonzales was to play the game. "We
can ratchet it up, or ratchet it down," is the way Carol explained
the standard procedure on border statistics at Main Justice.

Months later, Feinstein herself would write a letter to Gonzales.
"Despite high apprehension rates by border patrol agents," she
asserted, ". . . prosecutions by the U.S. Attorney's office appear to
lag behind."

Feinstein would take another tack entirely when, in the first
week of January, the Beltway was buzzing with news of the firings.
Later insisting that Lam had addressed the issues she'd raised,
Feinstein tentatively took on the role of our defender and wrote
yet another letter to Gonzales on January 11. It bore her signature,
along with those of Judiciary Committee chairman Senator Patrick
Leahy and Arkansas senator Mark Pryor, himself trying to parse
the local political aftermath of Bud Cummins's abrupt departure.

Of course, local politics was not the senator's only concern. Feinstein and her colleagues had discerned in our dismissals exactly the motivations that Kyle Sampson had voiced when he suggested installing Griffin as a test of the revised Section 546 of the Patriot Act, which so deftly dealt with the use of interim U.S. Attorney appointments to circumvent the consent of Congress.

"It has come to our attention," the letter began with a perceptible bristle, "that the Department of Justice has asked several U.S. Attorneys from around the country to resign their positions . . . prior to the end of their terms without cause. . . . We are very concerned about this allegation and we believe, if true, such actions would be intemperate and ill-advised." Intending to "look into changing the law to prevent such actions," the lawmakers demanded that Gonzales "desist from moving forward in these efforts and hold the requests in abeyance."

True to their word, two days later Feinstein, Leahy, and Pryor introduced legislation to "prevent circumvention of the Senate's constitutional prerogative." "The Bush Administration is pushing out U.S. Attorneys from across the country under the cloak of secrecy," a fired-up Feinstein was quoted as saying. "We know that this is not an isolated occurrence, but we don't know how many U.S. Attorneys have been asked to resign—it could be two, it could be ten, it could be more. No one knows . . . and we have no idea why this is happening."

Leahy, a former state prosecutor, offered one idea. "Political gerrymandering of these important posts is wrong," he thundered, "and an affront to our criminal justice system." Senator Pryor, bringing it back around to the local angle, added, "Arkansas has learned firsthand the unintended consequence of a little known provision in the Patriot Act."

But it didn't matter what perspective you viewed it from: our forced resignations were becoming big news. As a harbinger of a hopelessly politicized Justice Department, the cutting edge of a constitutional confrontation over separation of powers, a battle between the executive and the legislative branches of the U.S. government, or a wedge issue in local political warfare—the firings resonated on a lot of levels. Not the least of them was the very *strangeness* of the move, an act that on the face of it made no sense, politically, legally, or, it was becoming clear, ethically. From having worked their will as if on high, the architects of this grand changing of the guard were about to be faced with the necessity of explaining themselves.

"The attorney general could have legitimate reasons for asking for specific resignations," Feinstein observed, "or this could be motivated by political concerns or worse, derailing ongoing investigations."

Despite the fact that there was more than a little political expediency in the liberal Democratic senator from California trying to embarrass the administration, Feinstein, along with Leahy and Pryor, earned my respect by stepping forward with a cogent challenge to Gonzales's runaway DOJ. They were the first out of the gate, and their analysis of administration intent proved prescient. Yet in a way, I think they may have initially overestimated the degree of consideration and proactive planning that went into our firings. There were certainly those who saw the opportunity to test the new interim appointment rules in the revamped Patriot Act, but that could hardly have been the only reason for the massacre, or they would have stopped by removing Bud Cummins and replacing him with Tim Griffin. The logic of their precipitous actions would, in fact, inexorably unravel in the days and the weeks that followed.

It was no easy task, especially considering the legal issues involved. The president had, with very few exceptions, every right to hire and fire us at his pleasure.

The legal community saw it another way. "Tradition is a tremendously important consideration when you deal with power and its distribution," said Professor Jim Eisenstein. "What was being ignored here was, in large part, tradition, the ways things were done and the way they had been proven to work. Of course, the office of U.S. Attorney has a political dimension with all that that entails. You can't legislate away the potential for abuse, but you can respect the tradition that keeps that abuse in check." The complex system of nomination, appointment, and confirmation for U.S.

Attorneys encoded that tradition, and I've considered at length the irony of so avowedly conservative an administration being so willing or so careless to upset that carefully balanced applecart.

What was becoming clear from the alarmed inquiries of Senator Feinstein and her colleagues went deeper, however, than issues of protocol and the niceties that lawyers should extend to one another. The lawmakers quickly and correctly spotted the telltale signs of executive encroachment on the legislative branch of government. Feeling their way through the meager facts at hand, they had stumbled on a larger truth—the Department of Justice was in imminent danger of being fatally compromised.

On January 17, the story broke out of its regional bounds and went national with an article in the *New York Times*, focusing primarily on Lam's dismissal. The story also gave Feinstein a chance to stiffen her support for Carol, calling her "a straight shooter and a good prosecutor." More important, the article correctly identified the seven of us on a hit list for the first time. It was the opening episode in the twisted history of how that list came to be and how we came to be on it.

The source of the information in the *Times* piece had been a letter the Justice Department had sent to Feinstein, Leahy, and Pryor in reply to the senator's salvo on January 9. It was a work of accomplished tap dancing. "That on occasion in an organization as large as the Justice Department," it pointed out in a gently chiding tone, "some United States attorneys are removed or asked or encouraged to resign should come as no surprise." To the question of political motivation, the Justice Department scribe seemed to be swearing on a metaphorical stack of bibles that there had been no attempt in our firings "to retaliate against them or interfere with or inappropriately influence a particular investigation, criminal prosecution or civil case."

That was their story, and they were sticking to it. "We in no way politicize these decisions," Attorney General Gonzales had assured the Associated Press, driving the message home. It was the first utterance in an epic of stonewalling that would eventually serve to completely undermine the credibility of "the Judge." That erosion would begin in earnest on the morning of January 16 when the attorney general appeared before Feinstein and Leahy at a Judiciary Committee oversight hearing. From the opening moments, it became glaringly evident what level of cooperation would be forthcoming from Gonzales.

"How many U.S. Attorneys have been asked to resign in the past years?" Feinstein asked, at that point still trying to get an accurate head count.

Gonzales demurred, insisting that it was a personnel issue outside of her purview. "You're asking me to get into a public discussion," he replied.

"I'm asking you for a number," the senator shot back.

"I don't know how to answer that question," was the attorney general's mystified, and mystifying, response.

"I don't deny that," Gonzales would later assent when asked whether, in fact, U.S. Attorneys *had* been fired. "But that happens in every administration. . . . some people should view that as a sign of good management."

Management, and the lack thereof, would, of course, become a critical factor in the crumbling regard that Gonzales endured in the months to come. For the moment, however, he was possessed of the full authority of his high office when he told the senators that he would "never, ever make a change in a United States Attorney for political reasons or if it would in some way jeopardize an ongoing serious investigation. I just would not do it." The problem was, Gonzales didn't seem at all sure what the reasons for the firings actually might have been. In a front-page story in the *Washington Post* following the hearing, it was observed that the attorney general was "unaware of the specifics of the plan that [Chief of Staff Kyle] Sampson was orchestrating."

Good management at Main Justice had apparently devolved into a state of bemused neglect, as the unflappable attorney general made the claim that seven of his primary foot soldiers in the war against crime and terrorism and hordes of illegal immigrants, and by whom federal authority was represented on the streets of

America, had been summarily dismissed without his direct knowledge of the "plan" or its orchestration.

"Let me publicly preempt perhaps a question you're going to ask me," Gonzales concluded, "and that is: I am fully committed, as the administration's fully committed, to ensure that, with respect to every United States Attorney position in this country, we will have a presidentially appointed, Senate-confirmed United State Attorney. . . . I think he has a greater imprimatur of authority, if that person's been confirmed by the Senate."

The Judiciary Committee members were not reassured. When Senator Leahy was asked whether he thought anyone in the Bush administration might be committing perjury, he tersely replied, "We'll find that out."

Reading reports of the testimony of Attorney General Gonzales, I couldn't help but reflect on how far we'd come since the early days of his appointment and confirmation, when my hopes had ridden so high on the elevation of the first Hispanic to the nation's top law enforcement job. His hedging and hairsplitting were, to my mind, a distressing display of misplaced loyalty and, worse, an exercise in futility. Sooner or later, I felt certain, everything would have to come out, and the longer he delayed telling the whole truth and nothing but, the more damaging it would be for him and for the president he was so intent on protecting at all costs. His testimony gave me the impression of a tipping point that had been reached and then passed.

We were in uncharted territory here. If Alberto Gonzales was willing to try to conceal, however ineffectually, the inroads that partisan politics had made into his department, how far would he or his subordinates go to discredit those who were leveling the charges in the first place? My seven fellow fired U.S. Attorneys and I were directly in the line of fire, and I think we all shared a suspicion that Main Justice was quickly backing itself into a corner. If Main Justice officials couldn't come up with a good reason for firing us, they would have to make one up. Somehow, the Justice Department leadership attempted to shift the blame—we had to be held accountable for our own demise.

CHAPTER 9

Performance Related

February 2007 was ushered in on the rumors that Mike Battle, the reluctant enforcer of the dismissal decrees, had himself resigned his job as head of the Executive Office of United States Attorneys. It was not until a month later that the story was confirmed, with Fox News reporting that Mike "seemed unhappy" about the grim duty he had had to perform on December 7. He was also quoted as describing one of the conversations he'd had that day, in which he told one of us, "It's hard not to think you did something wrong when you get a call like this, but that's not always the case."

I think the same thing applied to Battle, except for him it was hard not to think he'd done something wrong when he *made* the call. He was simply too good an attorney and too decent a guy to fit comfortably into the role of executioner. I wonder whether, in the final analysis, Battle just couldn't find a way to dodge the collateral damage to his conscience. In any event, he was ready to put it behind him, and the press would get little more from him as he transitioned quickly into private practice. Main Justice, however, couldn't seem to refrain from a comment that, to my ears, damned Battle with the faintest of praise. "Mike Battle was not involved in the actual decision-making" behind the dismissals, a spokesperson laconically noted.

From the vantage point of well over a year since that day in December, I look back on early 2007 as a time when the personal crises in my life became national news events. Issues—constitutional, legal, and moral—trumped the career considerations that had been uppermost in my mind until then. However steep the emotional roller coaster Cyndy and I had been on, it was time to get off, get over it, and rise to the occasion. It was a process that felt a little like morphing from an actual flesh-and-blood person into a highly charged, somewhat two-dimensional symbol, one that could be interpreted and utilized in a number of ways, depending on one's political persuasion.

To some Republicans, I was a traitor, pure and simple. By refusing to go quietly, I had given the administration's enemies a weapon to wield and thus proved my disloyalty. In the Bush White House, as in the Gonzales Department of Justice, it was the unpardonable sin. To others in the GOP, I think my travails were seen as the first step in flushing out those within the administration who had themselves betrayed the principles of the party: the same conservative, fiscally responsible, small-government planks on which the Republican majority had stood since the Reagan eighties. It was a stake that the old guard could use to drive into the hearts of the neocons. To the Democrats, I was a valuable defector who'd seen the Justice Department Gone Wild from the inside and would certainly have some interesting stories to tell, if I could be persuaded to become a poster boy for the opposition.

I wasn't comfortable in any of those roles. It pained me to see how the scandal mushrooming in our midst had divided the Republican Party, disgraced the Justice Department, and become a political tool for Democrats. Once I had stopped worrying about my next job and started to focus on the one at hand—uncovering the truth—the last thing I wanted was to be exploited for political purposes. That had already happened to me, along with six others, and we had all determined to stay above the partisan fray as much as possible in the battle that was brewing.

The fact was, even as the story went from domestic to local to national, I never forgot its personal aspects, the way it had changed the lives of guys like Mike Battle and, I suspected, many more to come before it would all be over. My life had certainly been changed, but I couldn't have told you to what end. It was in God's hands, and for the moment God wasn't tipping his hand. All I could do was try to stay out ahead of events and keep my priorities straight.

The week of February 5 opened with a flurry of activity, as Leahy's Judiciary Committee announced that it would subpoena more Justice Department officials and legal experts in its widening investigation of the firings. Among them was Mary Jo White, a Clinton-appointed U.S. Attorney for the Southern District of New York, who had confirmed to the senators that the dismissals were wholly unprecedented, especially since they seemed to be "without significant cause." As to the DOJ's contention that in Bud Cummins's case, the removal of an outstanding federal prosecutor was simply to give someone else the opportunity to serve, White soberly assessed that rationale as "a threat to the independence of U.S. Attorneys."

It was an opinion shared by Laurie Levenson, a former Assistant U.S. Attorney and a professor at Loyola Law School, whose testimony marked the first time that legal scholars weighed in on the significance of the forced resignations. "The job of U.S. Attorney should not be a political prize," she informed the committee. "There is too much at stake for the district and the people who work in that office." Not to mention the sacrosanct principles of separation of powers, prosecutorial independence, and the integrity of the DOJ.

But witnesses like White and Levenson were just the warmup. From the beginning of the hearings, the main act was going to be Deputy Attorney General Paul McNulty, and, accordingly, a spectacular display of fireworks followed on his testimony. In sharp exchanges with the probing senators, McNulty laid out what would become the fallback position of Main Justice: the fired U.S. Attorneys had no one but themselves to blame. We had been forced out for "performance-related" issues. It was entirely our fault.

You could almost hear the other shoe drop from Washington to Little Rock to Seattle. Especially Seattle. McNulty's unblinking assertion of incompetence was exactly what John McKay had predicted and, in turn, was the trigger that he had promised would cause him to go public with his side of the story. It was, in fact, a flash point for several of us, especially after reading in no less an authoritative source than the *New York Times* of McNulty's claim that we had been "urged to leave because of poor performances." The number-two man at the DOJ exempted only Bud Cummins, who, he insisted, had just been asked to make way for the sake of Tim Griffin. New York Democratic senator Charles Schumer, a veteran Judiciary Committee member, was quick to point out the barn door–sized inconsistency in singling out Cummins from the rogue's gallery of ostensibly inept U.S. Attorneys whom McNulty had just identified. Was it accurate to say that Mr. Cummins had not done anything wrong to justify his removal? Schumer pointedly asked the deputy attorney general.

"I do not dispute that characterization," McNulty replied warily.

Had Cummins ever received a poor performance evaluation? Schumer persisted.

"I'm not aware of anything negative," McNulty responded with an equanimity that came to characterize the approach Main Justice would take through much of the subsequent scandal, serenely refusing to even acknowledge, much less admit, the logical lapses and transparent discrepancies in its version of reality. There were other jaw-dropping examples. After pronouncing himself, on behalf of Main Justice, "proud" of Carol Lam's prosecution in the Duke Cunningham case, McNulty went on to denounce political interference in the office of U.S. Attorney as "contrary to the most basic values of our system of justice";

then he promised to brief the committee members on the actual reasons behind the firings in private session.

Reading the account the next morning, I couldn't help but wonder what exactly was so sensitive about our firings that it had to be revealed away from the prying eyes of the public and the press. In any event, while I had no idea what McNulty might have told the senators behind closed doors, it apparently did little to impress them.

"It doesn't pass the smell test," Schumer contended on the issue of Bud's removal. "I can't even see how Mr. Griffin would be better qualified in any way than Bud Cummins, who had done a good job, who was well respected, who now had years of experience."

Within our circle, it was clear that the time had come to set the record straight. We were, in the simplest terms, being slandered, and there was a steely determination among Paul, John, Dan, Carol, and me to fight back. It was a lawyer's instinct as much as anything, I think. We relished good legal combat, all the more with so much on our side: the truth, the facts, our records, and a righteous indignation of almost biblical proportions.

Dan Bogden was first up to bat, granting an interview to the *Las Vegas Review-Journal* and announcing straight up that "to this date, no one from the department has previously identified any issues with my performance or the performances of my office."

In response to the inevitable question, he replied, "No, I was not given any explanation or reason for the request to step down." When asked to speculate, Dan said simply, "I'm not going to go there," but by the end of the interview, he had made certain to give a spirited defense of his tenure as U.S. Attorney. "We've done more gun cases, drug cases, child exploitation cases, identity theft cases," he counted off, "than any office has done in any five-year period of time." He had his facts straight, including the more than $55 million his staff had collected in forfeiture and fines.

It was in Dan's calm nature, in accordance with our common resolve to stay above the political skirmishes, that he would refuse to point fingers or name names. And the fact remained that of all the dismissals, Bogden's was still the most inexplicable. Perhaps, after all, there *were* no names. Perhaps the whole thing had been a glitch in the gears of Main Justice. It was an explanation that made about as much sense as a concerted conspiracy at the DOJ. Dan, however, wasn't about to make a guess in public, and I had to admire him for that, even as I respected his insistence on detailing his office's sterling performance in the public record.

The day after Bogden's story appeared, John McKay stepped up to bat with an account in the *Washington Post* by Dan Eggen, a staff writer who would be on top of several twists and turns in the developing story. "That is unfair," McKay said in a heroic show of self-restraint when Eggen quizzed him on McNulty's "performance-related" charge. "That reflects on my former colleagues in the office and the good work that we did and I know that's not true." He insisted that Battle, in his phone call to John, "said nothing about performance issues or management or anything else."

That was all McKay would allow for attribution, and I know from our correspondence that it was difficult for him to hold back from what he strongly suspected was the truth: that he had been let go for his refusal to take legal action during the 2004 Washington governor's race. Like Dan, however, John couldn't resist letting Eggen know that a few months before his December 7 call, he had gotten a letter from Mike Battle congratulating him for a laudatory Justice Department EARS report. As for what the specific performance issues that had been tried and found lacking might actually be, McKay was suggesting, the reader's guess was as good as his own.

Or, for that matter, as good as the guess of Judge Robert Lasnik, a respected Seattle jurist who, in a highly unusual move, claimed to be speaking for every federal judge in the Western District of Washington State, when he was quoted as saying, "We were dismayed to see that the Justice Department was suggesting there was something wrong with [McKay's] performance. . . . We unanimously agreed that he was absolutely superb." Even given such a blanket endorsement, it was hardly a surprise when McKay additionally revealed that four days after Battle's call, he had received word from the White House counsel's office that after being selected as one of three finalists for a Washington State federal judgeship, he was, as of now, being excluded from consideration.

The February 9 *Washington Post* piece on John's firing also had put several new elements into play, most significantly, a quick and decisive rejection by several key Republican Judiciary Committee members of the administration's strained account. A vote in the committee had been taken to recommend legislation limiting the attorney general's power to name interim replacements for the vacant U.S. Attorneys' posts. When the tally was counted, the motion carried, thirteen to six, with the help of three influential Republican senators: Arlen Specter of Pennsylvania, Charles Grassley of Iowa, and Orrin Hatch of Utah. It was not a good sign for the administration, and the Justice Department was quick to jump into the breach. Gonzales's right to appoint interim prosecutors was, insisted chief spokeswoman Tasia Scolinos, "good government and constitutionally sound." Main Justice, she continued, was "disappointed by congressional efforts to restrict our ability to appoint our own employees for temporary periods of time while a permanent nominee is selected."

It was a statement that spoke volumes, signaling as it did one distinctly possible explanation for our dismissals. With the interim appointment provision of the Patriot Act in place, the administration could put U.S. Attorneys in office across the country whose qualifications would have less to do with the demands of congressional confirmation than they would with adherence to a Bush White House ideological checklist. Removing eight of us in a *movida* (Spanish slang for "slick move"), opened the way for a wholesale elimination of the established precedents by which U.S. Attorneys were treated. It was possible that we were, in short, ousted to make way for the first wave of an oncoming phalanx of permanent interim appointees who would never have to pass the "smell test" of the legislative branch.

Having drawn a line in the sand with the performance-related alibi, Main Justice was forced to defend it and tried to stave off a furious effort by the media to dig up details of our alleged infractions. A platoon of DOJ spokespeople were put forward, most of them anonymously, citing the Privacy Act bar against discussing personnel issues. "'Performance-related' can mean many things," said one such nameless source to McClatchy investigative reporter Marisa Taylor, who, along with Eggen, would doggedly pursue the story in its developing stages. "Policy is set at a national level. Individual U.S. Attorneys around the country just can't make up their policy agendas."

True enough. What with the country at war, terrorism a top concern, and our border leaking like a sieve, U.S. Attorneys had, of necessity, to all be on the same page, a page that had initially been written by the Bush White House. The notion that we were somehow off creating problems of our own to solve suggested that we were not dealing with the nation's most urgent business, when in fact that was essentially all we had time for. Aside from being patently false and misleading, the remark also pointed out what the administration's evolving strategy would become in containing the firestorm it had started. If it could be shown that we had somehow neglected, or even ignored, the targets spelled out to us when we took office, the administration could make the performance-related charge stick.

Of course, the Bush White House would have to prove it first, and based on how Main Justice itself had measured our success, proof was increasingly difficult to come by. "He didn't get any dings," another DOJ source told Taylor, when asked to comment on Dan Bogden's EARS assessment. "The overall evaluation was very positive."

"We're not aware of any significant problems," said yet a third Main Justice source on the question of Carol Lam's record, and it was pointed out that Paul Charlton had been lauded for his "integrity, professionalism and competence" in a December 2005 EARS report.

Even at this early stage, there were voices in the Justice Department who found it difficult, or simply refused, to stay on message. I personally found the leaks supporting the exemplary performance records of my colleagues very heartening: it showed me that there were still people within the department for whom "integrity, professionalism, and competence" did indeed still matter. It was against the growing evidence in our favor, coming directly from within the DOJ, that spokeswoman Scolinos assured an increasingly skeptical press that the dismissal decision was a "careful and thoughtful" one. "This issue," she continued, "really boils down to the department's reasons for making internal management changes."

But an increasing number of citizens, senators, and scribes already *knew* that. It was a question of what those reasons might have been that remained a mystery—one that increasingly captivated official Washington and, slowly, the rest of the nation. There was indeed a smell in the air—the stench of a cover-up.

My turn to speak out came on February 9. Sitting in bumper-to-bumper traffic in downtown San Francisco, with Cyndy beside me in a rented minivan and the girls in the backseat, my cell phone vibrated, a mini-tectonic sensation that had by now become something of a dramatic cue in my life. We had come west for a family wedding and were on our way beneath overcast, drizzly skies to the downtown cathedral when a voice on the line identified himself as Dan Eggen. He had recently interviewed McKay and his byline had appeared that same day in the *Washington Post* under the headline: "Fired Prosecutor Disputes Justice Dept. Allegation."

Eggen got straight to the point. Did I know why I had been asked to resign?

If I hesitated, it was only for a heartbeat. There was no way to put back together what had come apart in the previous two months since I had last heard Mike Battle's voice on this same cell phone. Even if I'd wanted to, I couldn't stop the Justice Department from what it was about to do to itself and to the nation. There was only one way forward, to move through the scandal as it played out, hopefully toward a new beginning. "I think it was politically motivated," I told the reporter.

"Why is that?" Eggen asked, and I'm not sure whether he heard me take a deep breath. Cyndy certainly did, and she turned to look at me as the kids kept up a happy chatter in the back.

I glanced at my wife, and the unspoken message flashed between us. We had reached the point of no return. We were about to cross the Rubicon, and we knew it.

"Because I received inappropriate contacts from members of Congress," I replied, "asking me inappropriate questions."

I felt as if I was, in that moment, sharply attuned to what was appropriate and what could be construed as stepping over the line. Naming Pete Domenici and Heather Wilson was a step I was not willing to take—this was not the time or the place. But Eggen and, separately, Marisa Taylor didn't need permission to take that step themselves. Three weeks later, and during my final press conference, the two intrepid journalists began to place calls to every member of New Mexico's congressional delegation and even to other members of Congress to try to find out who had contacted me and for what reason. I had known that this Pandora's box would be opened when I made the allegation, but I also knew that I would not name Wilson and Domenici until I was under subpoena and testifying before Congress. An accusation that serious should not be made to the media but needed to be under oath and under penalty of perjury.

Events were moving quickly now, too quickly and in the wrong direction for the U.S. Attorney designate for Arkansas Tim Griffin. Bud's replacement seemed to justify Kyle Sampson's doubts about him, when Griffin announced the following week that he would not seek Senate confirmation for the post. There was a careful spin to this surprise development, with Griffin insisting that submitting his name for confirmation under the cloud of the mushrooming investigation would be tantamount to "volunteering to stand in front of a firing squad in the middle of a three-ring circus." It was an accurate-enough description, as far as it went, but Griffin went further, blaming "the partisanship that has been exhibited by Senator Pryor," the Arkansas lawmaker who had made common cause with Feinstein and Leahy in the initial Judiciary Committee probe. In fact, according to Griffin, the whole committee was out to get him. "I don't think there is any way I could get a fair hearing," he sniffed. Of course, Griffin volunteered to stay at his post until a replacement was found, which, according to the just-tweaked Patriot Act, could be a very long time or until Bush left office, whichever came first.

Meanwhile, more proof was piling up that the performance-related excuse was simply a dodge to get around the increasingly compromising question of why we had been let go at all. "They're entitled to make these changes for any reason or no reason or even for an idiotic reason," Bud was quoted as saying, with pointed irony, in the *Washington Post.* "But if they are trying to suggest that people have inferior performance to hide whatever their true agenda is, that is wrong. They should retract those statements."

As usual with Bud, he hit the nail right on the head. But there would be no retractions forthcoming. Rather, Main Justice stuck to its sputtering guns, with one spokesperson suggesting that the whole flap was simply a matter of "semantics." It was difficult for us to discern any linguistic variation in the phraseology that McNulty had chosen to use when he told the Judiciary Committee in early February that we had been "urged to leave because of poor performances." Maybe we were missing something. As a DOJ official told the *Washington Post's* Eggen, the decision to fire us related only to "policy differences between the Bush Administration and some of its employees," establishing for all time a classic new definition of a distinction without a difference.

Bud's blunt but eloquent remarks in the Sunday, February 18, edition of the *Washington Post* did not go unnoticed at Main Justice. The following Tuesday, Bud received a call from the department's designated enforcer, Mike Elston, the contents of which he made known to Dan, Paul, Carol, John, and me later that afternoon. As an indication of the mercurial mixture of emotions we shared at the time—anger and indignation, contempt and caution—Bud's e-mail to us is worth quoting at length.

The essence of Elston's message, Bud wrote, "was that they feel like they are taking unnecessary flak to avoid trashing each of us specifically or further, but if they feel like any of us continue to offer quotes to the press, or organize behind the scenes congressional pressure, then they would feel forced to somehow pull *their* gloves off and offer public criticisms to defend their actions more fully. . . . I was tempted to challenge him and say something movie-like such as 'are you threatening ME???', but instead I kind of shrugged it off. . . . He mentioned my quote on Sunday and I didn't apologize for it and pointed out to him that I had stopped short of calling them liars."

Bud's bare-knuckle confrontation with Elston was also the first time the subject was broached of the ever-more-distinct possibility that some or all of the seven dismissed U.S. Attorneys might be called upon to testify. "He reacted quite a bit," Bud continued, "to the idea of anyone voluntarily testifying, and it seemed clear that they would see that as a major escalation of the conflict, meriting some kind of unspecified form of retaliation. . . . I don't feel like I am betraying him by reporting this to you because I think that is probably what he wanted me to do. Of course, I would appreciate maximum opsec [operational security] regarding this e-mail."

Opsec was becoming increasingly hard to maintain and, to some of us, might even have seemed like an exercise in diminishing returns as we watched Main Justice ramp up its campaign of slander and intimidation. The way I saw it, silence and circumspection were becoming a liability, just as waiting for the administration to come clean was starting to seem like a waste of time. I began to understand that we had an opportunity to affect the outcome of these unfolding events, and I have to admit, it felt good. After two months of struggling to rise above victim status, I was eager to take the offensive. If I was going to go down, I was determined to go down swinging.

Accordingly, on February 28, my last full day as U.S. Attorney for the District of New Mexico, I called a press conference in the briefing room of the downtown offices that I would shortly be vacating. A large contingent of local press showed up.

I had to be careful. To a large extent, Albuquerque, like the rest of New Mexico, was Pete Domenici territory, and I knew there were people within the statewide media who would not look kindly on my implicit challenge to the senator and the Republican establishment that he had done so much to create. I was determined, as much as possible, to focus on defending my tenure as a U.S. Attorney, and I knew that any revelation of inappropriate contacts would trump that intent.

I got to work preparing a display of charts and graphs to illustrate the increased caseload and conviction rates of my office. It was my time to push back and push back hard. I was not going to hang there any longer, twisting like a piñata waiting for the next blow. It was a determination underscored by the fact that the same people who were now wielding the cudgels had been, until recently, colleagues of mine. I was not just a name on a list to Paul McNulty.

I was comfortable talking to the press, a skill I had developed over my tenure and an important tool for updating my district when it was crucial to speak directly to the citizens. This was one of those times, and although it made me uncomfortable to be in the middle of the story I was obliged to tell, I had long since come to realize that it was no longer really about me. The principles at stake had been only too starkly drawn, and, as much as anything, I believe it was because of my status as an up-and-comer in party politics that I now embodied what many saw as an ideological struggle taking shape. I didn't dispute that possibility; I just tried my best to keep it in context. My job was to tell the truth and let the chips fall where they may.

Naturally, there were people who had a wholly different interest in the direction of those falling chips. I was told before the press conference by my outstanding press officer Norm Cairns that a staffer from Domenici's Albuquerque office had watched the entire proceedings from the back of the room. I noticed that she took copious notes. Not that I cared. She would get what the local media got—a closing argument establishing the achievements of my office. Whether she showed up to try to intimidate me or just to take notes is something I'll probably never know.

A press conference is, of course, a kind of theater, and I deliberately chose it as a venue for stepping forward. I felt as if Dan and John before me had laid the groundwork. They'd been deliberately circumspect, letting others draw the conclusions we had all long since reached. Now it was time to spell it out, as plainly and simply as possible.

"I know my performance is not the real issue," I told the assembled press corps under the glare of television lights. "That leaves only one other possibility, and that's politics. . . . I would have no objection to someone calling me and saying I'd lost my political support. But they said it was performance, and I've got lots of data showing that's not the case."

Who was behind our ouster, one reporter asked? Would I be willing to take a guess?

I shrugged. "It could have been someone in the White House, someone at Justice, or someone in Congress," was my reply. "All political roads lead back to Washington." Then it was my turn to ask a question, inviting journalists to consider this: "From a political standpoint, why would they let go an evangelical, Hispanic veteran? I represent three major voting groups."

Why indeed? It was a puzzle that I hoped they would help to convey to those in the White House, Justice, or Congress who had engineered this betrayal. Actually, by then I had another term for it. Shortly before I announced my press conference, I had written an e-mail to an Albuquerque friend of mine, Mikey Weinstein, another former JAG who had taken on the military over charges of unconstitutional religious influence. In chronicling the latest developments, I described my dismissal to him as a political "fragging." I knew he'd get the reference: an ugly military term for a soldier murdering a comrade in arms. Mikey had passed the word on to a local blogger, and by the time my press conference had convened, it had become the common adjective that was attached to my situation. Soon, tpmmuckraker.com, the lead national scandal blog, picked up on the use of the incendiary e-mail to Mikey.

After my press conference, local investigative journalist Mike Gallagher followed me, uninvited, to my office. I agreed to talk to him off the record. He warned me that if I "outed" whoever was behind my forced resignation, they would "launch cruise missiles" against me. He did not say that his subsequent newspaper articles about me would facilitate those attacks.

Mike Elston's anxiety, as expressed to Bud Cummins, over the possibility that we might be called to testify, proved prescient. We had, in fact, been receiving initial inquiries from the staffs of both House and Senate Judiciary Committee members as early as the middle of February, and it seemed certain that after McNulty's testimony, we would be formally called on to offer our side of the story.

The only question for us was whether we would be testifying voluntarily or under subpoena. A subpoena came with an obligation to go to Washington. It was nice to have our expenses paid, but, more important, we would be required to go testify. We decided to wait for the subpoena. We also did not want to appear too eager, knowing that we would be accused of grandstanding if we volunteered.

The subpoena wasn't long in arriving. On March 1, the day after my press conference, I got a call from Preet Bharara, a former assistant U.S. Attorney for Manhattan, who was now serving on the legal staff of the Senate Judiciary Committee, under the direction of Senator Chuck Schumer. The New York lawmaker had taken the lead from Dianne Feinstein in the probe, and, Preet told me, we could expect a subpoena to Washington within days. As it turned out, the House beat the Senate to it, and even as I was talking to Bharara, the House Judiciary Committee was issuing subpoenas for Carol, Bud, John, and me.

The next seventy-two hours were spent hashing out the details of what would become our rare same-day testimony before both judiciary committees. It was agreed that the House would issue the subpoena, and we would appear voluntarily before the Senate. A date was decided on: March 6. Meanwhile, more names had been added to the witness list, including Paul Charlton and Dan Bogden, who were set to appear before the House Judiciary Subcommittee on Commercial and Administrative Law.

As we waited for the arrangements to be sorted out and a schedule finalized, the six of us talked extensively in telephone conference calls about what we agreed on and disagreed on. The circumstances, individually and collectively, were complex and not simply because we each had a different story to tell that led up to December 7. What we realized from our discussions was that we still hadn't reached a common understanding of the reasons behind our forced resignations.

On one end of the spectrum were Dan and Paul, who believed then that politics had no part in the decision. I think it was simply too hard for these career DOJ professionals to accept that the department had gone so far off the rails. On the other side were John and I, and we were all but convinced, based on the political flak we had experienced while trying to do our jobs, that we had been set up for purely partisan ends. I had said as much in my press conference and was ready and willing to say it again in sworn testimony. Absent an accord among us on the causality of this legal catastrophe, we determined that the best way forward was just to tell our stories, each in his or her own way, draw what conclusions we felt appropriate, and try, as much as possible, to carry no agenda with us into the hearing rooms.

It was a sober and considered approach, in keeping with the serious nature of what we had to reveal, but I can't say that, at least for me, emotion didn't enter in as I considered my upcoming testimony. I knew that we all would be facing a formidable effort by the administration to discredit us, and administration officials had already proved that they weren't above what Bud charitably refused to call lying to accomplish their ends. But there was also a very personal indication of how important it had become to destroy our credibility, and it came directly from my former mentor.

After I had tipped off Dan Eggen and Marsia Taylor about the inappropriate phone calls I had gotten back in October, the media had launched a furious search for the culprits.

"I don't have any comment," huffed Senator Pete Domenici, when an Associated Press reporter cornered him on the steps of the Capitol Building on the afternoon of March 1 to ask whether he had put political pressure on me. "I have no idea what he's talking about."

He knew exactly what I was talking about, and his angry denial would have sent a chill up my spine if I hadn't already taken the measure of the forces opposing my colleagues and me. As it was, Domenici's dismissive remark prompted a whole new determination to get the real story out. I later discovered, in the production of Justice Department documents, that Domenici and his chief of staff, Steve Bell, thought that it would be "a one-day story." What happened was just the opposite, and Domenici was hounded by the press in a way that he had never been subjected to, so much so that he described the experience as "hell."

For her part, Heather Wilson may have been less surly but was no more forthcoming. "You should contact the Department of Justice on that personnel matter," she told the Associated Press, once again trotting out the DOJ's all-purpose excuse for withholding information.

But Main Justice wasn't waiting for the media to come to it. The morning after Domenici and Wilson's nondenial denials, a new face appeared before the press to take the place of Tasia Scolinos. He was Brian Roehrkasse, a former Bush campaign staffer who would henceforth take up the heavy lifting on a story that was quickly reaching critical mass. For his remarkable ability to equivocate, dodge, fudge, pettifog, and spin the facts of the unfolding crisis, Roehrkasse was eventually named the DOJ's director of media affairs, the top public-relations post in the department. Bud Cummins would eventually write an article in the *Washington Monthly* magazine calling for Roehrkasse's firing due to his demonstrable pattern of lying.

In the weeks to come, he would earn it. He started by explaining, even as word of the politically charged phone calls began to spread, that I had actually been fired after much careful consideration. "We had a lengthy record from which to evaluate his performance as a manager," the spokesman went on, "and we made our decision not to further extend his services based on performance-related concerns." Roehrkasse proceeded to expand on that rationale, which now included "ineffectively prosecuting departmental priority areas, failure to follow departmental guidelines or just an overall inability to lead and effectively manage a U.S. Attorney's office."

Roehrkasse was also front and center when news broke of the thinly veiled threats that Mike Elston had made to Bud Cummins on February 20. After staunchly refuting a story about the calls, in which Bud remained an unnamed source, Roehrkasse went on to chide the press for choosing to "run an allegation from an anonymous source from a conversation that never took place."

It was against this backdrop of increasing escalation, desperate damage control, and the enveloping mist of a major scandal that I caught a plane to return to Washington on March 5 for the first time since I'd become a private citizen.

CHAPTER 10

The Justice League

It's not always easy to tell when history is happening. Moments of seemingly great consequence slip into obscurity, and insignificant events assume an outsized importance with the passage of time. It's especially true when you are in the midst of history as it is happening. At such a time, you can only do the best you can and leave it to others to judge the ultimate significance of your words and actions.

But at ten o'clock on the morning of March 6, 2007, as I raised my right hand and swore to tell the truth amid a battery of flashing cameras and the blinding glare of television lights, I had a pretty good idea that for the next few hours anyway, I would be privileged to be present at the unfolding of an authentically historic juncture. What had brought me to the august chambers of the Senate Judiciary Committee hearing room had been unprecedented. What would be revealed there could likely have an impact on the way Americans viewed the honesty and the integrity of their government, and the way that government would operate from that point on in the realms of law and justice. What resulted from the questions asked and the answers given that morning might well be understood by future jurists and scholars and those who enforce our laws as a dead end, a crossroads, or a way forward. There was a sense of weighty responsibility shared, I think, by all of us who had been called to that room, a solemn duty to do the best we could in the long view of history. Our words and actions mattered—now, perhaps, more than they ever had.

My initial nervousness evaporated as we sat down after our swearing in. I tried to ignore the unblinking eye of the C-SPAN camera that was dead ahead. On my notepad, I scrawled and underlined several things, "Stay above the fray" and "Isaiah 56:1," "Maintain justice and do what is right" and "Independence of the USAs [U.S. Attorneys] paramount."

It's hard to overstate the sense of awe that came over us as we stepped into that dark-paneled room and made our way to the green felt tables through a packed gallery to stand before a dais of the people's representatives, separated by a crowd of jostling photographers. It was, by design and intent, a place set aside for deliberating truth and falsehood, and as many courts as I had stood before in my career, I had never quite experienced what I can only call the majesty of the law in exactly that measure before. It was all the more memorable in light of what we had come to do: bring into the bright light of public scrutiny an abuse of power that struck at the heart of our criminal justice system, exposing an arrogance that would barter objectivity and impartiality for naked power and political gain.

The potential magnitude of what we had been summoned to bear witness to was clear enough to John, Paul, Dan, Carol, Bud, and me when we gathered the evening before at the historic Willard Hotel in the heart of Washington to reconnoiter one last time before our testimony. As we sat in the ornate lobby, a traditional watering hole for the capital's political and media elite, it became clear from the guarded and not-so-guarded looks cast our way that our new notoriety would require a heightened level of caution. The last thing we wanted was to be cornered by some eager journalist looking for a scoop or a senator or a congressman hoping to get a heads-up on tomorrow's proceedings. With a nod to one another, we left the Willard and walked several blocks in the frigid night air, looking for a sanctuary where we could talk privately. We found it in an anonymous diner off a side street, and we spent the next few hours together, eating a modest meal and sharing good company.

There was little serious strategizing that night, partly because we had been asked by the Judiciary Committee staff to keep our planned testimony confidential and partly because, I think, we really didn't want to dwell on or talk too much about the possible consequences of what was about to transpire. In that respect, our little gathering had the feel of an impromptu Last Supper. We laughed a lot and reminisced about our, perhaps more idealistic, earlier days together, but at the same time, we tried to avoid stating the obvious: like the country itself, we, too, had each come to what personally might be a dead end, a crossroads, or a way forward. It was a daunting prospect, more than a little intimidating in its implications, and we wanted to keep the mood light, to bask in the camaraderie we felt and appreciate the warmth of the moment. This warmth also encompassed Paul Charlton and Dan Bogden, who had come to Washington for testimony before the House and had joined our small circle in that cozy café. Together, we were soon to be dubbed the Justice League by a reporter for the *Washington Post*. The reference, of course, was to the comic book team of superheroes on a mission to protect truth, justice, and the American Way. It had a certain ring to it.

March 6 dawned clear and bitterly cold, the porcelain-blue skies an inept metaphor for the storm clouds that had been steadily gathering throughout early March. Several significant developments had, in fact, transpired even since the six of us had received our congressional subpoenas.

An article in the *New York Times* detailed allegations from the former U.S. Attorney for the District of Maryland, Thomas M. DiBiagio. He claimed that he had also been forced from office in early 2005, as a direct result of his probe into the administration of former governor Robert Ehrlich Jr. on charges of improperly funneling money from gambling interests to promote legalized gaming in the state. "There was direct pressure not to pursue these investigations," DiBiagio told reporters. He cited conversations he had had with prominent Maryland Republicans urging him to back off the corruption case, which subsequently grew to include links to the D.C. Madam scandal. So intense was the pressure, the ex-U.S. Attorney maintained, that when he was visited by a GOP lawyer, he reported it to the FBI as a threat. This charge took on sensational overtones in conjunction with the suspicious death in 2003 of one of DiBiagio's assistants, Jonathan Luna, who had been actively involved in the investigation.

"An absolute fairy tale," scoffed Department of Justice spokesman David Margolis about DiBiagio's charges. Margolis went on to categorically deny that DiBiagio's dismissal had anything to do with political pressure. "I clearly got the message that I had alienated my political sponsor," the combative DiBiagio shot back, referring to Governor Ehrlich, who had been a close friend before the investigation. "I would not have any support to stay another term. Clearly, they wanted me to leave."

It all sounded depressingly familiar, and although DiBiagio had had a turbulent tenure as a U.S. Attorney, I had no reason to doubt his account. He asserted that he had gone public with his dismissal only after connecting it to the forced resignations of my colleagues and myself. I knew firsthand what powerful politicians were capable of doing when they chose to exercise their influence, and I was also only too aware of how a tactic of constant, strident, and contemptuous denial could deflect even the most self-evident truth. Pete Domenici had vividly demonstrated this method by baldly claiming not to know what I was talking about on the subject of his inappropriate phone call.

But in the days following Domenici's out-of-hand dismissal, the senator's memory was apparently refreshed, along with that of Representative Heather Wilson. To this day, I'm not exactly sure what caused them to belatedly admit that they had, after all, made the calls that I had revealed to the press.

There is also the distinct possibility that Domenici and Wilson correctly calculated that I would reveal their identities under oath at the Judiciary Committee hearings. It was in such a venue, sworn to answer every question truthfully and to the best of my ability, that I would have no choice but to explain in detail the nature of the calls and from whom they had originated. It goes without saying that it was also in such a setting that maximum political damage would be inflicted. But such consequences were beyond my control and had been ever since Domenici and Wilson had chosen to conceal the truth. The situation had reached a crisis point of their own devising.

Whatever the reasons, on March 4, two days prior to our scheduled appearance before the Senate and House committees, Senator Domenici released a statement. In it, he acknowledged that he had indeed telephoned me at home in late October to obtain information about the ongoing courthouse corruption probe. "I asked Mr. Iglesias if he could tell me what was going on in that investigation," read the release from his office, "and give me an idea of the timeframe we were looking at. . . . In retrospect I regret making that call and I apologize."

But Domenici hardly let it go at that. The mea culpa was followed by several paragraphs in which he painstakingly laid out his dissatisfaction, and that of his constituents, with my overall performance. After insisting that "I never pressured him nor threatened him in any way," the senator went on to claim that in view of a caseload that had "become extremely heavy within our state," as well as his repeated attempts to "alleviate the situation," his "frustration with the U.S. Attorney's office mounted. . . . But public accounts indicated an inability within the office to move more quickly on cases. . . . This ongoing dialogue and experience led me, several months before my call with Mr. Iglesias, to conclude and recommend to the Department of Justice that New Mexico needed a new United States Attorney."

This was news to me—several levels of news. It began with the charge that "public accounts" had found my processing of cases to be inadequate. If such displeasure had been a matter of public record, it had utterly escaped my attention, and if it would have been brought to my attention, I would certainly have taken pains to point out my office's ratings for investigations, prosecutions, and convictions, one of the highest in the nation. In actuality, someone had released information showing that despite a growing caseload between 2001 and 2005, the average time that it took my office to process a case went from 4.8 months to 3.5 months. In other words, with fewer resources, my office had prosecuted more cases more quickly. A fair reading of Domenici's nonsensical press release was that he tried to get me more resources, he failed, and he fired me because he was unhappy that he couldn't get me more resources. The processing times, I knew, were a ruse. The only case's processing time he cared about was the courthouse corruption case involving Manny Aragon.

I was, of course, aware of the fact that there were certain people within the Republican Party who were less impressed with my performance than were the dozens of DOJ professionals who had prepared, written, and signed off on my EARS reports. But I never once considered that those voices in any way expressed the sentiments of the people of New Mexico, whose interests I had sworn to protect and uphold.

I was also surprised to learn that Domenici, without ever informing me of his rationale or intent, had recommended to the Department of Justice that I be replaced. When I first read his statement, I was immediately cast back to that moment of near panic after I had received Mike Battle's phone call and how, in complete bewilderment, I wondered what I had done wrong and how I could fix it. Apparently, there was no recourse and never had been. Notwithstanding the job I had done, the good reports I had received, or even what I assumed had been a cordial relationship with the man I considered my mentor, the decision had already been made, and for reasons I was not meant to know. It was a revelation that did a lot to clear up any lingering confusion I might have felt about who my friends and enemies really were and on what side of this issue I stood. A kind of cold rage came over me, as the last vestiges of victimhood dissolved into righteous indignation.

I was a little less angry but no less determined when, the next day, an article appeared in the *Washington Post* under the ubiquitous byline of Dan Eggen, in which Heather Wilson followed in Domenici's footsteps and admitted that she had made a call to me back on October 16. Like the senator, Wilson's overdue acknowledgment was a vigorous exercise in tap dancing. "I did not ask about the timing of any indictments," Wilson maintained to the *Post*, "and I did not tell Mr. Iglesias what course of action I thought he should take or pressure him in any way. The conversation was brief and professional." Again, my mind was cast back, and this time I recalled the irritation I felt at being on the receiving end of Wilson's probing into a matter that she knew as well as I did was none of her business. I wondered what part of "professional" she didn't understand.

Whatever it was, it did not stop at trying to do further damage to my reputation. In Eggen's article, he referred to a claim by Wilson that many of her constituents had complained about "the slow pace of federal prosecutions," and that one aggrieved but unidentified citizen had informed her that "Iglesias was intentionally delaying corruption investigations." As a result of this alarming development, Wilson went on, she wanted only for "Mr. Iglesias to receive this information and, if necessary, have the opportunity to clear his name.

"If the purpose of my call was somehow misperceived," she concluded with a figurative hand over her heart, "I am sorry for any confusion." She might just as well have announced that I owed her an apology for doubting her well-intentioned effort to clear my name. The reality was that Heather Wilson, at that point in her political career, could ill afford to be drawn into the scandal. Having won reelection by the narrowest of margins, her position as heir apparent to Pete Domenici—who, it was rumored, was considering retiring from public life soon—would inevitably be called into question. It was imperative for the ambitious congresswoman to deflect even the appearance of impropriety. In blunting her confession by impugning my record as a U.S. Attorney and my abilities as a prosecutor, she was killing two birds with one stone.

For its part, the Justice Department hardly jumped in to back up Domenici, much less Wilson. "The Department was unaware that such a conversation between the senator and the U.S. Attorney happened," intoned spokesman Brian Roehrkasse. The DOJ's reluctance to support the lawmakers' feeble justification for making their phone calls—that I was a poorly performing U.S. Attorney who needed help, guidance, or, simply, removal—was understandable. Main Justice had enough problems of its own devising.

On the day before our scheduled testimony, the McClatchy Group's Marisa Taylor broke the story of Mike Elston's ill-omened phone call to Bud Cummins. "The inference was that they were holding themselves back from saying more about why people were fired," Bud (identified only as one of the dismissed pros-ecutors) was quoted as saying. "It could have been construed as friendly advice or a casual prediction. . . . I took it to mean that negative, personal information would be released . . . that the gloves would come off and the Department of Justice would make us regret that we were talking."

By then, however, it was too late. We were already talking. And it seemed that the whole nation was now ready to listen.

The front row of seats in the hearing room gallery is reserved for the families and the colleagues of the witnesses, and it was a great comfort to see Cyndy sitting directly behind me as I took my place before the microphone. It was as if she literally had my back. Bud's wife, Jody, was also there, along with Carol's sister Eva, while, back home, my daughters were watching their dad on C-Span. I never thought that congressional testimony would be a family affair, but I knew there were people watching that morning who cared about us and about what we were doing, and I could feel their support. Even one of my Wheaton buddies, Brian Birdsall, a missionary in Ukraine, was represented by his nephew Judd Birdsall, who was working in the D.C. area and who sat in the audience to show his support.

Carol and I were to be the first witnesses, which was a sound legal tactic: lead with your strongest evidence. We had all seen the questions the Senate panel had prepared and had, in turn, given the senators an idea of what our responses would be. Nevertheless, it was fascinating to see these veteran lawmakers put together the first inchoate narrative of the story, keenly analyzing the political and legal implications of what was even then unfolding before them. Like press conferences, hearings can be a form of high theater, and the assembled senators were playing it for maximum dramatic effect.

Senator Charles Schumer opened the proceedings, titled "Preserving Prosecutorial Independence," with a barbed and stinging recap of what had brought us there that morning. "Most disturbing," he concluded after reading a long list of the DOJ's suspected ethical and legal lapses, "are the shocking allegations that Mr. Iglesias, far from being fired for performance reasons, was dismissed because he didn't 'play ball' after two members of Congress allegedly tried to pressure him."

The ranking Republican, Arlen Specter, in an ominous development for the administration, agreed that if the rumored accounts were correct, "there has been serious misconduct in what has occurred with the termination of these U.S. Attorneys." A former Philadelphia DA, Specter then went on to offer one of the most cogent summaries of what the stakes had become in the greater scheme of American judicial impartiality. "The prosecuting attorney has the keys to the jail," he said. "The prosecuting attorney has a quasi-judicial function, part judge, to decide whether cases ought to be brought and once having made that decision, to be an advocate, so that people in the position of U.S. Attorneys have to be allowed to do their job." They were powerful words, especially coming from a lion of the Republican Party.

Senator Dianne Feinstein used her opening statement, in part, to announce that the committee had recently approved and forwarded on a bill that would limit interim appointments for 120 days, in the process reminding us that there were currently thirteen vacant U.S. Attorney spots. The Justice Department needed what Feinstein termed "an incentive to go to the Senate" to fill those offices.

Then it was our turn. Carol stood and read a prepared statement that we had all worked on together, trading e-mail drafts back and forth in the days running up to the hearings. We had agreed on a joint statement to show our solidarity. "We respect the oversight responsibilities of the Senate Committee on the Judiciary over the [Justice] Department," Lam stated on our behalf and, in that role, wanted them to know that "[A]s the first U.S. Attorneys appointed after the terrible events of September 11, 2001, we took seriously the commitment of the president and the attorney general to lead our districts in the fight against terrorism."

It was also important, the four of us had concurred, to give the senators a sense of our abiding regard for the Justice Department, where we had believed that "new ideas and differing opinions . . . could be freely and openly debated within the halls of that great institution." It was the same institution that had summarily fired us and "given us little or no information about the reason." Yet whether there was to be a reckoning for wrongs done was not for us to decide. We didn't want the hearing to become a "forum to engage in speculation, and we decline to speculate about the reasons." Suffice it to say that we "today regret the circumstances that have brought us here to testify." Carol then concluded with what we had hoped would serve as a shot across the bow at anyone at Main Justice who persisted in pointing to our performances as a reason for the mass dismissal. "We leave with no regrets," she said, "because we served well and upheld the best traditions of the Department of Justice."

In a brief aside, committee chairman Patrick Leahy compared our forced resignations to the "Saturday Night Massacre" of the Nixon years, when Watergate prosecutor Archibald Cox was fired for his aggressive investigation of the break-in and the coverup. Leahy asserted that he had witnessed nothing of that magnitude until now. "I don't know of any precedent for it," the veteran legislator admitted.

Senator Schumer then began the formal questioning and cut straight to the chase, calling on me to describe in detail the phone calls I had received from Domenici and Wilson. I did exactly that, in as much detail as I could muster and naming them by name, although their own admissions had preceded me in the media two days earlier. Despite the fact that I was more than ready to do so, I was nonetheless grateful not to have to be the one who had to "out" the senator and the congresswoman.

Of course, there were limits on what I could actually tell the committee, especially regarding the status of the case about which Domenici had been fishing for information: the courthouse corruption investigation and its focus on Manny Aragon. No indictment had yet been handed down, and I was constrained from revealing information on the particulars of the probe. "We specifically cannot talk about a sealed indictment," I explained. "It's like calling up a scientist at Sandia Laboratories and saying, 'Let's talk about those launch codes.'" Regardless of the limitations, however, I was able to convey quite clearly what I considered to be the senator's intent. "I felt sick afterward," I told the committee when Schumer asked me about my reaction to the call. "I felt leaned on. I felt pressured to get these matters moving."

As the morning progressed, I began to discover new dimensions to the scandal, right along with the rest of the committee and the public. From John McKay, I heard for the first time of the phone call he had received from Ed Cassidy, the chief of staff for Congressman Doc Hastings, asking whether McKay planned to pursue a voter fraud investigation in the Washington governor's race. Given the sensitivity of the subject and his scruples as a former U.S. Attorney, John had not revealed the information to any of us before that moment.

Hastings, on the other hand, hardly waited a heartbeat to respond. Almost before the hearing was over, he had released a statement characterizing Cassidy's call as "entirely appropriate. It was a simple inquiry and nothing more and it was the only call to any federal official from my office on this subject either during or after the recount ordeal." One was left to wonder whether

Hastings was trying to claim credit for not calling *more* federal officials in an attempt to interfere with their duties.

"I was concerned and dismayed by the call," John testified, anticipating the senator's possible questions about why the contact hadn't been reported to Main Justice. "I immediately summoned the First Assistant U.S. Attorney and the criminal chief for my office and briefed them on the details of the call. We all agreed that I stopped Mr. Cassidy before he entered clearly inappropriate territory, and it was not necessary to take the matter any further."

I also got additional insight during the hearings into the heavy-handed call that Mike Elston had placed to Bud Cummins on February 20, attempting to silence us through intimidation. "It might have been a threat," Bud acknowledged to the committee. "It might have been a warning or an observation or a prediction. You can characterize it. I'm going to leave it up to you."

It was vintage Cummins, wry and measured, with just the slightest ironic edge. "The inference was clear," he told the senators. "I thought about it for a while, and I felt like it had been a confidential conversation. . . . On the other hand, I was very concerned about my colleagues. . . . I would not feel comfortable having one of them give an interview the next day and then the world falls on top of them."

"The message I took was that we better tone it down," I told Senator Schumer when he asked me about my impression of Elston's call. I might have been a bit bolder than Bud in my estimation, but I was also intent on letting the lawmakers know why. "They wanted us to stop talking or there would be embarrassing things revealed about our records," I said. "It didn't intimidate me. It made me angry. So, hence, my presence here."

But one of the most intriguing new facts I accumulated that day occurred later in the afternoon when we moved to the House of Representatives for an appearance at the Committee on the Judiciary. There, we were joined by Paul Charlton and Dan Bogden, who both revealed that the DOJ's number-three official, Bill Mercer, had contacted them. Mercer, who bore the lengthy title of principal associate deputy attorney general at Main Justice, had a simple, albeit belated, message to pass along to Pablo and Dan several days after their abrupt termination: despite the department's studied silence on the subject, he wanted them to know, after all, that they had been asked to resign to make way for someone else to get at shot at the job. It was essentially the same questionable pretext that had been offered to Bud when Tim Griffin arrived in Little Rock.

Bill Mercer himself played an intriguing, if tangential, role in the quickly expanding controversy. As U.S. Attorney for the District of Montana, he had run afoul of his constituents by spending an inordinate amount of time in Washington instead of back at his home base. One account stated that Mercer spent only two days per month in Montana, even though he was still the U.S. Attorney there. The DOJ leaped to his defense with the assertion that Mercer was "in compliance with the residency requirement" and then promptly altered the same requirement specifically to suit Mercer's situation, with a specially written provision in the Patriot Act reauthorization package. In fact, Mercer himself was put in charge of shepherding the provision—which would have applied retroactively to his own residency, or lack thereof, in Montana—through the congressional approval process. Despite this legislative legerdemain, Mercer would ultimately become yet one more top-level Justice Department leader whose career flatlined in the aftermath of the scandal. He would return to Montana as a full-time, in-state U.S. Attorney. It was a smart move on his part, as he would have never been confirmed as principal associate deputy attorney general.

Aside from such revelations, there was a concerted effort on our part simply to set the record straight. Carol Lam, for instance, had entered into a spirited defense of her office's prosecutorial performance, especially in the area of border enforcement. She directed her remarks to Senator Feinstein. I'm sure that Carol had not for a moment forgotten that Feinstein herself once voiced her displeasure over Carol's illegal immigration caseload. For her part, the senator went out of her way to assure Carol, and the watching nation, whose side she was now on. Lam, Feinstein let it be known, "was very well respected by judges, by investigators, and by others in the district."

In the battle that was taking shape, Democrats lined up early in our support, and as much as I appreciated it, I was also well aware of the fact that thanks to us, they had just laid hold of a powerful new weapon with which to bludgeon the administration.

The attitude of Republicans, as might be expected, was considerably more ambivalent. Of the nine GOP committee members, only Arlen Specter took an active part in the questioning. Five never made an appearance at all, while senators Jon Kyl, Jeff Sessions, and Lindsey Graham were notable either for their silence or for the frequency with which they ducked in and out of the proceedings.

Not that it mattered much. As our morning session in the Senate hearing room continued, the four of us were able to score some telling rebuttals against the DOJ's poor-performance charges. Along with Carol's statistically dense but passionate vindication of her office, I, at one point, was able to enter into the record a snippet of a letter that Mike Battle had sent to me on January 24, 2006, in which I was lauded for "exemplary leadership in the Department's priority programs, including anti-terrorism, weed and seed, and the Law Enforcement Coordinating Committee."

Carol, meanwhile, sounded a note of concern when she spoke out on what the consequences of our dismissals, intended or otherwise, might be for the remaining U.S. Attorneys. "When there is no notice or awareness, and therefore it becomes a guessing game to how it is that the Department is displeased," she ventured, "that's the chilling effect: perhaps I should just play it safe and try not to displease anybody. I don't think that's in the best interests of the country to have U.S. Attorneys who just want to play it safe."

The term *chilling effect* was one that was often used to describe the potential for the scandal to stifle the work of U.S. Attorneys. Indeed, in the days immediately following our forced resignations, you could almost feel the frost forming in U.S.

Attorneys' offices across the nation. It was hardly surprising, considering the revelation that there had been other names on the dismissal list, added and subtracted seemingly at whim, and that indeed, at one time, all ninety-three U.S. Attorneys had been on the chopping block.

Eventually, in the aftermath of the hearings and the events they precipitated, there was a sense of palpable liberation among my former colleagues. The administration was mortally embarrassed by the pure caprice and incompetence of the dismissals; now it seemed that the last thing administration officials wanted was to let another U.S. Attorney go, for cause or otherwise. It was a feeling best summed up by one U.S. Attorney who had prepared a potentially controversial case and, worried about the repercussions, had approached David Margolis, a forty-year veteran of the DOJ. At one time, Margolis had been chief of the Organized Crime and Racketeering Section, supervising no less than seventeen Organized Crime Strike Forces. "Don't worry," the crotchety Margolis reportedly assured the fretful U.S. Attorney. "These days, you could pee on the president's leg and not get fired."

As free from the fear of retaliation as the remaining U.S. Attorneys might have felt, there was no such assurance within Main Justice. Indeed, the legal impact of the hearings themselves, especially as it might apply to possible sanctions and penalties, was never far from anyone's mind. Senator Sheldon Whitehouse clearly articulated what many of us were thinking when he posed the question of how we might hypothetically respond if, during the course of an investigation, we had gotten word of witness intimidation along the lines of Mike Elston's phone call to Bud Cummins.

"I would be discussing it," replied John McKay, "with regard to possible obstruction of justice."

I agreed. "I would probably contact the FBI," I told Senator Whitehouse, "and talk about what evidence we had to move forward on an obstruction investigation."

Ultimately, however, it was left to the eloquent Bud Cummins to best sum up the very real damage that the scandal was capable of inflicting on the psychology and the morale of U.S. Attorneys and, in turn, on their ability to serve the people of their districts. "When I got this job," he testified, "I was explaining with some excitement to my wife, Jody, how it was really neat and that you might have to go out and make really tough decisions and pros-ecute powerful people and that if I did it right, we might not have a friend left in town. And she looked at me kind of funny, as if to say, 'And why do you want this job?'

"But it never occurred to me in that dialogue," Bud continued with quiet intensity, "that the Department wouldn't insulate me, even if I became unpopular . . . that as long as they were con-vinced that I was following the book and I was doing my duty, that they would insulate me from that criticism even if we didn't get into the country club."

It was shortly after a noon break, near the end of the three-hour Senate Judiciary Committee session, that Senator Schumer let drop an indication of just how rough a game of hardball Main Justice and the administration was prepared to play in order to dis-credit us by any means necessary. In a question to me, he referred to the secret briefing that senators had been given by Deputy Attorney General Paul McNulty back in the first week of February. "One of the reasons the Justice Department said you had a perfor-mance problem," Schumer revealed, "was that you were an 'absen-tee landlord.'"

I couldn't quite believe what I was hearing. Were they saying that because of my navy reserve duties, which I was undertaking in a time of war and national emergency, I was actually neglecting my responsibilities as a citizen?

That's what Schumer seemed to surmise. "Isn't it true," he continued, "that you are required to serve your country in the reserves approximately forty days a year?"

"That's correct, sir," I nodded, adding, "Sometimes I add a lit-tle extra duty so it probably averages a little more per year."

"How do you feel," Schumer prompted, "when they accuse you of absenteeism and you know that the primary reason that you were out of your office was to be in the reserve?"

"It's very ironic," I responded, "since the Department of Justice enforces the Uniform Services Employment and Reemployment Act, that ensures reserve members have full employment rights." I didn't feel that it was necessary to add that I was never more than a phone call or an e-mail away from my office while on reserve duty. Instead, I focused on tamping down the sense of outrage I had managed to contain all morning. The notion that I was somehow derelict in my district duties by fulfilling my obligation to the armed forces was hard for me to comprehend. It was deeply troubling that in a crucial time in our nation's history, the Justice Department apparently held it against me that I was in the U.S. Navy Reserve.

In the days immediately following our testimony, the steady drip of innuendo and insinuation concerning the reasons for our firings began to issue from mostly anonymous sources within Main Justice. I heard, for example, that I was accused of being "aloof and remote" and that I delegated too much of my authority. Such charges, to my mind, were simply not worth answering. Given the workload my office regularly operated under, delegation was never merely an option: it was a necessity. In fact, I made it a point to practice "walk-around management," which simply meant that I dropped in on people at their offices on a regular basis to see what was going on. I also made it a point to send people get-well cards, newborn baby cards, and condolence cards. Suffice it to say, I had great confidence in the staff I had assembled, and to the degree that I delegated to them the important work of investigation and prosecution, it was a reflection of that confidence.

By the same token, no one had ever informed me that I had to win a popularity contest to be a successful U.S. Attorney. If there was any truth to being called aloof and remote, I'll chalk it up to being preoccupied instead. In the pressure-cooker atmosphere under which we all worked, there was a palpable virtue in cutting to the chase, and to this day, I am proud of the personal relationships I maintained with the dedicated professionals under my authority, despite the heavy caseload.

McNulty, it turned out, had initiated the smear campaign when he appeared behind closed doors for the Judiciary Committee and offered up a plethora of excuses for our firings. That much was evident as our Senate testimony continued, and Schumer asked John McKay what might be construed as the ultimate leading question, revealing in the process that Main Justice had used McKay's passionate advocacy of the cutting-edge criminal information–sharing system called LInX (Law Enforcement Information Exchange) as a reason for forcing him out. "It would make no sense," the senator prompted, "to fire you because you thought you were arguing that LInX would be a good system for you or others to use."

I shared a quick, flabbergasted look with John. Was being a champion of a proven system such as LInX, like my service in the U.S. Navy Reserve, the best they could come up with as a rationale for forcing us out? Were these the egregious "performance-related" issues to which they obsessively referred? It seemed entirely possible, especially when, soon after the hearing, a Main Justice official gave reporters the best explanation he could think of in the moment for such an action. "You can't have multiple information-sharing systems," the unnamed source staunchly maintained.

For his part, John McKay, like the rest us, was by now unwilling to dismiss the possibility of even the most questionable pretexts being ponied up by Main Justice. "I accept what they say today," McKay told reporters outside the hearing room. "I wonder what they're going to say tomorrow."

What they would say tomorrow, and the day after, making adroit use of the Beltway grapevine, was even more underhanded. In what had to be a low point of a scandal already marked by a steep downward spiral, shadowy sources within Main Justice let it be known that another reason for forcing John McKay's resignation, aside from his voter fraud failures, had to do with the tragic 2001 murder of Tom Wales, an Assistant U.S. Attorney for the Western District of Washington. A respected prosecutor and a passionate advocate of gun control, Wales was shot to death while sitting in his Seattle home office. The resultant investigation was just getting under way when McKay was confirmed as U.S. Attorney. Wales is believed to be the only Assistant U.S.

Attorney killed in the line of duty. Because Wales worked in the U.S. Attorney's office, McKay and his staff were, of necessity, recused from involvement in what might potentially be a death penalty case.

"You couldn't have Tom's friends in the office making those kinds of decisions," McKay told journalist Jeffrey Toobin in a lengthy article in the *New Yorker*. But as the case dragged on with no resolution, it became apparent to members of McKay's staff—who subsequently made their concerns known directly to McKay, and in no uncertain terms—that inadequate assets were being deployed to find Wales's killer. "I decided that it should really be my job to advocate for appropriate resources to be devoted to the Wales case," McKay said to Toobin. It was this advocacy, according to well-placed leaks within Main Justice, that added another shovelful of dirt in the attempt to bury McKay.

That McKay would be removed for too actively pursuing the means to bring the killer of a dedicated public servant to justice moved all of us beyond anger to a kind of deep remorse, a shared sorrow for just how low the partisan powers within the Justice Department were willing to stoop. "It was very sad," McKay later reflected. "It didn't matter, of course, whether by pushing for more manpower to find Tom's killer I was actually contributing to my own firing, or whether, in their desperation to justify their actions, they had simply used it as an excuse. Either way, it was beneath contempt."

Contemptuous behavior, it appeared, was a judgment call, as the ethical foundations on which the Justice Department was established had suddenly become permeable, and the truth was twisted to suit an increasingly tortured cover-up. It would be suggested, for example, that among the reasons that Paul Charlton had been let go was a run-in he'd had with FBI director Robert Mueller over, of all things, taped confessions by the Bureau. "For some reason, they had a policy that discouraged taping confessions, relying on written reports instead," Paul explained. "They were essentially using technology that had been around since the Code of Hammurabi, and it was hurting our chances for successful prosecutions."

Charlton's push for a forensic upgrade in the district quickly drew the ire of FBI bureaucrats—in particular, Mueller, who expressed his unhappiness over Charlton's efforts to introduce taping. "I offered to resign," Paul explained, "but they talked me out of it and eventually gave me a pilot program." He smiled ruefully. "I was willing to leave over my issues with the FBI," he said. "They talked me out of it. Then they told me to leave and pointed to my issues with the FBI as the reason. You figure it out."

The hearings changed everything: the shape and the size of the scandal; the way each of us would live our lives going forward; the political landscape of the country. In the middle of the whirlwind, we all tried to keep our perspective. Whatever happened from here on, it was out of our hands. We had done our duty and shared a sense of pride in one another and ourselves. In a very real way, the House and Senate Judiciary Committee hearings came as a vindication for us. We had been provided with a forum to tell our side of the story, to refute the charges, ranging from malicious to absurd, of the Justice Department, and, through it all, to speak out for what we really believed in: the rule of law, prosecutorial independence, and the integrity of the legal system.

Other things remained the same. "The Department stands by its decision," Deputy Attorney General William Moschella testified before the House Committee on Commercial and Administrative law. "To be clear, it was for reasons related to policy, priorities, and management that these U.S. Attorneys were asked to resign." And, of course, the administration was not without its allies on Capitol Hill. Among them was Utah representative Chris Cannon, a Republican who had won 100 percent ratings from the American Conservative Union for two years running. Cannon's testimony was taken under the high ceiling of the House hearing room—larger, but just as packed as the Senate's—and his job that afternoon was to try to shake our stories.

"Mr. Iglesias," he asked me pointedly, "did you report the contacts from Ms. Wilson and Mr. Domenici?" When I answered that I hadn't, he wanted to know why. "Were they unimportant?"

"They were very important," I replied. "They were very important to my career. Mr. Domenici was a mentor and a friend. Heather Wilson was also a friend. . . . I felt terribly conflicted about having to report it."

The exchange escalated quickly as Cannon accused me of "using the media as a mechanism for communicating with the Department of Justice." After I reminded him that I had not named Domenici and Wilson until that day, Cannon pushed home his point, telling me that "loyalty was a two-way street" and that I had felt "justified in lashing back." I didn't argue.

"I will tell you that I know Mr. Domenici," Cannon said, in an attempt to scold me. "He is really smart and really tough, and I just don't believe your characterization of how the phone call happened. I don't think he would have called you and done something that should have been reported to the Department of Justice." Once again, I let it pass. It wasn't worth reminding the congressman that two days earlier, Domenici had admitted to and apologized for making the same call that Cannon was now fervently defending. Cannon would later state on a cable TV news show in July 2007 that I was fired because I was an "idiot." The Salt Lake media called me for a comment. I stated that it was beneath the dignity of his office for him to use such language. Cannon would later take some heat from the Utah press because of his use of this sophomoric and intemperate language. It pained me to see my party launch into ad hominen attacks when they did not have the facts to rebut our testimony.

"God bless you," Cannon concluded enigmatically when his time was up. "You were a U.S. Attorney and you talked to the press about it."

To borrow a line from Paul McNulty, I did not dispute that characterization. I *had* been a U.S. Attorney. But what neither of us could have anticipated was that my days of talking to the press had only just begun.

Actually, I remember them starting even before the hearing concluded that afternoon, as the winter sky darkened with an early snowfall. During the break, I had made my way to the restrooms in a hallway behind the dais. It was there that I encountered senior *Newsweek* political writer Michael Isikoff, who had somehow managed to break away from the horde of reporters waiting in the corridor on the far side of the hearing room.

Would I agree to an interview? Isikoff wanted to know. There were a lot of questions he wanted to ask, a lot of details he needed to acquaint himself with.

"Hey, Mike," I said, backing away slowly. "Can I go to the restroom first?"

CHAPTER 11

All Roads
Lead to Rove

I was bone weary and emotionally drained when Cyndy and
I arrived back at our Washington hotel room that evening
after a full day of intense testimony. At that juncture, the last
thing I wanted to do was to attempt to parse the political and personal implications of the day's events. More than anything else,
I was looking forward to having a nice, quiet dinner with my wife,
calling my daughters at home, and then turning in for a good
night's sleep.

But almost as soon as we opened the door, the phone started
ringing, and as I answered it, Cyndy looked at my e-mail in-box,
which was already piling up with requests for interviews. When the
first reporter got off the phone, another quickly rang in, and after
him, another. I told them all the same thing: I was too exhausted to
make any sense that night. If they still wanted to talk to me tomorrow, I'd be available.

The requests and the entreaties followed us back to Albuquerque, and I soon established a busy routine simply responding
to the press and its seemingly insatiable appetite for the scandal.
For the next three months, my life was a whirlwind of television

and talk show appearances, op-ed pieces, Q&As, and photo sessions from Fox, CNN, and the major networks to newspapers and current events programs from across the nation and around the world.

What seemed to have emerged from the hearings was a need for the media to focus on one member of the Justice League as a quick and symbolic reference point for everything the U.S. Attorneys' firings had come to represent. I was that person, and I tried to use whatever telegenic and press-worthy appeal I might have had to keep the story in the national spotlight. It was perhaps because my particular case was one of the most blatant of any of the eight of us, with a more easily understood narrative of pressure and intimidation from high places.

My status as de facto spokesman may have also had to do with the fact that I was simply *available*. Most of my colleagues had already gotten jobs with private firms or in the corporate realm, and I certainly needed work myself. But it would be seven months before I picked up my next paycheck. Instead of rushing into the next stage of my career, I held back purposely. I granted myself an impromptu sabbatical and waited to weigh whatever options came my way. Giving my side of the story, along with the stories of the other fired attorneys, had become my job, and I had found purpose in it. Aside from all the attention, I had the rare opportunity to speak about an issue that could well have a lasting impact on our national discourse, a chance to stand up for what I thought mattered, and the ability, as least potentially, to influence the course of great events.

It was my first chance to "speak truth to power." I had thought, however, that I would be speaking out for a matter of days and not for the months that ensued. Following up on the first flash of notoriety, I settled into my new task of relentlessly pursuing vindication. I was comfortable in the role of commentator, especially as it pertained to the momentous aftermath of the congressional hearings. I eventually wrote two op-eds, one for the *New York Times* and one for the *Los Angeles Times*, opportunities that helped me to understand just what kind of platform I had been given.

The Justice Department could hardly have ignored the black eyes it had sustained as a result of our testimony. Accordingly, it moved quickly into a maximum spin cycle. On March 7, in a sidebar of an editorial headlined "Political Pressure Taints Firing of Top Prosecutors," readers of *USA Today* found a brief, to-the-point editorial on the subject from no less an authority than Attorney General Alberto Gonzales himself, in which he fervently expressed the hope that "this episode will ultimately be recognized for what it is: an overblown personal matter." Out of respect for the fired U.S. Attorneys, Gonzales went on, "The Justice Department . . . would have preferred not to talk publicly" about the reasons for our "performance-related dismissals." I wondered how the attorney general might then have characterized all the chatter on the airwaves and in the dozens of newspaper columns.

In a telling counterpoint to the attorney general's insistence that all of this was strictly a matter for the DOJ's Human Resources department and not properly the purview of either the press or politicians, his second in command, Deputy Attorney General Paul McNulty, was doing exactly what his boss had cautioned against in yet another executive session, this time before both House and Senate Judiciary Committee members, the day after our appearances. But far from backing up Gonzales on the claim that the spreading mess was nobody's affair but Main Justice's, McNulty now seemed intent on limiting the damage to his own career. He told lawmakers that, in fact, he had had very little to do with the firing process and had not even participated in selecting those on the hit list.

It was a remarkable admission from the number-two man at the DOJ. Could he really have been totally unaware of how the list of names of nine U.S. Attorneys who were to be forced out of their jobs had come into existence in the first place? But the startling revelations did not stop there. McNulty also told the joint committee that he had even been left out of the loop in the planning stages of the firings, preparations that been going on for the better part of two years. Aides in the attorney general's office, specifically the chief of staff, Kyle Sampson, who had been the first to interview me when I applied for the U.S. Attorney job back in 2000, had handled all that, according to McNulty. Joining Sampson in developing the dismissal strategy was the department's thirty-four-year-old counsel to the attorney general and White House liaison, Monica Goodling, who brought to the task her strong ties with the West Wing.

Formerly teamed with Tim Griffin, who would step into Bud Cummins's place as interim U.S. Attorney for Arkansas, Goodling worked on opposition research for the Republican National Committee during Bush's 2000 presidential campaign. A cum laude graduate of the newly established Regent University Law School, she subsequently moved quickly up the Justice Department career ladder. "She is the embodiment of a hardworking young conservative who believes strongly in the president and his mission," was the way former attorney general John Ashcroft described some of her most salient qualifications.

With such endorsements, it was hardly a surprise that Goodling became deputy director of the Executive Office of United States Attorneys, where, among other duties, she helped to oversee personnel management and evaluation. Less than a year later, she was promoted again, this time directly into the attorney general's office, where she served as the department's liaison to the White House. It was this connection that caught the attention of the legislators questioning McNulty. "If the top folks at DOJ weren't the key decision-makers," Senator Schumer posited, "it's . . . much more likely that the people in the White House were making major decisions."

Perhaps, but there was no proof as yet that the operation had been directed from outside the DOJ, a critical consideration when factoring in possible political influence. It was not for lack of trying by Senate and House Democrats to dig up such proof, however. Aside from McNulty, a plethora of interview summonses were issued by the Senate Judiciary Committee, including requests to talk with Mike Battle, Bill Mercer, and Mike Elston. Even as Pete Domenici took the proactive step on March 8 of hiring a top Washington criminal defense lawyer to deal with an ethics probe, the lawmakers were increasing their demands on Main Justice.

Schumer, remarking on a second get-together that the committee had that same day with Attorney General Gonzales, revealed that "While we didn't get any better explanation for these unprecedented firings," an important development had nonetheless come from the meeting. "The attorney general told us the administration would not oppose our legislation requiring Senate confirmation of all U.S. Attorneys."

As Senator Dianne Feinstein, the author of the provision, put it, U.S. Attorneys "may be hired by the president, but they serve the people and they should not be subjected to political pressure." Under the circumstances, it seemed as if the abandonment of the concept of the permanent interim appointment was little more than a belated attempt by Main Justice to cut its losses.

That was becoming increasingly difficult to accomplish, with administration missteps mounting and support eroding. Capitol Hill, Republicans and Democrats alike, expressed outrage over both the facts of the firings and the DOJ's inept handling of the resulting conflagration. "I hardly think it's a personnel matter," huffed Arlen Specter, referring to the glib *USA Today* editorial about our forced resignations. "And I hardly think it's overblown. One day there will be a new attorney general," he added darkly, "maybe sooner rather than later."

It was a day that both Main Justice and, increasingly, the White House were doing all they could to forestall. March 9 marked the deployment of major administration assets, when Bush's senior political adviser Karl Rove spoke for the first time on the spreading scandal during a University of Arkansas event. "My view," Rove offered, "is that this is unfortunately a very big attempt by some in Congress to make a political stink about it."

There was no question about that, just as there was little doubt that attempts to contain the stench were increasingly ineffectual, particularly when it came to the familiar odor of putrefying politics. On March 11, just five days after our congressional testimony, New Mexico Republican Party chairman Allen Weh, in an interview with McClatchy's Marisa Taylor, unwittingly cinched up the partisan link between the White House and the Justice

Department by announcing that in late 2005, he had complained about my performance in the voter fraud investigation to an aide of Karl Rove's. A year later, during a 2006 White House holiday party, shortly after Mike Battle had been handed the task of terminating us, Weh spoke directly to Rove himself.

"Is anything ever going to happen to that guy?" Weh, a retired U.S. Marine Corps Reserve colonel, asked Rove, again expressing his dissatisfaction with me.

"He's gone," Rove told Weh, and the New Mexico Republican Party chairman's response was "something close to 'Hallelujah,'" Weh told Taylor. "There's nothing we've done that's wrong," Weh went on to insist, in response to a question that hadn't been asked, "It wasn't that Iglesias wasn't looking out for Republicans. He just wasn't doing his job, period."

Someone hadn't been doing their job; that much was beyond dispute. Even as the House Judiciary Committee announced its intention to issue subpoenas to top administration officials, starting with Rove himself and including Harriet Miers and William Kelley—the president's counsel and deputy counsel, respectively—the White House, through spokeswoman Dana Perino, acknowledged Rove's role in passing directly to the Justice Department such complaints about U.S. Attorneys as the ones lodged by Alan Weh. Among the names that Rove specifically recalled mentioning to Main Justice was my name.

The fact that the taint of scandal had reached so high, so fast, suggested that there was a lack of a suitable scapegoat to take the fall. One was quickly found. The following day, March 12, Kyle Sampson, the chief of staff for the attorney general, abruptly announced his resignation after ostensibly acknowledging that he had not told key Justice Department officials of the extent to which he was in contact with the White House over the dismissals, which allowed Gonzales, McNulty, and others to provide inadequate information to the investigating committees. I found out while attending a Wheaton Board of Visitors meeting, when Bud Cummins called me in the early evening as the darkness gathered over suburban Chicago. That was my first indication that not only would this affair be, at best, a Pyrrhic victory for the administration, but, more likely, a Pyrrhic loss.

Sampson's departure was the first in a series of tumbling dominoes. It also marked a sad chapter in what had been his notable career in the Justice Department, including stints as Assistant U.S. Attorney and counselor to Attorney General John Ashcroft. On March 29, 2007, Sampson, under intense questioning by Senator Chuck Schumer and before the Senate Judiciary Committee, finally admitted that he would not have put my name on the list of fired U.S. Attorneys. That night, Larry King asked me about this 180-degree turn. It was the beginning of the end for the house of cards that the Justice Department had so hastily thrown together about our forced resignations. Based on Sampson's testimony, Schumer wrote Attorney General Gonzales a letter seeking an apology for me. And Senator Arlen Specter said on a Sunday morning talk show that if I had been improperly fired, I should have been reinstated.

I took no joy in Sampson's fall from grace or that of any of the others who would follow him. The ugliest side to the scandal that had engulfed, and would continue to engulf, so many was the toll it exacted on so many lives. I knew what Kyle and the others were feeling: I had felt it, too, and to that degree, I felt empathy. Like Gonzales himself, leading by example, these were men and women who had lost their way.

Questions about the content and the quantity of communications between the White House and Main Justice immediately became a matter of intense interest. Sampson's last act before his effective-immediately resignation was to hand over a sheaf of e-mail correspondences between him and key White House officials, including Harriet Miers, dating back to early 2005. It was an action that could hardly be construed as throwing himself on a sword to protect the attorney general and others. Instead, Sampson's document dump served to spread the blame, providing, for the first time, a look at the Machiavellian maneuvering that had taken place around the mass firings.

It made for fascinating reading and was followed, the next day, by the release of further documents by Main Justice. Over the course of several more days, the House Judiciary Committee received thousands of pages of letters, memos, and e-mails, which in turn widened the perimeters of the scandal that much further and fed the demand for more documents.

Through March and early April, the lawmakers made numerous attempts to pry more data from the White House—in particular, any Karl Rove e-mail traffic regarding the firing plan. They got everything but. It serves a bureaucracy that feels itself under threat to delay and obfuscate as much as possible, and when Main Justice was forced to release its first round of correspondence, some three thousand pages in all, it larded the package with much irrelevant material, including, for some reason, the fifty-plus charts and graphs I had shown in a Power Point presentation at my February press conference. Yet interspersed with the dross were dates, times, and places that played themselves out into a political tragedy, unfolding chapter by chapter in Capitol Hill's hearing rooms and across the front pages and TV screens of America.

As good a place to start as any in the saga that was being pieced together by the press and the politicians would be in late 2004, when John McKay first came under scrutiny for insufficient zeal in prosecuting voter fraud. As the pressure for retaliation increased, Washington State Republican National Committee chairman Chris Vance was in regular touch with Karl Rove, to whom he freely vented his frustration, along with that of other state Republicans, over John's perceived intransigence. Also complaining frequently to Rove was Seattle businessman Tom McCabe, who demanded that McKay be fired forthwith. I had also attracted notice around that time, but of a different kind. In a terse e-mail reference, Kyle Sampson had characterized me as a "diverse up-and-comer; solid."

By the early weeks of 2005, the first signs that the Gonzales Justice Department was actively considering a mass firing came when Colin Newman, an aide to then White House counsel Harriet Miers, passed a message up to Kyle Sampson. "Karl Rove," he wrote, "stopped by to ask how we planned to proceed regarding U.S. Attorneys, whether we are going to allow any of them to stay, request resignations from all and accept only some of them, or selectively replace them."

The origins and the intent of Rove's inquiry have never been clearly delineated, primarily because the Bush administration, claiming executive privilege, repeatedly refused to make Rove's e-mail correspondence on the subject available to the committees. In point of fact, there were allegations that the White House was hiding a good deal of relevant material by having aides and officials use their private e-mail accounts instead of sending messages through the official, and traceable, channels. If true, this is in violation of federal law. Whatever the case, from its very inception, it seems, the name of Karl Rove appears in close proximity to the plan to fire some, all, or a few U.S. Attorneys. *Why* still remains a mystery. Was the intent to purge any or all obstreperous U.S. Attorneys in order to give a new batch of underlings a chance at the plum job, or something altogether more sinister?

"The vast majority of U.S. Attorneys," Kyle Sampson wrote on January 9, 2005, "are doing a great job, are loyal Bushies, etc." Passing over, for the moment, the fact that we were apparently being judged by our loyalty to the president, Sampson's e-mail made it clear that a purge was already in the works. He and the "Judge"—Alberto Gonzales—had discussed it and had determined that "we would like to replace 15–20 percent of the current U.S. Attorneys—the underperforming ones."

No mention was made of how, exactly, "underperforming" might be defined. Were we underperforming prosecutors or underperforming Bushies? Sampson did, however, raise a red flag. "When push comes to shove," he warned, "home state Senators likely would resist wholesale (or even piecemeal) replacement of U.S. Attorneys." But he was, in the end, upbeat. "That said," he concluded in his response to Colin Newman's e-mail, "if Karl thinks there would be political will to do it, then so do I."

This time, there was no passing over the fact that Sampson had all but acknowledged that the decision was to be made on a purely political basis. It was solely a matter for Rove's consideration and judgment.

Meanwhile, against a backdrop of increased calls for McKay's dismissal and the dissatisfaction of New Mexico Republicans over my own decision not to file any voter fraud charges, Carol Lam appeared for the first time in the Main Justice crosshairs for her handling of immigration cases. Over much of the remainder of 2005, the administration and the Justice Department continued to lay the groundwork for their coup against the office of U.S. Attorney, abolishing Senate oversight with Section 502 of the Patriot Act Reauthorization and thereby establishing the post of permanent interim appointee. It was perhaps the last piece of the puzzle, removing in unison the final obstacle to selecting U.S. Attorneys by strict ideological standards alone.

In any event, in January 2006, Kyle Sampson and Harriet Miers, representing the DOJ and the White House, respectively, entered into a lengthy e-mail exchange to hash out the next step in the scheme. In a confidential memo dated January 9, Sampson laid out the potential pitfalls in a widespread dismissal of U.S. Attorneys. Concerned that it would "cause a significant disruption in the work of the Department of Justice," the attorney general's chief of staff assured Miers that "none of the obstacles are insuperable" and discussed ways of "mitigating the shock to the system." He concluded his e-mail with a list of those who "might be considered for removal and replacement:" Margaret Chiara, Bud Cummins, Kevin Ryan, and Carol Lam.

It was a list that would change several times over the course of months, with names being added and subtracted and my own not appearing until Election Day, November 7, 2006. On the last day of January 2006, Senator Pete Domenici contacted Kyle Sampson on the subject of my unsuitability. He had previously made such contacts, to both Sampson and McNulty, and they were later characterized by Justice Department spokesman Brian Roehrkasse as expressing "general concerns about the performance of U.S. Attorney Iglesias and questioning whether he was up to the job."

In April, Domenici made yet another call to complain, this time in conference with, among others, Monica Goodling. The presence of the well-placed White House liaison was the direct result of a secret order that Attorney General Gonzales had issued in March that gave both Goodling and Sampson the authority to hire and fire DOJ appointees, such as—and perhaps primarily— U.S. Attorneys. Apparently unbeknownst to their immediate superiors, most notably, Paul McNulty, the ambitious young aides had now effectively taken over the process of selecting candidates for summary dismissal.

Goodling and Sampson quickly assumed a take-charge attitude, and Monica quietly met with disgruntled New Mexico Republicans Mickey Barnett and Pat Rogers, at the behest of Scott Jennings, the White House deputy director of political affairs, who was directly under Karl Rove. Topic A: David Iglesias. Meanwhile, the furor surrounding Carol Lam and her border-enforcement policies, along with her prosecution of Duke Cunningham, took center stage in the spring and the early summer of that year, mostly fueled by her vilification by the vociferous congressman Darryl Issa.

In July, Deputy Attorney General Bill Mercer joked with NcNulty's chief of staff, Mike Elston, that Lam may not go so easily. "She won't just say 'OK, you got me,'" he wrote in an e-mail on the eighth of that month. "'You're right, I've ignored national priorities and obvious local needs.'" Sampson also seemed to have it in for Carol, asking Mercer whether anyone at the DOJ had ever "woodshedded her re: immigration enforcement."

Yet for all the rich-target environment of the politically vulnerable U.S. Attorneys, the actual heads on the chopping block seemed less significant to Goodling, Sampson, and company than the procedural dynamics of the group firing. Back in April, Sampson had circulated a second list of potential contenders, singling out only Margaret, Bud, and Carol. "If you pushed me," Sampson wrote to Associate White House Counsel Dabney Freidrich, "I'd have 3–5 additional names that the White House might want to consider." Once again, the ultimate tally, like the names that would appear on it, seemed to be a decision that the Gonzales Justice Department was comfortable to leave to the discretion of the White House.

Goodling and Sampson spent late August ironing out last-minute wrinkles in the installation of Tim Griffins to replace Bud

Cummins, who had served as a test case for the firing strategy when Mike Battle had given him his walking papers two months earlier. Their solution to the objections of two Democratic lawmakers, who were questioning the inexplicable switch in the Arkansas U.S. Attorney, was simplicity itself, given the recent passage of Section 502 of the Patriot Act Reauthorization: Griffin would be named as an interim replacement, the first under the recalibrated law.

But by early fall, the master plan still had not jelled. On September 13, Goodling e-mailed Sampson with yet another revised list, this one including, for the first time, John McKay, Paul Charlton, and Dan Bogden. In reference to Paul and Dan, Sampson had received a message from DOJ official and anti-obscenity activist Brent Ward that claimed, "We have two U.S. Attorneys who are unwilling to take good cases we have presented to them." It was the first time anyone had offered anything like a rationale for firing Charlton and Bogden, but, apparently, Sampson took it as proof positive that they, too, should be shown the door.

Once again, I was conspicuous in my absence, especially considering that Domenici would soon contact McNulty yet again with his grievances over my prosecutorial assessments. A few weeks later, President George W. Bush himself had a conversation with Attorney General Gonzales regarding the clamor around voter fraud investigations in New Mexico, Washington, and elsewhere. Months later, when confronted with evidence of the exchange, administration spokeswomen Dana Perino artfully hedged its implications when she allowed that Bush "may have informally mentioned it to the AG during a meeting on other matters," but the press and the public should rest assured that "it doesn't appear that the president was told about a list or shown a list." In short, Bush did not "direct the DOJ to make any specific action with regards to a specific U.S. Attorney."

Perino's protestation may have, for the moment, stopped the stain of the scandal from spreading into the Oval Office, but it was obvious, even from Goodling's and Sampson's increasingly flexible roles as interchangeable White House and DOJ operatives, that the administration was knee deep in the muck. Congressional investigators seemed convinced of the connection as well and had been badgering the White House for additional data dumps, as they incessantly demanded access to Rove's e-mails.

By late October, right around the time I had received the improper phone calls from Senator Domenici and Congress-woman Wilson, Goodling and Sampson were at last putting the finishing touches on both the final firing tally and the strategy to implement it. Immediately after the November 7 election, when my name appeared for the first time on the hit list, Sampson unveiled his five-step "Plan for Replacing Certain United States Attorneys." In it, the complete list—Paul Charlton, Carol Lam, Kevin Ryan, Margaret Chiara, Dan Bogden, John McKay, and David Iglesias—was presented, along with bullet-pointed answers to what was assumed would be Frequently Asked Questions—such as "Who Decided?" and "Why Me?"—that Mike Battle would likely hear throughout the day on December 7.

Sampson sent a copy of the plan to White House counsel Harriet Miers, letting her know that he and his team would "stand by for a green light from you." Then he added a note of concern: "We must all be on the same page," he insisted, "and be steeled to withstand any political upheaval that might result . . . if we start caving to complaining U.S. Attorneys and Senators then we shouldn't do it—it'll be more trouble than it's worth." That would prove to be the understatement of the year.

There was one senator who I knew for sure would not be complaining. Sure enough, when news of my forced resignation reached Domenici's chief of staff, Steve Bell, he declared himself "happy as a clam." I naturally assumed that he was speaking for Saint Pete.

"We're a go for the U.S. Attorney plan," Bill Kelley e-mailed Kyle Sampson and Harriet Miers on the afternoon of December 4, three days before Battle would swing into action. "WH [White House] legal, political and communications have signed off and acknowledged that we have to be committed to following through once the pressure comes."

But when the pressure came, those who had masterminded the plot found themselves in utter disarray. It was perhaps that lethal combination of what John McKay had described as "incompetence and arrogance" that led Sampson, Goodling, and, one might presume, Karl Rove himself to so utterly underestimate the outrage and the indignation that would follow on their meticulously planned miscalculation. Except, of course, that Rove was widely considered one of the savviest political operatives ever to sit in the counsels of power, which would effectively eliminate the "incompetence" element of John's equation.

That leaves "arrogance," and, as a prosecutor, it's a charge I think I could have easily made stick. From virtually the first day, the Bush administration seemed to have wrapped itself in an impenetrable aura of hubris, stiffened, as its members were, by ideological rigor and dedicated to Rove's own goal of a permanent Republican majority. Under the ineluctable sway of that grand goal, those who expressed dissent or demonstrated disloyalty or were simply suspected of doing either were judged expendable. My fellow fired U.S. Attorneys and I were just collateral damage in a larger battle to refashion government to reflect the ideals and the values of a single partisan agenda.

Of course, like the rest of America, I can only infer such motivations based on circumstantial evidence. A good rule of thumb in any investigation is to follow the money, but in this case, it is the information trail that is most instructive. And that trail led right through the threshold of Karl Rove's West Wing office. We might yet find that information trail if attempts to pry loose his correspondence in the weeks and the months leading up to December 7 are ever successful. All that's left to do in the meantime is sift through the rubble in the search for clues about one of the most explosive and destructive scandals in the history of American justice.

To do that, it is first necessary to excavate the mound of prevarication, obfuscation, and simple evasion that Main Justice and the White House erected in the immediate aftermath of the firings. Far from being "committed to following through once the pressures comes," the cast of characters who had played their shadowy roles in our forced resignations scattered to the four corners under the harsh light of scrutiny. Their vows of solidarity quickly turned into a search for a scapegoat, preferably one far enough down the ladder to keep their superiors safe from the spreading contagion of scandal.

It didn't work out that way. In a belated bit of the-buck-stops-here bravado, Attorney General Gonzales called a press conference on March 13, a week after our two Judiciary Committee appearances, in which he admitted that "mistakes were made here." "I accept that responsibility," he continued, "and my pledge to the American people is to find out what went wrong here, to access accountability and to make improvements."

It was a statement that did not bode well for those who had actually implemented the firings. But what was left unsaid by the attorney general was that the ultimate accountability did, in fact, rest with him. There was nothing that still needed to be accessed. Instead, Gonzales went to considerable lengths to distance himself from the decision. "As we can all imagine in an organization of 110,000 people, I am not aware of every bit of information that passes through the halls of the Department of Justice. . . . obviously there are going to be decisions that I'm not aware of in real time. Many decisions are delegated."

It was an astonishing admission by any measure. The attorney general, the most powerful law enforcement official in government, was effectively acknowledging that he had delegated the job of firing eight U.S. Attorneys, those men and women who represented the will and the wish of the federal government throughout the country and, as such, were among the most significant appointees in his entire 110,000-person strong structure. Once the decision was delegated, Gonzales went on to all but admit that he had allowed himself to be effectively left outside the loop, in willful ignorance of the means and the methods of the machine that had been set in motion, not to mention the men and the women who would be ground in its gears. There were, however, those who were anything but uninformed—the individuals within the White House who, by the attorney general's own admission, had initiated the plan. "As a general matter," he told reporters, "some two years ago, I was made aware of a request from the White House as to the possibility of replacing all the United States Attorneys."

Wherever the buck was stopping, it was apparently bypassing the desk of Alberto Gonzales, at least according to his own convoluted account. At one and the same time, he was asking reporters and the public to believe that "accountability" for the firings rested on those beneath him to whom the job had been delegated, as well as on those above him who had "requested" that the axing take place. The attorney general filled the role of a genial, bemused, and generally ineffectual middleman, passing along information and willingly leaving others to decide how his department would operate and on what principles.

The next day, March 14, President Bush himself weighed in on the mounting political crisis during his own press conference while on a state visit to Mexico. "The Justice Department recommended a list of U.S. Attorneys," he explained, before going on to endorse the crumbling performance-related rationale. "I believe the reasons why were entirely appropriate." But the fact remained, the president acknowledged, that the "issue was mishandled to the point now that you're asking me questions about it in Mexico. . . . Mistakes were made and frankly, I'm not happy about it."

He wasn't the only one. In the days leading up to the president's and the attorney general's public comments, e-mail in-boxes at Main Justice and the White House had been bulging with panicked communiqués from many of the principles behind the firings. The flurry of alarm, recriminations, and second-guessing had begun almost immediately after the December 7 calls. "Heads up about disgruntlement in Nevada," deputy White House counsel Bill Kelley wrote to Kyle Sampson on December 8, going on to describe how Republican senator John Ensign was "very unhappy about the decision to let Bogden go. . . . I explained our thinking to him at some length," Kelley continued, but Ensign had insisted on calling the attorney general himself "to make sure that Bogden, who they say has done a great job for Nevada, gets a fair shake."

Ensign's indignation, soon to be joined by that of Arizona senator Jon Kyl on behalf of Paul Charlton, pointed up a fatal flaw that Sampson, Goodling, and the others had committed from the onset. Step one of Kyl's planning document directed operatives to contact Republican home-state senators or "Bush political leads," on December 7, the actual day of the phone calls. The idea that important lawmakers and supporters, who were directly involved in the outcome of the imminent firings, would not be consulted or even contacted until it was too late for them to object is further proof of McKay's "incompetence and arrogance" theorem. By the very next day, they were reaping the whirlwind.

Less than a week later, Sampson found himself putting out another brushfire fanned by the spreading inferno. On December 13, he wrote an e-mail reviewing the escalating chaos and copied, among others, Johnny Sutton, whose help I had sought in the days immediately following my forced resignation. They were, he informed his team, "weathering two main complaints: in making the calls Battle (1) wasn't clear whether the USAs [U.S. Attorneys] in question would be permitted to resign or instead were being fired; and (2) was too abrupt."

Although Sampson had once encouraged others to "be steeled to withstand any political upheaval," he now wondered whether an effort might not be made to soothe ruffled feathers. "Perhaps a second round" from Battle might be in order. "Talkers" provided for Battle's benefit included, "I wanted to be sure you understood that DOJ intends not to say anything about our leaving. . . . We want to work with you over the next six weeks to ensure a smooth transition. . . . It's in our interest for you to land on your feet— how can I help?" Yet by the end of his memo, Sampson seemed uncertain whether fence-mending would even work. "Perhaps this is a bad idea?" he concluded plaintively. "Thoughts?"

Offers to help Bogden with landing on his feet, smooth transitions, and a promise of silence were already too little, too late. No such offers of assistance were made to any of the rest of us. But Sampson and Goodling and their assorted White House and Main Justice minions were only beginning to catch heavy incoming flak. Just before the Christmas break, Democratic Arkansas senator Blanche Lincoln cut to the chase by characterizing the interim appointment of Tim Griffin, whom she dubbed a Karl Rove protégé, as "very unfortunate." "This is a person who's going to be implementing the law of the land," she continued, "and I have concern from what I read in terms of his political nature."

"I think we should gum this to death," Sampson cynically wrote to Goodling on December 19. "Ask the Senator to give Tim a chance. . . . If she ultimately says 'no, never,' (and the longer we can forestall that, the better), then we can tell them we'll look for other candidates . . . and otherwise run out the clock. All this should be done in 'good faith' of course."

After the holidays, the gloomy portents continued. Even as Pete Domenici was busy naming four new candidates for my former job (which eventually went to my first assistant, Larry Gomez, as, ironically, an interim appointment), the beleaguered confederates were engaged in fighting off demands from the investigating committees for more documentation, including copies of relevant EARS reports. They also floated a half-inflated trial balloon by suggesting that the real reason for the firings was the fact that at least three of us—Paul Charlton, Carol Lam, and I—all came from border districts. Obviously, the move was a reflection of the administration's determination to solve the immigration problem. It was a contention that was quickly countered by a look at our respective records.

But what had really caught their attention was the increasing likelihood that some or all of the eight fired U.S. Attorneys would be called upon to testify. When that day dawned, our appearance was closely monitored by, among others, Billy Kelley and White House spokeswoman Dana Perino, who were exchanging rapid-fire e-mails even as we answered questions in the hearing room.

"How do I answer whether we think it was inappropriate for lawmakers to call U.S. Attorneys?" Perino needed to know after hearing my accounts of the Domenici and Wilson phone calls.

"Can't we just say that we'll leave it to Congress to examine those questions?" replied Kelley.

"I could try," was Perino's doubtful response, but by that time she had other concerns: Bud Cummins had revealed details of the loaded exchange he had had with Mike Elston on February 20 and the e-mail he had sent to us describing it. "What about this Bud Cummins e-mail?" she continued to Kelley. "This is bad."

"Very bad," agreed Tasia Scolinos, the DOJ spokesperson who was also in the e-mail chain. "We are clearing a strongly worded statement now to get out as soon as we can." Before the lunch break that day, the statement, by Brian Roehrkasse, was released. It insisted that "A private and collegial conversation between Mike Elston and Bud Cummins is now somehow being twisted into a perceived threat by former disgruntled employees grandstanding before Congress." There was something slightly hysterical in the bluster, as if, in a last-ditch attempt to put a lid on the crisis, they had thrown caution to the wind with rhetorical overkill.

But, of course, by then it was too late. Less than a week later, Kyle Sampson would be gone, the first in a series of sacrificial offerings thrown into the maw of a monster of their own creation. It was a monster that would prove to have an insatiable appetite.

CHAPTER 12

Fredo

B y the end of March 2007, the scandal that had engulfed
my life and the lives of my colleagues had transitioned
from the personal realm into a larger historical context.
I would, of course, continue my involvement in getting the story
out, even as I recognized that my days as a point person for the
Justice League were drawing to a close. My wife and children
once again become my top priority: I needed to find a job.

Not all of the attention that I received was favorable or even
pleasant. My role as betrayer of the Republican Party was writ
large for some, especially in the tight, fierce circles of New Mexico
politics. Members of a shadowy group calling itself New Mexicans
for Honest Courts took it upon themselves to launch a one-minute
radio ad campaign excoriating me for taking "taxpayer-funded jun-
kets around the world." "David Iglesias," the spot concluded. "He
still can't figure out why he was fired. Come on, David. Isn't it
obvious?"

It seemed to me a wasteful expedient to express disdain for an
ex-public official. I wasn't running for office. I wasn't suing anybody. I was, for all intents and purposes, out of commission. What

was the point? My comment to this attack ad was simple: "This is the first time I've heard of an unemployed, former government official not running for office being attacked. They must be desperate."

If the point was to intimidate me into a cowed silence, they were wasting their time. The fact was, the story had grown way beyond me or any of us, for that matter. It was a struggle now over principles and politics and their inevitable points of contact, and from that perspective, it was a tale as old as the hills. Pride comes before the fall. No one needed me to tell them that, and with the rest of the nation, I watched, while spring fought its way through the slowly retreating winter, as the immemorial drama played itself out. It was an awful sight to behold, as, one after the other, important people in powerful positions struggled to save their reputations. But it was also a greatly satisfying purge of the political bloodstream, which had been poisoned by partisanship. Despite the best efforts of those at Main Justice and the White House to prove otherwise, the system was actually working.

Like many historical accounts, the dénouement of this unhappy chapter in the annals of American law and justice became a series of footnotes that trailed off without reaching a final, formal conclusion. Calls for the resignation of Attorney General Alberto Gonzales, beginning with such staunch Republican legislators as John Sununu, Gordon Smith, Dana Rohrbacher, and Paul Gillmor, resounded within two weeks of our committee appearances. Before the month was out, the White House had presented to the restive lawmakers a startling compromise to their demand for records and testimony from key administration officials, including William Kelley, Harriet Miers, and, most urgently, Karl Rove. The conditions for their cooperation were, simply put, stunning: all testimony would be in closed-door sessions; no transcript would be kept of the meeting; and the White House staff members would not be sworn in. Any trial lawyer will tell you that this type of testimony is worthless since you cannot use it to challenge a later statement.

This unprecedented act of political chutzpah was underscored the same day, March 20, when President George W. Bush held a press conference to, among other things, reaffirm his support for the attorney general and vow to resist any subpoenas of his staff by the House or Senate Judiciary Committees. He also, in passing, thanked the fired U.S. Attorneys for their service. "I appreciate his gratitude," I noted in my *New York Times* editorial the next day, "—this marks the first time I have been thanked. But only a written retraction by the Justice Department setting the record straight . . . would settle the issue for me."

That apology, an essential step in repairing the damage to my reputation, would of necessity have had to come from Alberto Gonzales himself, but the attorney general was, for the moment, preoccupied. In April he would appear again before the Senate Judiciary Committee, standing virtually alone to face the wrath of the politicians and the public. Monica Goodling had previously announced that she would exercise her Fifth Amendment rights in her own appearance before the committee. She had taken an indefinite leave of absence from the Justice Department, then later resigned. News accounts stated that this was the first time in American history that a sitting Justice Department official had taken the Fifth Amendment. Eventually granted limited immunity in exchange for her testimony, Goodling told House members that the hapless deputy attorney general Paul McNulty had been less than candid with them by claiming that she had largely handled the firings. The truth about the detailed planning of the dismissals with the White House would be extremely difficult to pinpoint, given that McNulty himself had jumped ship. He had announced his resignation on May 14. Simply put, the attorney general was running out of scapegoats.

Of all those swept away in the floodtide of this scandal, it's Alberto Gonzales who most elicits an odd mix of empathy and anger in me. It may be our shared Hispanic heritage or the common thread that runs through our life stories or just the fact that he had initially seemed to me to be a man earnestly committed to the rule of law and his sworn duty to uphold that rule. In short, I liked the man and maybe, in different circumstances, we could have even been friends.

Ultimately, perhaps, my expectations were too high. Maybe my hope that the first Latino attorney general in our nation's history would comport himself with the wisdom and the dignity that came with the office blinded me to the truth of where the judge's real loyalties lay. Whatever the case, Gonzales's fate moved me, perhaps even more so considering that his destruction was entirely self-inflicted.

One of the most commonly asked questions heard in the aftermath of the scandal was whether Gonzales was actually responsible for what happened on his watch or was, rather, only an obedient pawn in political machinations that reached, perhaps, into the Oval Office itself. I certainly can understand the reasons behind such speculation, as part of the deep and lingering mistrust of government since the Watergate era, when suspicions of presidential involvement in criminal activity ran deep and it was imperative to pin down what the chief executive knew and when he knew it.

But the correlation goes only so far. Who was really guilty of this concerted attempt to co-opt the Justice Department for political ends? It's certainly easy, as far as it goes, to point the finger at the hapless attorney general. It was his job to protect the integrity of the institution he led, and in that respect, Alberto Gonzales was a miserable failure. But does that analysis go far enough? In the case of Karl Rove—who was charged with the weighty responsibility of being the president's domestic policy adviser—certainly not.

But what about Bush himself? There is no question that he had been apprised of complaints by Republican politicians regarding many of the U.S. Attorneys who were subsequently fired. But was it his responsibility to investigate such matters? Of course not. That was the attorney general's job. Yet was Bush, by hiring someone as pliant and blindly loyal as Gonzales, somehow culpable in the resulting catastrophe? I think it depends on when, exactly, benign neglect becomes malicious intent. Bush set a standard that placed allegiance to him above all else, and Gonzales met that standard at every turn. From that fundamental premise, all else proceeded.

As personal as my emotions might have been regarding my former superior, I know that I had in common the same feelings as most Americans when I watched the dismaying, deceiving, and ultimately depressing performance the attorney general of the United States gave before the Senate Judiciary Committee on April 19, 2007. It became, in its aftermath, an enduring moment of deep embarrassment, even shame, for our nation to watch its chief law enforcement officer dodge and deny the truth, even as he willingly cast himself as both incompetent and arrogant in order to protect an administration that, in the final reckoning, did not deserve his fealty. Yet his appearance that day was as infuriating as it was mortifying. Gonzales greeted even the sharpest attacks on his honesty and integrity with the same bland, slightly bemused expression, as if, for the life of him, he couldn't figure out what all the fuss was about. The increasing frustration and utter disbelief expressed by his questioners were deflected by a kind of search-me smirk that never wavered. In some unfathomable way, Gonzales had made peace with the process of being torn apart, secure in the knowledge that at the end of the day, his most important allegiance—to the president—had remained inviolate.

Even as the nation was still reeling from the shocking mass murders at Virginia Tech earlier that week—a tragedy that had put the hearing briefly on hold—the attorney general nodded while listening to the injunctions of Senator Jeff Sessions, a former U.S. Attorney, at the hearing's opening. "Be alert and honest and direct with the committee," the Alabama lawmaker abjured him. "Give it your best shot. You are a good man, and I think that will show through."

What showed through instead was an utter disregard, bordering on contempt, for the committee, its authority, and its mission. Before the hearing broke for lunch, Gonzales had answered nearly sixty questions posed to him in exactly the same way: "I do not recall." When pressed by Senator Ted Kennedy as to the procedure for the firings, Gonzales suggested with a long-suffering air that since the committee had already interviewed most of his aides, the senators now knew more about the dismissals than he did.

To the end, the attorney general stuck to the script. "U.S. Attorneys serve at the pleasure of the president," he reminded the committee in his opening statement. "There is nothing improper in making a change for poor management, policy differences or questionable judgment. . . . While reasonable people might decide different things differently, my decision to ask for the resignations of these U.S. Attorneys is justified and should stand." At the same time, he asked his interlocutors to mitigate his responsibility for that decision by "recognizing my limited involvement in the process."

So it went. Under intense questioning from Chairman Pat Leahy about the timing and the intent of my forced resignation, the attorney general, while admitting that he "accepted the recommendation," at the same time insisted that he was "not responsible for compiling the list." "I was not surprised," he added, "that Mr. Iglesias was recommended to me, because I had heard about concerns . . . from Senator Domenici."

"And Karl Rove?" Leahy pressed.

Yes, Gonzales admitted, "I heard concerns raised by Mr. Rove."

When asked to elaborate on the reasons I had lost the attorney general's confidence, as he had stated in his *USA Today* editorial on March 7, the judge recalled a conversation he'd had in the fall of 2005 with Pete Domenici. "[H]e called me and said something to the effect that Mr. Iglesias was in over his head."

"My question," interrupted Leahy, "was when and why did he lose *your* confidence."

"What I instructed Mr. Sampson to do was consult with people in the department . . . ," Gonzales stammered.

"When and why did he lose your confidence?" the senator asked for the third time.

He never did get an answer, and it's hard to discount the possibility that there was no answer to get. The attorney general didn't have the faintest idea when and why he had lost confidence in me. Nor was he willing to admit that any of the reasons proffered to date had been insufficient." Clearly, I had not lost the confidence of Gonzales, as evidenced by his nonresponsive answers. He clearly had not expressed any concerns when he visited my office in August 2006, just months before my name was added to the list. I had lost the confidence of Domenici, who had taken the counsel of what author J. R. R. Tolkien would have called his "worm tongues."

"When, how, and by whom did the 'absentee landlord' rationale for replacing Mr. Iglesias arise?" Leahy continued.

"That rationale was not in my mind," Gonzales responded, "when I accepted the recommendation.

Later that day, when Senator Kennedy asked the attorney general to cast his mind back to the moment when he made his "judgment and decision" to approve the firings, Gonzales this time expressed uncertainty both as to the reasons for the actions and to whom, exactly, those reasons might apply. "Senator," he said, "There are two that I do not recall knowing in my mind what I understood to be the reasons for the removal." The twisted locution was an almost palpable manifestation of the knots that he was willing to tie himself into for the sake of obscuring the truth.

There was a deeply offensive element to the attorney general's assertion that he couldn't really recall the actual reasons why he had "accepted the recommendations" made by Kyle Sampson, Monica Goodling, and the rest. When asked by Republican senator Sam Brownback of Kansas why, specifically, Dan Bogden had been terminated, Gonzales threw logic and coherence completely out the window. "This is probably the one that, to me, was the closest call," he mused before adding, "I do not recall that I knew about Mr. Bogden on December 7. . . . That's not to say that I wasn't given a reason; I just don't recall the reason. I didn't have an independent basis or recollection of knowing about Mr. Bogden's performance."

There was certainly an "independent basis" for evaluating the performance of the cabinet officer whom President Bush had playfully nicknamed "Fredo." That basis was candor and sincerity and, in the end, simple honesty. "In thinking about it," the attorney general concluded on the subject of Dan's dismissal, "I believe it was still the right decision."

Occasionally, Gonzales professed to be in the dark even about whether he made a decision or not. When asked by Democratic senator Herb Kohl whether the U.S. Attorney for the Eastern District of Wisconsin, Steve Biskupic—who had taught alongside me at the DOJ's "voting integrity symposium"—had ever made the firing list, the attorney general fished around for a response before stating, more or less unequivocally, "[T]his was a process that was ongoing that I did not have transparency into."

Transparency was at a premium that day in the Senate Judiciary Committee hearing room. "I have no recollection," "I do not recall," "I have no memory": the same enervating litany was repeated over and over as the afternoon session wore on. Before it was done, as if sensing that his amnesiac prevarications were wearing thin, the attorney general tried out a variety of other bobs and weaves. "There were a lot of other weighty issues I was dealing with," he told Senator Sessions when asked about his inattention to the firings. When quizzed on incriminating statements that Kyle Sampson gave before the committee, Gonzales refused to "characterize others' testimony." When Senator Lindsey Graham asked about inconsistencies in the testimony of key witnesses, Gonzales pleaded, "it's difficult for me to reconcile the conversations."

The attorney general later declaimed, "I'm trying to inform the Congress that I don't have anything to hide."

"Right," Senator Graham replied laconically.

By the conclusion of that long and exasperating day, Senator Charles Schumer attempted, as best he could, to sum up the dispiriting juggling act the committee had just witnessed. "[We] laid out the burden of proof for you to meet, to answer questions directly and fully," the lawmaker commenced, "You've answered 'I don't know' or 'I can't recall' to close to a hundred questions. You're not familiar with much of the workings of your own department. And we still don't have convincing explanations of the who, why, and when in regard to the firings. . . . You haven't met any of these three tests. I don't see the point of another round of questions. And I urge you to reexamine your performance and, for the good of the department and the good of the country, step down."

"May I respond?" Gonzales equitably asked and, when granted permission, began first by acknowledging, "I have the burden of proof of providing to you the reasons why I made my decisions." He then, with extraordinary aplomb, shifted that burden back to the committee and, by extension, to the American people. "I think in terms of whether or not something improper has happened here, respectfully, Senator, that the burden lies upon you and others who are making the allegations."

Schumer was having none of it, nor, I suspect, was the witnessing nation. "That would be true if there were a criminal trial, sir," he shot back. "But our standard for attorney general is . . . a much higher standard than that."

Fredo was silent, and it was left to Leahy to gavel the hearing to a close. It had all petered out in dozens of false starts and dead ends, which seemed to terminate in Fredo's implacable expression. The chairman thanked the attorney general for attending and observed, more in sorrow than in jest, "This is not the day I think you wanted." To paraphrase T. S. Eliot, the hearing ended not with a bang but with a whimper. In the many years of watching C-SPAN hearings, I had never seen such a wretched performance.

It was a day none of us wanted, one that exposed a shocking lapse of integrity and honesty at the highest levels of our government. Watching it unfold, I was reminded of the old fable of the emperor's new clothes. The attorney general, supposedly garbed in all the gravitas of his office, had paraded naked for the world to see. It was both a sad and a sobering sight.

"Every day," Alberto Gonzales told the committee members near the conclusion of his testimony, "I ask myself the question, 'Can I continue to be effective as leader of this department?' The moment I believe I can no longer be effective, I will resign."

That moment of realization would, in due course, arrive, albeit much earlier for most Americans than for the attorney general himself. Four months later, and much longer than any who had witnessed the debacle in the hearing room might have given him, Attorney General Alberto Gonzales announced his resignation. The pleasure of the president was no longer served, and the highest-ranking official to lose his job in the aftermath of the scandal was cut loose as the administration circled its wagons a little tighter.

All that was left was the summing up, the speculation and the commentary, the lessons learned, and, perhaps, the wisdom gained. "I once said that I found Gonzales to be a personal inspiration," I wrote a month after the hearings in a *Los Angeles Times* editorial titled "Cowboy Up, Alberto Gonzales"—ranch slang for doing the right thing despite the cost. I wrote, "No one can deny him his life story, which is the American dream writ large. It began in Humble, Texas, born of impoverished Mexican American parents. He, like me, is a veteran of the U.S. military. He went to some of the best schools in America, including Harvard law. Yet somewhere along the way, he drank the loyalty Kool-Aid. Watching him testify was painful for me. He had been a trailblazer for the Latino community, and then, in the space of a few hours of tortured testimony, he became just another morally rudderless operative."

James Comey, the former deputy attorney general under both Ashcroft and Gonzales, saw it from another perspective. His riveting testimony on May 15 before a Senate Judiciary Committee—still immersed in the investigation and the efforts to shake loose more information from Main Justice and the White House—was one of the most damning indictments yet, not only of Gonzales, but of an entire administration that had indeed lost its moral rudder. With the possible exception of DOJ accusations against John McKay for "pushing" the Tom Wales murder case too hard, there was perhaps no lower ebb in the whole story than Comey's description of the attempt by Gonzales, who was then White House counsel, to get John Ashcroft to sign off on a controversial warrantless surveillance program, while the attorney general lay virtually at death's door in a hospital intensive-care room. It seemed that men who would stoop to such levels would hardly have qualms about firing dedicated public servants, an observation that Jim Comey stirringly underscored by telling the committee that he was unwilling to "sit by and watch good people smeared."

One by one, and for the record, Senator Arlen Specter sounded off our names.

"Dan Bogden."

"Dan Bogden was an excellent U.S. Attorney."

"As to John McKay and the competency of his performance?"

"Again, it was excellent in my experience."

"And as to Paul Charlton, Arizona U.S. Attorney?"

"The same." Comey paused. "I don't want to make it look like I love everybody, but I did like him a great deal."

Senator Specter waited for the laughter to die down before continuing his role call. "And David Iglesias, U.S. Attorney for New Mexico."

"Same thing. I dealt with him quite a bit, both as a peer and as his superior, and had a high opinion of him. I thought he did a very good job."

Comey later recalled to me the moment when he first knew that his beloved Justice Department had been hijacked. "I was sitting with my wife watching Paul McNulty's testimony on TV," he told me. "When he claimed that everyone had been let go for performance-related reasons, I turned to her and said, 'They just lit a powder keg.'"

The fuse to that keg may have been long, but it came to an end that April day in the hearing room when Fredo fell on his sword as the nation watched aghast. But to hear John McKay tell it, the fuse still has a ways to go. McKay, who currently teaches constitutional law, law of terrorism, and national security law at Seattle University, recently prepared an article for the school law review, titled "Train Wreck at the Justice Department." In it, he presents a compelling case for obstruction of justice charges to be brought against Gonzales. Focusing on Carol Lam's dismissal as she was overseeing the bribery case against Duke Cunningham, McKay argued that the former attorney general, along with Paul McNulty and Kyle Sampson, be made to "demonstrate that their complicity in the removal of Lam had nothing to do with her aggressive prosecution of powerful Republicans for public corruption."

Calling for the appointment of a special prosecutor, McKay went on to detail additional possible criminal charges against Gonzales, including an "explicit effort to utilize United States Attorneys to obtain advantage in . . . questionable election fraud" and "the possibility that one or more Justice Department official has lied to Congress." To prove his point, McKay quoted Arkansas senator David Pryor. "The attorney general not only lied to me as a person," Pryor stated at the hearing, "but when he lied to me, he lied to the Senate and he lied to the people I represent."

But McKay ended his scathing analysis on a hopeful note. "The resignation of the Attorney General," he wrote, "has undoubtedly been a relief to those who have observed the faulty memories, political maneuvering and outright incompetence at the Justice Department. . . . The President and the Senate now have the opportunity to restore leadership . . . and hold accountable Justice Department employees who have failed, or in the future fail to uphold the values of independence, truthfulness, non-partisanship and the non-political pursuit of justice."

What McKay left unsaid was that such a pursuit might well lead beyond the halls of the Justice Department and into other, more secretive, realms of government. It's hard to know whether the damage done by our forced resignations was a factor in the departure of Karl Rove four days after Gonzales made his own farewell announcement. In the Byzantine labyrinths of power through which Rove moved, there may never be anything as simple as cause and effect. But it doesn't really matter. Comey's analogy of the lit fuse may extend a little further still. Out of office, Rove is hardly off the minds of the lawmakers who are still seeking answers to those "mysteries without any clues." Even as the Office of the Inspector General prepares its long-gestating report on the possible legal and ethical violations of the firings, Democrats on the Senate Judiciary Committee, as recently as December 2007, pushed forward with a resolution to hold the White House in contempt of Congress for failing to provide a long list of subpoenaed information and witnesses in the investigation.

At that top of that list is Karl Rove, and for him and others, the final verdict has yet to be rendered. Within days of the one-year anniversary of our firings, the Senate Judiciary Committee voted to hold Rove in contempt of Congress for refusing to cooperate in its probe of the firings, in the process rejecting the administration's claim of executive privilege for withholding documents and testimony. It's the opening salvo in the next stage of an ongoing battle being waged over one of the fundamental principals of the American experiment: the separation of powers.

It is, of course, in the success or the failure of that experiment that the true significance of the scandal lies. It was not about me losing my job, however painful that might have been; nor was it about the unprecedented act of forcing out a group of highly competent and ethical federal prosecutors for base political reasons, however unfair that might have been. The deepest implications of the disaster at Main Justice are not of partisan politics, nor are they of transient liberal or conservative issues. Rather, at their molecular core, they are issues of illegality and unconstitutionality. I spoke out because I could never get over the insurmountable fact that what had happened to me was wrong and that it would be repeated to future U.S. Attorneys unless I spoke out.

The scandal was a wrenching but necessary object lesson about the need to maintain the independence of the prosecutor and the consequences of attempting to politicize the criminal justice system at the highest levels. A politicized prosecutor is anathema to anyone who has read the Constitution or studied American history. As McKay eloquently stated in an analysis for the *Washington State Bar Association* magazine, "What's at stake here is prosecutorial independence from partisan politics and renewed dedication to fair and impartial justice which is tempered by compassion."

The framers of our Constitution were leery of concentrating too much power—they had seen the abuses of England's King George, which led to the American Revolution. The framers split power into three parts. As any fifth-grader who has studied American civics will tell you, the legislative branch makes the laws (Article I), the executive branch enforces the law (Article II), and the judicial branch interprets the law (Article III). Judges and prosecutors are expected to stay out of politics, and the sanction for breaking that historic shibboleth is impeachment for the judge and job termination or disbarment for the prosecutor. It is un-American and unconstitutional to act otherwise.

America stands for many inspiring principles, the rule of law being one of the pillars in our noble experiment in democracy. Failed states don't recognize this principle—in some countries, prosecutors and judges are mere pawns of the corrupt elected officials. Justice cannot flow from such a polluted source. On the other hand, the American public has the absolute right to believe that when someone is charged with a crime, it is based on the evidence alone.

Every president makes hundreds, if not thousands, of appointments during the course of his four- or eight-year term. Alone among this legion of appointees is the U.S. Attorney—only he or she can take a citizen's life, property, and liberty away. Former U.S. attorney general and Supreme Court justice Robert Jackson recognized this vast power when he gave a speech to U.S. Attorneys in 1940, saying, "[A]ssembled in this room is one of the most powerful peacetime forces known to our country. The prosecutor has more power over life, liberty and reputation than any person in America."

That power is not one to trifle with. Historically, U.S. Attorneys were free to independently evaluate the evidence and proceed if they thought it supported a prosecution. Again, Robert Jackson alluded to this polestar requirement of the prosecutor when speaking to a group of U.S. Attorneys: "Your positions are of such independence and importance that while you are being diligent, strict, and vigorous in law enforcement you can also afford to be just."

Anyone associated with law enforcement will affirm that it is no science, despite the whiz-bang technology now available, to investigate cases. The honest prosecutor must be motivated by seeking a fair redress to a crime, not by racking up convictions. The goal is a just, fair result, not a symbolic notch in a courtroom gunslinger's belt. The Justice Department, under the failed leadership of Alberto Gonzales, lost sight of this core principle. Having never served as prosecutors, both Gonzales and his deputy, Paul McNulty, did not understand this key requirement. Perhaps going to horrific crime scenes, talking to the emotionally distraught family members of victims, or hearing the accounts of hard-bitten agents or police officers would have helped them to better understand. But in the antiseptic confines of Main Justice or the White House's West Wing, they did not know this truth to be self-evident; it was simply outside the realm of their experience.

To the Gonzales Justice Department, U.S. Attorneys were mere political appointees, not impartial and nonpolitical agents of justice to be protected from the capricious winds of Capitol Hill. It was as if we were mere summer help with law degrees, to be moved about the appointment chessboard by the likes of Karl Rove as he sought the Holy Grail of a permanent Republican majority in government.

In the end, the Justice Department debacle proved the resiliency of the American system of checks and balances. An emboldened House and Senate sought to reveal just how much partisan politics contaminated a department with a long and proud history of staying out of politics. The results were ugly. If the executive privilege claim will be resolved, Congress should get a full accounting of who actually ordered the terminations and why. Only then will the system's checks and balances be seen for what they truly are—not inconvenient obstacles to political ends, but a necessary expedient against an ascendant executive branch that was bent on expanding its wartime powers to areas that have nothing to do with the legitimate role of the commander in chief of the armed forces.

Power is a terrible thing to behold if it is not restrained by fairness and decency. Former attorney general and Supreme Court justice Robert Jackson said it best, "[T]he citizen's safety lies in the prosecutor who tempers zeal with human kindness, who seeks truth and not victims, who serves the law and not factional purposes, and who approaches his task with humility."

This administration's Justice Department was driven by political hubris, not by the basic concepts of fairness and fair play that are precious to us all. The leadership was not committed to the rule of law, but to the rule of politics. And in the gladiatorial world of Washington, D.C., politics, the leadership at the Justice Department found out the hard truth to this eternal principle: you reap what you sow.

Epilogue

Shortly before Deputy Attorney General Jim Comey left office in 2005, he visited Paul Charlton and me in Window Rock, Arizona, capital of the Navajo nation. After leaving the Navajos, he met with me on top of Acoma Pueblo, otherwise known as Sky City. Established in the twelfth century, it is considered to be the oldest continuously inhabited community in the United States. Set on top of a 367-foot mesa, it has a commanding view of the gigantic red stone valley and huge mesas in the distance.

It was a warm and sunny day in that dramatic and otherworldly place. I had a hard time getting Comey off Sky City. Standing near the edge of the precipice, he just kept staring at the horizon, apparently lost in his thoughts. When we finally reached my office in Albuquerque, he gave a sobering speech to my staff about the "reservoir of trust" that the Justice Department must maintain. He said that it takes years to fill the reservoir and just seconds to drain it, causing immeasurable harm to the trust in our criminal justice system. The next week he announced his resignation.

The reservoir metaphor is an apt one. It will take time for the damage done to the Justice Department to be completely remedied. In the meanwhile, life goes on. My girls are getting older, and the job of raising a family is ever more over-scheduled. After seven months of unpaid sabbatical, I finally found a job, like many of my colleagues, in the private sector. I'm now advising on law-enforcement issues for a respected global consulting firm, which allows me to stay planted in my beloved New Mexico. I even hung on to the hot tub that had seemed like such an unnecessary extravagance in the days immediately following December 7. I still regularly attend to my duties in the U.S. Navy Reserve, proud to serve my country and the armed service branch that first offered me an opportunity to give something back to the country that had given me so much. I am grateful to have been inculcated with the service's core values of honor, courage, and commitment. Those principles, along with the support of Cyndy and the prayers of hundreds of people helped me make it through the vociferous blowback from the local Republican zealots.

I can't say I don't miss the excitement and sense of accomplishment that came with being a U.S. Attorney. I was able to make a difference in a job filled with purpose. I brought clarity to a vexing Indian Country jurisdiction problem by calling for and facilitating new congressional legislation that was signed into law, oversaw the biggest corruption cases in state history, and brought the cutting-edge LInX information-sharing system to New Mexico. I accomplished virtually everything I set out to do. I am grateful to the many people in the U.S. Attorney's office who helped make it happen. Like the people I met, the work I did while a U.S. Attorney defined, in large part, my own sense of purpose and destiny and did much to make me the person I am today.

In a similar way, losing that job was also essential in building my character. Romans 8:28 says, "All things work together for good to those who love God and are called according to His purposes." There was a time when I wasn't sure I believed that. Now, I know it's true.

In December 2007, a few of my colleagues and I got together to mark the one-year anniversary of our December 7 phone calls. As several of us gathered under the warm California sun for a weekend in beautiful Coronado, it was tremendously gratifying to realize that we were doing well, both personally and professionally. Dan Bogden and Paul Charlton had joined prestigious law firms in Nevada and Arizona, respectively, while Margaret Chiara had found meaningful work on a federal prison commission. Bud Cummins was instrumental in helping to build an important bio-fuel refinery in Nebraska, John Mckay is a professor at Seattle University Law School, Carol Lam was doing an exemplary job as a senior vice president and counsel at Qualcomm, Todd Graves had started his own law firm, and Kevin Ryan had established a practice in San Francisco specializing in sports law. What had been meant to destroy us had instead been turned to our benefit, and we all gained in stature among the public and our peers for the ordeal we had suffered. That's not something you can say of those who went down in disrepute when their incompetence and arrogance were finally brought to light.

Our opponents did not fare so well. My former mentor Pete Domenici's approval ratings hit 41 percent, the lowest in his thirty-five-year career, just a few months after my testimony. The public interest group CREW filed an ethics complaint against him which was still on-going as of early 2008. He announced he would not be running for office again in October 2007, citing an incurable brain disease. I suspect that disease may have led to his highly improper phone call to me, but I also believe that had he not been ensnared in the scandal, he would have found a way to stay in office, despite his health concerns. Time will tell whether Heather Wilson faces formal ethics charges and whether she is successful in her bid to become New Mexico's next U.S. Senator. Domenici's departure set off a chain reaction that led to all three New Mexico Congresspersons running for his vacancy. I saw the rule of law in action here as well as the rule of unintended consequences.

In early 2008, there were no fewer than six separate investigations into the scandal. The Senate and House ethics and judiciary committees had inquiries, as did the Department of Justice's Office of Inspector General and Office of Professional Responsibility. Also, the Office of Special Counsel was looking into whether my reserve military status was a basis for my forced resignation. On February 14, 2008, the House voted to hold Josh Bolton and Harriet Miers in contempt for failure to appear and testify about our firings. The last time the House had issued a contempt citation was in 1983. I hope that the executive privilege claim is resolved. American citizens have a right to know if there was an unconstitutional attempt to politicize the Justice Department—there are documents and e-mails in the White House that will shed light on this pressing matter. On March 10, 2008, the House of Representatives' Judiciary Committee filed a civil action against former White House counsel Harriet Miers and White House chief of staff Josh Bolten to compel their testimony over our firings.

As for the future, everywhere I go I hear suggestions that my prospects for elected office have been greatly enhanced by my notoriety. Both Democrats and Republicans, liberals and conservatives, have urged me to take a run at it. But that's for another day, if ever. Maybe I've seen too much—or maybe not enough. I still believe that it's possible to do good works in political office. But I also believe that something fundamental needs to change to attract principled and ethical people into the political arena. The need for reform is real. That is one lesson I learned, along with the rest of America, through the darkest days of this scandal.

But optimism and idealism are real, too. Despite my original doubts early in the scandal, the rule of law is alive and well in America. U.S. Attorneys are independent in a way they have not been for years. Politicians will, for a season, leave prosecutors alone. America is truly a great nation of "laws not men," to which I owe so much. It has made me who I am. Who I will become is in God's hands.

Letter from Senator Charles Schumer to Alberto Gonzales

United States Senate

WASHINGTON, DC 20510

March 30, 2007

The Honorable Alberto Gonzales
Attorney General of the United States
Department of Justice
950 Pennsylvania Ave, NW
Washington, DC 20530

Dear Attorney General Gonzales:

As you know, your former Chief of Staff, D. Kyle Sampson, testified voluntarily before
the Senate Judiciary Committee yesterday as a part of our ongoing investigation into the
Department of Justice's dismissal of eight U.S. attorneys last year. We regarded Mr.
Sampson as a key witness given that, in your press conference on March 13, you said that
Mr. Sampson was "charged with directing the process" of identifying U.S. attorneys for
dismissal.

Yesterday, in response to my questioning, Mr. Sampson admitted that he did not do any
independent research into the performance of the U.S. attorneys who were dismissed. He
also admitted that, in hindsight, he would not have recommended Mr. Iglesias for
dismissal given the information that Mr. Sampson now knows.

In light of these startling admissions by your former chief of staff, it is imperative that
you restore Mr. Iglesias's tarnished reputation by confirming that his performance as a
U.S. attorney did not warrant dismissal. I urge you to take this step immediately, in order
to clear the name of this dedicated public servant.

Sincerely,

Charles E. Schumer
United States Senator

APPENDIX B

Excerpt from the National Association of Former United States Attorneys Resolution

Recognizing the importance of the position of the
United States Attorney

Now, therefore, it is Resolved:

That the President, the Congress, the Attorney General and the Department of Justice are best served and, in turn, best serve the nation and the fair administration of justice, by insuring: that United States Attorneys are appointed by the President, with the advice and consent of the Senate; that the institutions of government recognize and fully support integrity and independence of United States Attorneys in prosecutorial and litigative judgment as fundamental to the fair operation of the federal criminal and civil justice system; and that United States Attorneys must be free from even the appearance of improper political considerations in the exercise of their prosecutorial and litigative responsibilities.

NAFUSA is a bipartisan organization composed of former U.S. Attorneys from administrations going back to President John F. Kennedy. At their annual meeting in 2007, they publicly released this resolution condemning the firings of my colleagues and me.

That there have been a series of resignations and terminations of United States Attorneys who were performing their duties in an outstanding, professional manner in the finest tradition of United States Attorneys. It is imperative that all Executive and Legislative Branch officials respect these rules of conduct which are written to promote the essential independence of United States Attorneys in their districts and to promote the fair and impartial administration of justice.

1. Decisions by United States Attorneys regarding bringing a case should be made without regard to political issues and should be made in an impartial manner.
2. United States Attorneys should never be asked to conduct or not conduct an investigation or bring or not bring charges to assist any candidate or any party in an election.
3. Cases should never be brought by a United States Attorney in an attempt to assist a candidate or a party to win an election.
4. Decisions regarding indictments or prosecutions should be made without regard to the position of United States Senators or United States Representatives on those cases.
5. No Senator or Congressman should attempt to influence a United States Attorney regarding an investigation or prosecution.
6. A United States Attorney should never be asked to resign or be terminated from his or her position because a Senator or Representative has complained to the Department of Justice or White House regarding the U.S. Attorney's decisions regarding indictments or prosecutions.
7. United States Attorneys should never be asked to resign or be terminated from their position unless they have had an opportunity to present their position to the Attorney General and without the Attorney General and President approving this decision, barring a change of administration or exigent circumstances.

Adopted this 10 day of November, 2007 by the members of the National Association of Former United States Attorneys, Miami, Florida.

INDEX